EVERYMAN'S DATABASE PRIMER

FEATURING dBASE III PLUS™

ISBN: 0-912677-85-6

Copyright (c) 1986 Ashton-Tate

Published by Ashton-Tate Publishing Group
20101 Hamilton Avenue, Torrance, California 90502-1319

The software, computer, and product names mentioned in *Everyman's Database Primer Featuring dBASE III PLUS* are manufacturer and publisher trademarks and are used only for the purpose of identification.

dBASE, dBASE III, and Ashton-Tate are a registered trademarks of Ashton-Tate. *1-2-3* is a trademark of Lotus Development Corporation. PFS:FILE is a trademark of Software Publishing Corporation. VisiCalc is a trademark of VisiCorp. WordStar and MailMerge are a registered trademarks of MicroPro. Multiplan is a trademark of Multimate International Corporation.

Senior Editor: Brenda Johnson-Grau
Assistant Editor: Shaista Ali
Associate Editor: James Bradbury
Production Manager: B.T. Miyake
Designer: Thomas Clark

10 9 8 7 6 5 4 3

TABLE OF CONTENTS

Acknowledgements

This is the second major revision of *Everyman's Database Primer*. Over the years, many people have contributed, each adding a little of themselves. The book was born in George Tate's garage at the very beginning of dBASE II and Ashton-Tate. With the help and encouragement of George Tate and the author of dBASE, Wayne Ratliff, an idea became a manuscript. The skillful editing of Virginia Bare transformed the manuscript into a book. And then, the enthusiasm and support of the entire Ashton-Tate family turned the book into a success.

The first major revision of the *Primer* was caused by the introduction of dBASE III, the big brother of dBASE II. Again, the Ashton-Tate product formed the backdrop for the manuscript while the publications group — particularly Monet Thomson and Robert Hoffman — transformed that manuscript into a successful book.

Now we have another bigger and better dBASE — and another major revision to the *Primer*. The attractive new book design is the work of Tom Clark and Bruce Miyake of Ashton-Tate. Preparation of most of the screens and figures was accomplished by Anton Byers of Softwords; he also performed much of the technical review. Brenda Johnson-Grau polished this manuscript with unusual skill and a wry style. This is my third book with Brenda, who has always been a real joy to work with.

SECTION ONE
GETTING STARTED

Section One introduces *databases* and acquaints you with how they work. Databases are common in daily life; we rarely think twice about their part in our routine activities. A *database management system* is simply the way in which these familiar databases are contained and manipulated by a computer.

We will take a close look at some common database examples and analyze the pieces in order to understand how a database system works to provide us with organized information. The process is simple: We will start right away, turn our computer on, and design our first computer databases.

CHAPTER ONE

DATABASE

*D*atabase is computer jargon for a familiar and essential item in our everyday lives. A database is a collection of information organized and presented to serve a specific purpose.

One of the more familiar database examples is the *telephone directory*. This common printed database contains the names, addresses, and telephone numbers of individuals, businesses, and governmental agencies. The addresses and telephone numbers have little value by themselves. They are useful only when they are *related* to a name.

The number of databases in common use is astonishing. Some common databases are a dictionary, a cookbook, a mail-order catalog, an encyclopedia, a library's card catalog, your checkbook, and so on. Other familiar databases are stock market reports in the newspaper, an accounts receivable ledger, and a personnel file.

Why are these examples databases? Why isn't the newspaper or a nonfiction book considered a database? After all, these also contain information. The reason is specific. In each of the examples given above, information is presented in a manner which makes it easy for you to locate some particular piece of information.

In the telephone directory, the telephone numbers and addresses are related to the name. The names are presented in alphabetical order so you can find them easily. Find the name and you find both the address and the phone number. The name is the *key* to using the phone book. A dictionary works similarly: There is a word and a definition. The words are listed alphabetically so that they can be found, and the definition is related to the word. The *key* to using the dictionary is the word.

The common element in all of the examples is *organized* information presented in a way that makes it easy to *find* by the use of a key. In other words, information that can be presented as tables (rows and columns) can be a database. Some examples of column headings in tables that could be considered databases are shown in Figure 1-1.

Examples	Column Headings				
PHONE BOOK:	NAME	ADDRESS	PHONE NUMBER		
DICTIONARY:	WORD	DEFINITION			
CATALOG:	ITEM	DESCRIPTION	SIZE	PRT NO.	COST
STOCK REPORT:	STOCK	SHARES TRADED	HIGH	LOW	

Figure 1-1

By now, you should have a general concept of a database and you might be asking, "Okay, but what's a *computer* database? What can I do with it that I can't do without it?" The computer database can't do anything you couldn't do yourself from a printed database. However, many things are just more practical with a computer than without a computer.

We have all found a scrap of paper with a phone number on it — no name, just a number. If we want to discover the name that belongs to the number, the telephone book isn't much help. If, however, the telephone directory is a computer database, we can ask the computer to check the phone number and the name will promptly appear.

Suppose you want the phone number of someone named Smith who lives on Santa Monica Boulevard in Los Angeles. You can ask the computer's Los Angeles phonebook file (perhaps called "LAPHONE") for the names, addresses, and phone numbers of all the Smiths on Santa Monica Boulevard. It may not give you a single name and number, but it will surely narrow the search down.

The computer is no panacea. It can't do anything you can't. But, it can *help* you do the things you want to do quickly and easily. It is a tool to help you accomplish things that are simply not practical without it.

Using a personal phone book as an example, a simple database might resemble the one shown in Figure 1-2.

Of course, a real database can contain many, many more items of information. In fact, this database is much better kept in a small notebook than in a computer. You can carry it around with you, make notes in it, and it's a lot cheaper. To get value from a computer you need to have a lot of information — in general, so much information that you can't efficiently use it without the computer.

Conceptually, a computer database is just like one that you could create from paper and pencil. Since both a paper database and a computer database exist to be *used*, an appropriate question is: What do you actually *do* with your phone book?

You write in new acquaintances, perhaps change the addresses or phone numbers of people who move or get a new phone. Maybe you cross some people out (or erase them, if you've had

Chapter One

NAME	ADDRESS	PHONE NUMBER
Byers, Robert A Sr	9999 Glencrest, Standale	555-9242
Byers, Robert A Jr	48 N. Catalina, Pasadena	555-9540
Cassidy, Butch	4800 Rimrock Ct., Sunland	878-1121
Evans, Sydney H.	398 S. Calif. Blvd., Encino	998-1234
Goose, Sil E.	21809 Cottage Ln., Montecito	675-1212
Hedman, Gene	139 Luxury Dr., Bev. Hills	987-6543
Maori, Stanislas	2800 Oak St. #344, Red. Bch.	324-8529
Robertson, James	5892 Glencrest, Standale	997-2741

Figure 1-2

enough foresight to keep your records in pencil). When you want to use the information stored there, you may be trying to make a call, going to a party, or mailing a letter. Thus your phone book — if you keep it up-to-date — reflects a process of change and, at any given time, will supply you with the information you're looking for. The same is true of a computer database. You can easily add, remove, or change the information in a computer database. Likewise, you can easily view information from your database.

In your everyday activities, you are always adding and subtracting from information at hand, changing it, selecting what you want to see, and ignoring what you don't want to see. This activity is basic to the thinking process. But, we are going to put all this information that we're so accustomed to having strewn about us — where we can see it and touch it — into a computer database.

Now, there will be something holding this information — something between us and the data. Once we begin to use the computer we need to become comfortable with the idea that the data is inside of the "blinking box." Even though you can no longer "touch" the information, it is there when you need it. After you become comfortable with this knowledge, you'll be amazed at how many ways a computer database can fulfill your information needs.

Using your computer will become as easy as using your phone book. It will take some thought, some planning, and some *how-to* knowledge. You need to know how to create, how to use, and how to change your store of information. In the learning process, you won't have to reinvent the wheel. You are only learning a new function — a new set of mechanics for a new machine — designed to support your efforts to perceive and process information already familiar to you.

The purpose of this book is to teach you about databases and how to use them. To make your learning manageable, we'll use very small databases for our examples. The same database principles apply to both large and small databases. Exactly the same principles apply to our personal phone book example and to the white pages for Los Angeles County. The only difference is that there are many more entries in the white pages. To better acquaint you with computer databases, that is,

- how to plan them
- how to make them
- how to use them
- how to change them

Database

we are going to build a computer database from a simple telephone book example. To help us do this, we'll use the popular database management system dBASE III. A database management system is software that takes care of all the details involved with a database, and lets you use, manipulate, and change the database contents.

Let's look at a simple example to illustrate the concepts behind a database management system. Suppose you need to replace a part in your car. You go to an auto parts store and tell the clerk which part you need. The clerk looks up the part in a set of parts catalogs.

- The first book gives the clerk an identifying number for the part.
- The clerk then looks up this part number in another book. This book shows where the part is located within the store.
- After locating the part, the clerk again uses the number to find the cost of the part from a price list.

In this example, the actual automotive parts correspond to the data items in the database. The clerk, catalogs, lists, and storage bins, correspond to the database management system. To use this *automotive parts management system*, you tell the clerk what you want in a language that you both understand (English) and with terminology related to cars. "I need a carburetor for a 76 Belchfire 8," you say. The clerk takes care of all the business of getting the parts, keeping the books current, knowing how to use the books, and so forth. All you need to have is a reasonable idea of what you want. The clerk, the books, and catalogs take care of the rest.

The same is true for the computer *database management system* (DBMS). As soon as a DBMS is installed on a computer, the computer becomes an expert at all the details involved in storing, cataloging, and retrieving data. All you need to do is have a reasonable idea of what you want and know a little computer terminology. This book provides you with the computer terminology you need. The computer and the database management system take care of the rest.

Another example of a database management system is a large library. In many large libraries, particularly university research libraries, you are not usually allowed access to the shelves where the books are stored. To acquire a book, you must consult the card catalog, copy information from the index card on a slip of paper, and hand the paper to a librarian. Then — unseen by you, a "gnome" will "scuttle" through dark passageways to retrieve the book and deliver it to the librarian, who in turn delivers it to you.

When you return the book, much of this process is reversed. The librarian gives the book to a "gnome" who "scuttles" back to place the book in its original location. Again, the card catalog, the librarian, the "gnomes," and the storage facilities, correspond to the computer database management system. The book corresponds to the data item. All that is required of you is a little knowledge of how to use this system; the system does all the work.

OUR FIRST COMPUTER DATABASE

We have talked at length about our personal phone book, which makes a good basis for our first computer database. We will use it as an example and, as we proceed, you'll see that the process isn't much different from putting the information on a sheet of paper with an ordinary typewriter.

If we were going to type this information on a piece of paper, the person typing the information *might*

- Type a page title
- Determine how wide to make the column (how many spaces)
- Type column headings such as name, address, and phone number

With a computer database, these activities are *not* optional:

- You *must* give the database a title
- You *must* determine the size of each column
- You *must* assign each column a column title

In addition, you must tell the database what *kind* of information will be stored in each column.

DATABASE TERMINOLOGY

The personal phone book in Figure 1-2 is arranged as a table of rows and columns. The rows are called *records* and the columns are called *fields*. The column titles are *fieldnames*. The kind of information stored in a field is its *fieldtype*. The database title is the *filename*.

The Record

This entry is a RECORD:

Byers, Robert A Sr   9999 Glencrest, Standale   555-9242

Pieces of information that make up a RECORD are seen horizontally, displayed in rows across the page. Our phone book has eight rows — eight RECORDS — eight sets of name + address + phone number.

The Field

If we draw vertical lines between the names and addresses and between the addresses and phone numbers, we would isolate columns of similar information. We separate three groups of vertically arranged data — a column of names, a column of addresses, and a column of phone numbers. These columns are called FIELDS. Our phone book has three FIELDS.

The Fieldname

The column titles — Name, Address, and Phone Number — are called FIELDNAMES.

The Fieldtype

The columns in this database all contain ordinary *character* data. The *fieldtype* for each field is CHARACTER.

We are almost ready to start building our computerized version of a personal phone book. Before proceeding, you should know that computers have definite rules and surprising limitations.

Rules For Filenames

If we make a typewritten version of our personal phone book, we *might* give it a title. The title can be *anything* we want it to be: "Phone Book" or "Telephone List." The computer version *must* have a title. The title is its FILENAME. The FILENAME must conform to these rules:

- It can contain only letters and numbers
- It cannot be longer than 8 characters
- It cannot contain embedded blank spaces

In addition, the FILENAME is often preceded by an additional symbol to identify the disk drive which is to be used. A disk drive is identified by a letter followed by a colon, A:, for example.

Some possible titles (FILENAMES) for our computerized telephone book (database) are shown in Figure 1-3. You can give the database any name you choose as long as you follow the rules shown above.

```
                                          A:TELEFONE
              (for disk drive A)          A:FONEBOOK
                                          A:FONELIST


                       OR


                                          B:TELEFONE
              (for disk drive B)          B:FONEBOOK
                                          B:FONELIST
```

Figure 1-3

It is a good idea to choose filenames that help you to remember what is in the database. Like the filenames in Figure 1-3, these are examples of mnemonic (that is, intended to aid the memory) filenames:

CLIENTS   INVENTRY   PAYROLL   PERSONNL   QTRLYTAX

FIELDNAME

Column headings (FIELDNAMES) must be assigned to each of the columns (FIELDS) in the database. FIELDNAMES have rules similar to those for FILENAMES. A FIELDNAME:

- cannot have more than ten letters and numbers
- cannot contain embedded blank spaces
- *must* begin with a letter

Our simple phone list has three column headings (that is, three FIELDNAMES): Name, Address, and Phone Number. The first two (Name and Address) can be used as FIELDNAMES, but Phone Number can not. It has more than ten letters and contains an embedded blank space. So, we have to give this column a name such as FONENUMBER or PHONE or NUMBER to conform to the rules.

FIELDTYPE

The computer handles different kinds of data in different ways. So, we need to tell it which kind of data is contained in each column. This is called the FIELDTYPE or data type. Each field can be one of five types:

    CHARACTER
    DATE
    MEMO
    LOGICAL
    NUMERIC

In our example, all the FIELDS are CHARACTER FIELDS and may contain letters, numbers, spaces, and other standard typewriter symbols. Other fieldtypes — numeric, date, memo, and logical — will be explained fully in later examples.

FIELDWIDTH

We must tell the computer how "wide" the column is. The width is the number of typewriter spaces the field will contain.

Each time a record is entered the computer automatically gives it a number. It calls the first row (which is the first record) RECORD 1, the second RECORD 2, and so on. You could, indeed, work with databases for a long time and do some very involved work without ever using a record number. They are, however, convenient for some things, and we will discuss their usefulness later.

We have covered, then, some basic, pertinent terminology. Make sure you are comfortable with the concepts because we will now construct a simple database. Remember:

- Rows are RECORDS, automatically numbered by the computer.
- Columns are fields; they need titles called FIELDNAMES (ten characters maximum, no spaces, beginning with a letter).
- Each field must have a FIELDNAME, a FIELDTYPE, and a FIELDWIDTH.
- You must give the database a title, its FILENAME (eight characters maximum — no spaces).
- You should tell the computer where (which disk drive) to put the data (for example, A:FONEBOOK places the data on the A drive).

OUR FIRST EXERCISE

In this first exercise we will start from scratch. When the computer is first turned on, the video display should be similar to Figure 1-4. You are in your computer's *operating system*.

```
Current date is Tue  1-01-1980
Enter new date: 07/17/85
Current time is  0:02:44.28
Enter new time: 10:35


The IBM Personal Computer DOS
Version 2.00 (C)Copyright IBM Corp 1981, 1982, 1983

A>
```

Figure 1-4

THE OPERATING SYSTEM

Your computer has an operating system that helps you to control the computer. Database management systems such as dBASE III use the operating system to perform routine tasks. Although the operating system sometimes imposes specific ways of doing things on the database system, you will not need to learn the details of the operating system to use a database management system.

The A> is a *prompt*. It is the operating system's way of telling you "I'm ready, tell me what to do." The A designates the *logged* disk drive. The symbol to the right of the A> is called the cursor. The cursor is a light marker to show you where you are on the screen. It is the computer's equivalent of a pencil point. When you press a key on the keyboard, the character you pressed will appear on screen just where the cursor is. As each letter is typed, the cursor moves to the right.

The first examples in this book assume a computer with two floppy disk drives. If your computer is equipped with a fixed (or hard) disk, the screen will probably show a C> instead of the A> of Figure 1-4. *If you are using a fixed disk, substitute C: for B: as the disk drive identifier in the examples.* Appendix A contains information about how to copy dBASE onto the fixed disk drive.

GETTING YOUR COMPUTER TO USE dBASE

dBASE comes on two floppy disks labeled SYSTEM DISK #1 and SYSTEM DISK #2. Place the floppy disk labeled SYSTEM DISK #1 into the A disk drive. To use dBASE, you must load it into the computer's memory: Type **DBASE** at the A> prompt. The video display should be similar to Figure 1-5. Press the Return key.

```
Current date is Tue  1-01-1980
Enter new date: 07/17/85
Current time is  0:02:44.28
Enter new time: 10:35


The IBM Personal Computer DOS
Version 2.00 (C)Copyright IBM Corp 1981, 1982, 1983

A>dbase
```

Figure 1-5

dBASE takes several seconds to load; while the program is loading, the red light on the disk drive will be lit. When SYSTEM DISK #1 has loaded, the computer will tell you to remove SYSTEM DISK #1 and to insert SYSTEM DISK #2 into the A disk drive. When you have done so, press Return. Again, this disk will take several seconds to load. *Leave SYSTEM DISK #2 in the A disk drive during the entire time you are using dBASE.*

The screen will resemble Figure 1-6. The top line on the screen tells you exactly what you have installed. dBASE III PLUS is the name of the database management system. "Version 1.0" tells you the particular edition of dBASE III PLUS. The date that follows is the release date of the particular version. A version number is similar to a model identifier, and usually each new version has all the features of earlier versions, plus new and/or improved features.

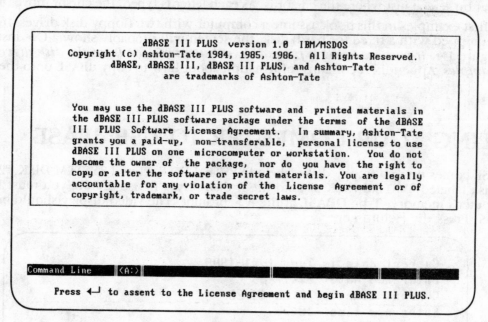

Figure 1-6

What happens next will depend on the version of dBASE and how it has been *installed*. For many readers, the screen will resemble Figure 1-7. This is the dBASE Assistant — a special subprogram of dBASE that is intended to make dBASE easier to use for a beginner. The Assistant lets you use dBASE through a menu of database options. We'll cover the Assistant in detail later on in this book. For some readers, the screen may look like that shown in Figure 1-8. This is the command mode of dBASE. In this mode you use simple commands to tell dBASE what you want it to do.

Most modern database managers have both command and menu modes of operation. Which you choose will depend a great deal upon the complexity of your task and how often you use the database.

To give you a better feel for using a database management system, we will be using the command mode of dBASE. If the screen shows the Assistant, press the Esc key. This will take you out of the Assistant and place you in the command mode.

The screen should now look like that shown in Figure 1-8. The cursor is located above the *status bar* and just to the right of a DOT. This DOT is called the DOT PROMPT. The DOT PROMPT is dBASE's way of telling you "I'm ready, tell me to do something." You tell it what to do with COMMANDS. In dBASE, the commands are simple English words and phrases.

Earlier versions of dBASE do not have the status bar. You can turn the status bar off by typing SET STATUS OFF after a dot prompt.

. SET STATUS OFF

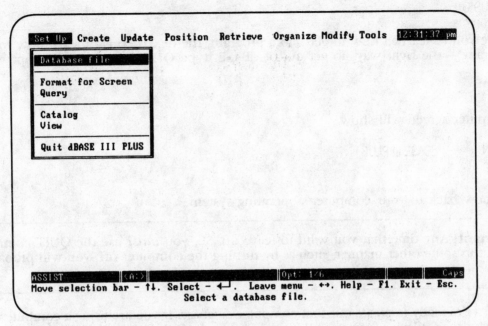

Figure 1-7

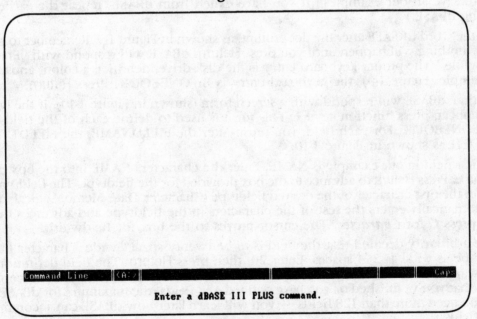

Figure 1-8

Then press the Return key. SET STATUS OFF is a command. After each command you must press Return. Pressing the Return key tells dBASE "Do it now!" To turn the status bar back on, type:

Database

. SET STATUS ON

Once you've learned how to get into a program, the next step is to learn how to get out of the program — the right way. To get out of dBASE, type **QUIT** after a dot prompt.

. QUIT

The computer screen will show

***END RUN   dBASE III PLUS
A>

You are now back to your computer's operating system.

Important: Any time that you want to leave dBASE, you *must* use the QUIT command. If you exit in some other manner, such as by turning the computer off, you will probably lose data.

Now we're ready to create our first computer database. If you are using a computer with only floppy disk drives, place a formatted floppy disk into the B disk drive (see Appendix B). We'll use this disk to save all our examples. (If you have exited from dBASE, repeat the earlier directions for entering dBASE.)

Type the word CREATE after the dot prompt, as shown in Figure 1-9. Remember to press **Return**. Absolutely nothing will happen until you press **Return**. dBASE will respond with "Enter the name of the new file." The proper keyboard entry is the disk-drive identifier, a colon, and the filename. In our example (Figure 1-9), the keyboard entry is B:FONEBOOK. Press **Return**.

This time dBASE will respond with a screen form (shown in Figure 1-10). If the boxed legend does not appear, press function key F1. This form is used to define each of the fields in the new database FONEBOOK. For each field, you must enter the FIELDNAME, the FIELDTYPE, and the FIELDWIDTH as shown in Figure 1-10.

The first field in our example is NAME. Enter the characters NAME into the box provided for the fieldname. Press **Return** to advance to the box provided for the fieldtype. The fieldtype is selected by typing in the first character of the desired fieldtype (Character, Date, Memo, Logical, or Numeric). dBASE automatically enters the rest of the characters in the fieldtype and advances the cursor. In this case, press C for *Character*. The cursor moves to the box for fieldwidth.

We've arbitrarily decided that the field is to be twenty spaces wide. Character fields such as NAME can be as wide as 254 spaces. Enter 20, then press **Return**. The field definition for NAME is complete, and dBASE is ready to accept the next field definition. This process continues until you signal that you've finished or you have defined 128 fields (the maximum for dBASE III). (Don't worry if you need more than 128 fields — you will learn later how dBASE can accommodate more than 128 fields.)

To tell dBASE that you've finished with the field definition process, press the Return key when prompted to define another field. In this example, the Return key was pressed when the computer asked for the fieldname for field four — because this database has only three fields (NAME, AD-DRESS, PHONE). Once you've defined the fields in your database, you're ready to begin entering the data.

Chapter One

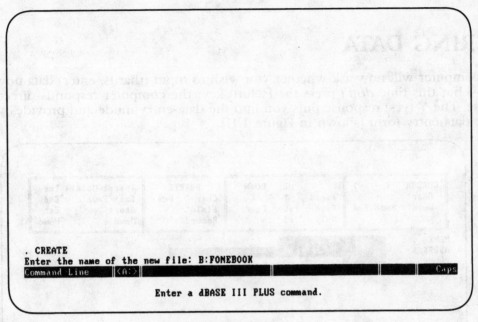

. CREATE
Enter the name of the new file: B:FONEBOOK
Command Line   ⟨A:⟩   Caps

Enter a dBASE III PLUS command.

Figure 1-9

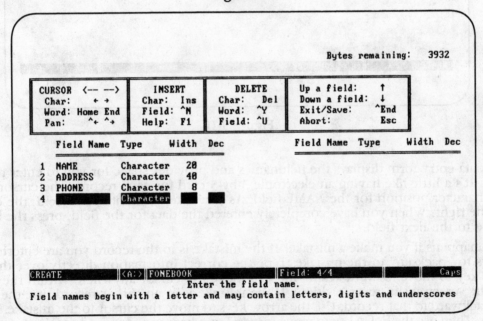

```
                                                        Bytes remaining:   3932


     CURSOR  <-- -->      INSERT          DELETE        Up a field:     ↑
     Char:     ← →     Char:  Ins      Char:   Del      Down a field:   ↓
     Word: Home End    Field: ^N       Word:   ^Y       Exit/Save:      ^End
     Pan:    ^← ^→     Help:  F1       Field:  ^U       Abort:          Esc

         Field Name  Type     Width  Dec       Field Name  Type    Width  Dec

      1  NAME        Character   20
      2  ADDRESS     Character   40
      3  PHONE       Character    8
      4              Character


 CREATE            ⟨A:⟩ FONEBOOK                    Field: 4/4                Caps
                     Enter the field name.
 Field names begin with a letter and may contain letters, digits and underscores
```

Figure 1-10

Database

ENTERING DATA

The computer will now ask whether you wish to input (that is, enter) data now. Enter a Y (for yes) — but this time *don't* press the Return key; the computer responds directly to the Y in this case. The Y (yes) response puts you into the data-entry mode and provides you with an electronic data-entry form (shown in Figure 1-11).

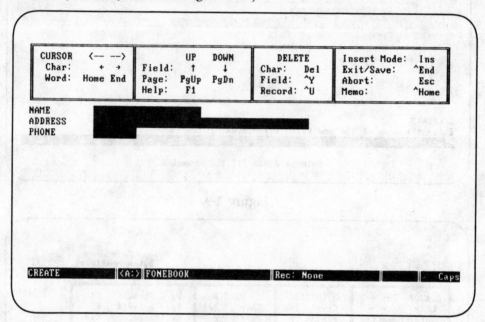

```
CURSOR    <-- -->      UP   DOWN      DELETE         Insert Mode: Ins
Char:       ←   →   Field:  ↑     ↓   Char:   Del    Exit/Save:   ^End
Word:   Home End    Page: PgUp PgDn   Field:  ^Y     Abort:       Esc
                    Help:  F1         Record: ^U     Memo:        ^Home

NAME
ADDRESS
PHONE




CREATE        <A:> FONEBOOK              Rec: None             Caps
```

Figure 1-11

This data-entry form displays the fieldnames and provides space for you to enter the data for each field. It's a little like having an electronic 3-by-5 card for each record. The cursor will be in the first character position for the NAME field. As you enter data into each field, the cursor will move to the right. When you have completely entered the data for the field, press the Return key to advance to the next field.

What happens if you make a mistake? If the mistake is in the record you are entering, use the arrow keys to "back up" to the mistake. Type the correct information directly over the old. Use the arrow key to move forward again. You can move the cursor anywhere within the data-entry area (on the screen it's in reverse video). If the mistake is in an earlier record, use the PgUp key to move backward to that record. Use the arrow keys to move the cursor to the mistake. Make your correction. Then use the PgDn key to move forward to where you were and continue entering data.

When you have entered all of the data for a record (Figure 1-12), the computer clears the screen and provides you with a new, blank data-entry form for the next record. This process continues until you signal dBASE that you're finished.

To tell dBASE that you're finished, press the Return key — with the cursor positioned to the beginning of a new, blank record. dBASE will exit from CREATE and respond with a dot prompt, indicating that it is ready to accept further commands.

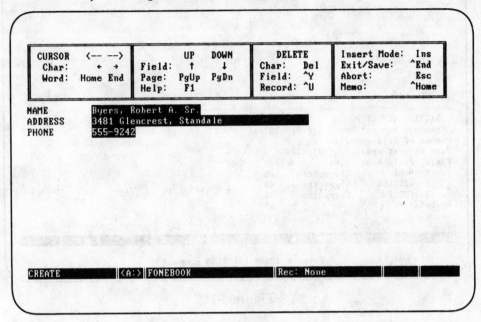

Figure 1-12

Earlier, we identified fields as *vertical columns*. Now the data for the vertical columns is entered as consecutive rows on the screen — for convenience in entering the data. The computer places each field entry into a *vertical column* in the database.

USING THE DATABASE

We now have a database. It has eight records and three fields; NAME, ADDRESS, PHONE. Its filename is FONEBOOK, and it is on the B drive. We can use this database at any time by typing USE B:FONEBOOK (and a Return) after a dot prompt.

. USE B:FONEBOOK

The computer responds with another dot prompt on the next line. The database B:FONEBOOK is now ready for use. You may have many databases available on your computer. By specifying "B:FONEBOOK," you tell the computer you wish to work with the database located on the B drive whose FILENAME is FONEBOOK. USE B:FONEBOOK is similar to saying to your assistant, "Chatsworth, please get me the phone book in my study."

Let's "use" it first to look at our newly created structure. The structure of the database is really determined by the definition of the fields (columns). To review the structure, type DISPLAY STRUCTURE following a dot prompt. The computer will respond with the display shown in Figure 1-13.

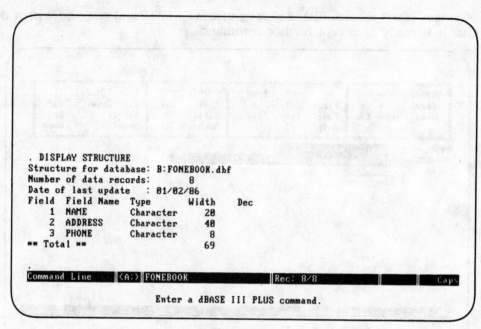

```
. DISPLAY STRUCTURE
Structure for database: B:FONEBOOK.dbf
Number of data records:       8
Date of last update   : 01/02/86
Field  Field Name  Type        Width    Dec
    1  NAME        Character      20
    2  ADDRESS     Character      40
    3  PHONE       Character       8
** Total **                       69
.
```

| Command Line | ⟨A:⟩ FONEBOOK | | Rec: 8/8 | | | Caps |

Enter a dBASE III PLUS command.

Figure 1-13

Notice that the dBASE has added a .DBF to the FILENAME of the database. This is the filetype. The filetype tells dBASE how to deal with a specific file — as we'll see later, dBASE uses several different kinds of files. The *Date of last update* is the date of the last change to this database file. This date is taken from your computer's internal clock calendar. The *Total* at the bottom indicates the number of characters in a record. Note that the "TOTAL" is one more than the number of characters used onscreen. dBASE uses one character of "overhead" for each database record.

Once you've created your database, you can add new records at any time by simply using it (USE), and typing the command APPEND after a dot prompt. APPEND is the dBASE command to add records to an existing database. APPEND works just like the part of dBASE that adds records to a newly created database.

Now that we have "used" B:FONEBOOK and viewed its structure, let's move on to the major "use" for databases: the retrieval of stored information. Perhaps we wish to retrieve some of the information we have stored so that we can look at it. One way to look at the information is to type DISPLAY ALL after a dot prompt. DISPLAY ALL is the dBASE command that displays the entire contents of the database. The result of this command is shown in Figure 1-14.

The left-hand column displays the automatically assigned RECORD NUMBER we discussed previously. If you do not want the record number displayed, type DISPLAY ALL OFF instead of DISPLAY ALL. The computer will generate the same display — except the record numbers will not be shown.

You can specify *which* records are to be displayed. Earlier, we talked about searching through the phone book to find the owner of a particular phone number. To demonstrate how to select records, let's tell dBASE to display the record containing the particular phone number 998-1234. The command looks like:

Chapter One

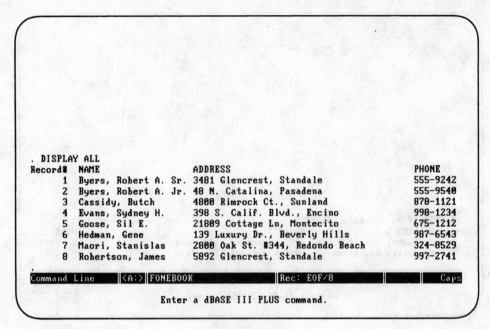

```
. DISPLAY ALL
Record#  NAME                   ADDRESS                             PHONE
      1  Byers, Robert A. Sr.   3481 Glencrest, Standale            555-9242
      2  Byers, Robert A. Jr.   48 N. Catalina, Pasadena            555-9540
      3  Cassidy, Butch         4800 Rimrock Ct., Sunland           878-1121
      4  Evans, Sydney H.       398 S. Calif. Blvd., Encino         998-1234
      5  Goose, Sil E.          21809 Cottage Ln, Montecito         675-1212
      6  Hedman, Gene           139 Luxury Dr., Beverly Hills       987-6543
      7  Maori, Stanislas       2800 Oak St. #344, Redondo Beach    324-8529
      8  Robertson, James       5892 Glencrest, Standale            997-2741
.
Command Line     |<A:>|FONEBOOK          |Rec: EOF/8      |      |   Caps
```

Enter a dBASE III PLUS command.

Figure 1-14

```
. DISPLAY FOR PHONE='998-1234'
    RECORD#    NAME                ADDRESS                       PHONE
    4          Evans, Sydney H.    398 S. Calif Blvd., Encino, CA    998-1234
```

This command looks straightforward and it is. The word FOR tells dBASE that we want to select records. We also have to tell it what to look for (the actual phone number) and the name of the field to be searched (PHONE). This short instruction tells dBASE to *look through* the entire database and *display* each record containing the characters *998-1234* in the phone column.

The single quotation marks around the phone number in the command are called DELIMITERS. They identify the beginning and the end of what is called a CHARACTER STRING. The characters between the quotes are exactly — to the letter and the space — what dBASE is to search for.

The phone number must be identified as a character string because the phone number field (PHONE) is a character field. As we mentioned earlier, dBASE has numeric fields. Why isn't the phone number stored in a numeric field? After all, it's all numbers. Numbers are interesting. We can treat them as either numbers or as a symbol such as a comma or the letter A. A good rule of thumb is to store numbers as simple characters unless they are to be used in arithmetic calculations. There is a host of "numeric" data that is usually treated in this way: phone numbers, zip codes, social security numbers, and so on. Almost never do we use these "numbers" in calculations.

When we use numbers in a command, as in the above example, the delimiters tell dBASE to treat the number as a character string. Digits enclosed by quotes are considered to be characters. Digits that are not enclosed by quotes are considered to be numbers. 555 is a number. '555' is a character string. All character strings — not just those containing numbers — are enclosed by quotes when used in a command.

Now, let's tell dBASE to show us everyone who lives in Standale:

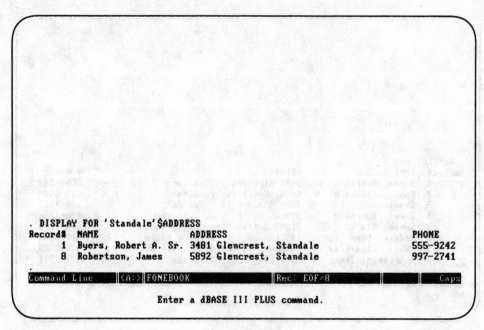

```
. DISPLAY FOR 'Standale'$ADDRESS
Record#  NAME                     ADDRESS                          PHONE
      1  Byers, Robert A. Sr.  3481 Glencrest, Standale            555-9242
      8  Robertson, James      5892 Glencrest, Standale            997-2741

Command Line    <A:> FONEBOOK              Rec: EOF/8                  Caps
                   Enter a dBASE III PLUS command.
```

Figure 1-15

Just as before, the character string is enclosed in single quotes. This example, however, looks a little more exotic. The dollar sign ($) is shorthand for *contained in*. This command tells dBASE to look through the entire database and display every record that contains the characters "Standale" anywhere in the address column. Suppose that we issue *almost* the same command — except we use all uppercase letters for STANDALE — as in Figure 1-16.

This time the computer responds with a dot prompt: This means that there are no records with the character string STANDALE in the address field. The character strings Standale and STANDALE are different. The first uses uppercase and lowercase letters, the second uses all uppercase letters. You and I would know they mean the same thing, but the computer doesn't. The computer takes these instructions literally. Computers are fast, but they're not particularly bright.

As another example of the computer's literal interpretation, let's tell it to display all the records containing the character string "Robert". The computer's response is shown in Figure 1-17. This is an example of a character-string search where the computer gave more information than we thought we asked it for. The point here is that *it did exactly what it was told to do*. In this case, we wanted a display of everyone whose first name was Robert. This would have been obtained by using ' ,Robert' instead of 'Robert' in the instructions. This is because 'Robert' as a first name always follows a comma.

To remove a little more of the mystique for you from computer database operations, let's take a look at the process that goes on when we say DISPLAY FOR 'Standale'$ADDRESS.

- The computer goes to the beginning of the database (Record 1) and looks through the ADDRESS field of Record 1 to see whether the CHARACTER STRING 'Standale' is there.
- If it is there, the computer will display all of Record 1.
- If it is not there, the computer will not display any part of Record 1.

Chapter One

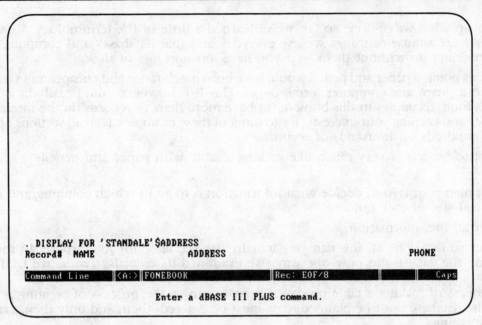

Figure 1-16

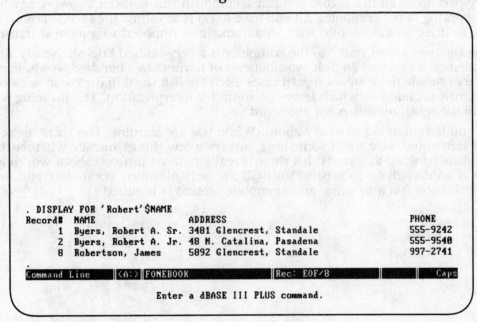

Figure 1-17

- When Record 1 has been examined and either displayed on the terminal or not, the computer will proceed to examine Record 2 in exactly the same manner.
- This record-by-record examination of the ADDRESS field continues until every record has been examined.

Database

Let's recap what we've done so far. We've learned a little of the terminology. We've learned that databases are similar to things we use everyday and that databases and computers can't do anything you can't do without them — if you have lots and lots of time.

Up to this point, a paper and pencil would have been much faster and cheaper and you wouldn't have needed to learn any computer terminology. This list, however, could easily be 80, 800, or 8000 names long. Examples in this book never have more than 15 records (in the interest of conserving paper and keeping your interest). Try to think of these examples as small sections of databases containing hundreds or thousands of records.

The entire process is very much like making a table with paper and pencil:

- You must plan your layout, decide what information is to go in which columns, and determine the physical size of each column.
- You enter all the information.
- Only after you've done all this can you actually use the table for its purpose. In this chapter we "used" the database in only one way: We examined its records; that is, we DISPLAYed it.

The process of making a table on paper is analogous to the process of creating a computer database: The database must be planned; data must be entered; then, and only then, can you use it to do something.

The nice part about all this is that you can accomplish this without knowing anything about the internal working of the computer. All you have to do is to follow the (dBASE) rules. It's a little like learning to drive an automobile with an automatic as opposed to a manual transmission.

The language you use to "talk" to the computer is a *very* limited English. Nearly all commercially available databases have "English" vocabularies of fewer than a hundred words. Furthermore, unlike ordinary English, there are no special cases. Each English word in the computer's vocabulary has a very narrow meaning — which leaves no room for interpretation. The meaning will be *one* of the common English meanings for the word.

Finally, you have nothing to worry about. While you are learning, you *can't* break the computer. If you aren't quite sure about something, just try a few things and see whether they work. Probably the hardest thing to learn is that there is really nothing difficult about working with the computer; it is an easy thing to master. You will use only a limited vocabulary and no difficult physical coordination (such as using an automobile clutch) is required.

CHAPTER TWO

A SIMPLE DATABASE EXAMPLE

Now that you're familiar with what a computerized database is, we are ready to move on and investigate more facets of database capability. Although the personal telephone book exercise used a familiar example to cover the creation of a database, the example didn't offer enough material to demonstrate the full range of computer database management.

So, it is time to begin our second database project. Our new project will use the computer with its database management system to conduct an inventory of a retail store. We've chosen this example because most readers will be familiar with the concept of conducting an inventory. In addition, it will allow us to work with *numeric* fields as well as character fields, and with records that can be grouped into categories. For the chapter finale, we will prepare the report shown in Figure 2-1.

For the subject of our inventory we have chosen to use a *very* small liquor store. This store is *so* small that it carries only fifteen items in stock. Nevertheless, this is more than enough to demonstrate database concepts.

To be useful, our inventory database must contain data that will be of interest to the store owner. Likely items include:

Type of liquor
Brand name
Container size
Amount of stock on hand
Wholesale cost
Retail price

```
Page No.      1
08/31/85

                     LIQUOR STORE INVENTRY


    BRAND NAME              SIZE      QTY      COST     INVEST

**   BOURBON
    SOUTHERN ARISTOCRACY    1/2 GAL     3      6.89      20.67
    SOUTHERN ARISTOCRACY    QUART      21      3.50      73.50
    SOUTHERN ARISTOCRACY    FIFTH      22      1.78      39.16
    SOUTHERN ARISTOCRACY    PINT        5      0.99       4.95
    SOUTHERN ARISTOCRACY    2 LITER     5      6.47      32.35
**  Subtotal **
                                      56                170.63


**   SCOTCH
    AULD COUNTRY            2 LITER     7      9.78      68.46
    AULD COUNTRY            PINT       88      2.74     241.12
    AULD COUNTRY            QUART      23      5.59     128.57
**  Subtotal **
                                     118                438.15

**   VODKA
    REAL RUSSIAN            PINT       75      1.49     111.75
    REAL RUSSIAN            2 LITER     9      7.95      71.55
    REAL RUSSIAN            QUART      35      3.78     132.30
**  Subtotal **
                                     119                315.60

**   WHISKEY
    OLD WYOMING            QUART      19      5.29     100.51
    OLD WYOMING            PINT       44      1.98      87.12
    SOUTHERN RYE           QUART      32      5.11     163.52
**  Subtotal **
                                      95                351.15

*** Total ***
                                     388               1275.53
```

Figure 2-1: A sample report

Chapter Two

These items become the columns (fields) in our new database. Just as in the personal book example, we use the CREATE command to create the database and define its structure.

```
. CREATE
Enter the name of the new file: B:INVENTRY
```

The first step is to assign our new database a filename. We have chosen the filename INVENTRY. "Liquor Store Inventory" is too large and contains embedded blank spaces. INVENTRY is descriptive and is only eight characters long. We have placed this database file on the B disk drive.

Next, we define each of the fields for our new database. The field definitions form the *structure* for the database. Each field definition consists of a *fieldname*, a *fieldtype*, and a *fieldwidth*. The completed field definitions are shown in Figure 2-2.

- LIQUOR is the fieldname for the column to contain the *kind of* liquor. It is a character field that is 10 spaces wide.
- BRAND is the fieldname for the column to contain the brand names. This is a character field 20 spaces wide.
- SIZE is the fieldname for the *container size*. It is a character field 7 spaces wide.
- QUANTITY is the fieldname for the column to contain the amount of stock on hand. This is a numeric field which is 3 digits wide. This field width allows values of up to 999 for each item in the inventory.
- COST and PRICE are numeric fields for *unit cost* and *price*. Unlike QUANTITY, they have decimal places. We want to allow for prices up to 999.99. This is a decimal number with 2 decimal places. The field size is 6 bytes — 5 digits plus the decimal point.

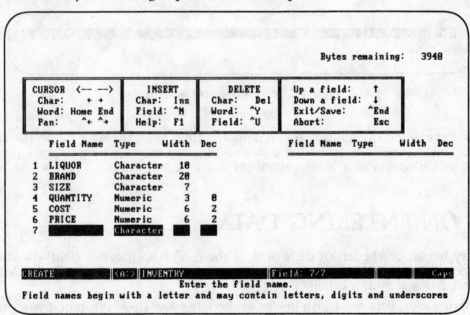

Figure 2-2: Field sizes

Simple Database Example

When the data to define the INVENTRY database has been entered, the screen will resemble Figure 2-2. To tell dBASE that we've finished, we simply press the Return key when prompted to enter the fieldname for field 7. This action *saves* the structure of our new database on the disk. dBASE will then ask

Input data records now? (Y/N)

With your Y (yes) response, you will be presented with a screen "form" like that shown in Figure 2-3. You can enter data into this form just as you would if you were using a typewriter. A representative record for this database is shown as Figure 2-4.

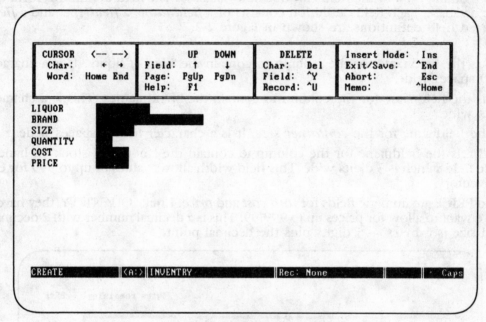

Figure 2-3: Data-entry screen

The data-entry process continues, one record at a time, until the data for all the records has been entered. This database has only fifteen records. To stop entering new records, press the Esc key when presented with a new blank record (in this case, record 16).

NOTES ON ENTERING DATA

Data entry begins on the left of each field. If the field is a character field, the data remains at the left edge, just as it would if you were typing on a piece of paper. This is called *left justification*. Character fields are left-justified.

For numeric fields, data entry also begins at the left edge. However, when you press Return (telling dBASE that you have finished entering data into the field), the number will automatically move to the right edge of the field. This is called *right justification*. Numeric fields are right-justified.

Chapter Two

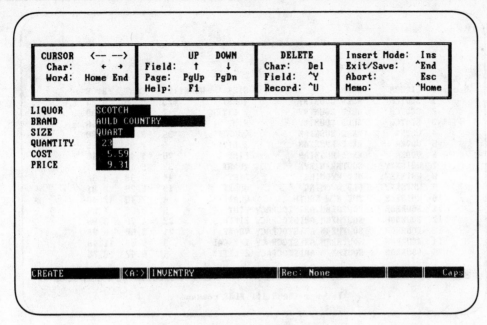

Figure 2-4: A sample record

You will not be allowed to enter a letter into a numeric field. The letter will not be accepted and the computer will beep.

While entering data, you can use the *arrow keys* to move the cursor anywhere in the data-entry area. This lets you "back up" to a previous character or digit and "reenter" it by simply typing the new value over the old. You can even "back up" to a previous record by pressing the PgUp key. If you do so, you can return to your new record with the PgDn key. If for any reason you exit from entering new records before you intended, you can resume adding records by typing APPEND after a dot prompt.

. APPEND

When we exit from the data-entry mode we are still "using" our database. To view the contents of INVENTRY, type the command LIST after a dot prompt. This command will display the complete contents of the INVENTRY database (as shown in Figure 2-5).

One of the objectives of an inventory is to find out how much money we have tied up in inventory. When we finish an inventory in the conventional way — that is, with paper and pencil — we haul out the calculator and begin to compute the value of the inventory. The inventory value is obtained by multiplying each quantity by the corresponding cost and then adding the results. Each step in this process provides an opportunity for *error*. If, on the other hand, we have done the inventory with dBASE, we can get an *error-free* result immediately. With the dBASE computerized database, our only chance for error is during the initial data entry. With the manual method, we could make a mistake every time we use a number.

Simple Database Example

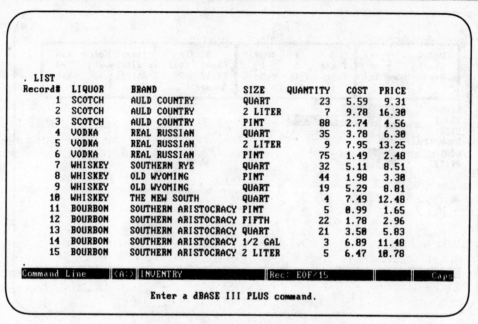

```
. LIST
Record#  LIQUOR    BRAND                 SIZE      QUANTITY   COST   PRICE
      1  SCOTCH    AULD COUNTRY          QUART          23    5.59   9.31
      2  SCOTCH    AULD COUNTRY          2 LITER         7    9.78  16.30
      3  SCOTCH    AULD COUNTRY          PINT           88    2.74   4.56
      4  VODKA     REAL RUSSIAN          QUART          35    3.78   6.30
      5  VODKA     REAL RUSSIAN          2 LITER         9    7.95  13.25
      6  VODKA     REAL RUSSIAN          PINT           75    1.49   2.48
      7  WHISKEY   SOUTHERN RYE          QUART          32    5.11   8.51
      8  WHISKEY   OLD WYOMING           PINT           44    1.98   3.30
      9  WHISKEY   OLD WYOMING           QUART          19    5.29   8.81
     10  WHISKEY   THE NEW SOUTH         QUART           4    7.49  12.48
     11  BOURBON   SOUTHERN ARISTOCRACY  PINT            5    0.99   1.65
     12  BOURBON   SOUTHERN ARISTOCRACY  FIFTH          22    1.78   2.96
     13  BOURBON   SOUTHERN ARISTOCRACY  QUART          21    3.50   5.83
     14  BOURBON   SOUTHERN ARISTOCRACY  1/2 GAL         3    6.89  11.48
     15  BOURBON   SOUTHERN ARISTOCRACY  2 LITER         5    6.47  10.78
.
Command Line    <A:> INVENTRY             Rec: EOF/15             Caps
Enter a dBASE III PLUS command.
```

Figure 2-5: Contents of INVENTRY

EXTRACTING INFORMATION

The dBASE command to request the value of the inventory looks like:

```
. SUM COST * QUANTITY
       15 records summed
   COST * QUANTITY
       1305.49
```

This command tells dBASE to multiply the COST by QUANTITY for each record in the database and to *total* the results. The result (1305.49) is printed just below the command. The asterisk (*) is the symbol used to indicate multiplication in dBASE.

Suppose we want to know how much we have invested in Scotch. We can limit the command to just the Scotch records by adding a *condition* as shown below.

```
. SUM COST * QUANTITY FOR LIQUOR = 'SCOTCH'
       3 records summed
   COST * QUANTITY
       438.15
```

Now, let's find the investment in *quarts* of Scotch. The command and its result are shown below. Note how much these commands resemble ordinary English. The word "and" has periods at both ends. Although it looks like the English "and," it is a special .AND. called a *Boolean* operator.

```
. SUM COST * QUANTITY FOR LIQUOR = 'SCOTCH' .AND. SIZE = 'QUART'
        1 record summed
     COST * QUANTITY
           128.57
```

Simple computations like these only scratch the surface of the tools that dBASE provides to extract information from a database. You can actually obtain entire formal reports that organize and display your information in just the way that you want it — with only two commands.

STANDARD REPORTS

Most database management systems have a built-in *report generator* to help you prepare reports from your database. Figure 2-1 is an example of a report prepared by the dBASE report generator. A dBASE report is prepared from the database with a *report form*. A report form is prepared with the CREATE REPORT command. A report form is saved on the disk and can be used over and over again. A report form can be changed with MODIFY REPORT.

To show you how this works, we will create the report form used to prepare the report shown in Figure 2-1. Type CREATE REPORT at the dot prompt.

```
. CREATE REPORT
Enter report file name: B:INVENTRY
```

A report form is a disk file and, therefore, must have a filename. The rules for report form filenames are the same as for database filenames. They can be up to eight characters long, and they may not contain embedded blank spaces. To help us remember which database file the report form "belongs to," we will name it after the database — INVENTRY.

You might wonder how the computer can tell the difference between INVENTRY (the database) and INVENTRY (the report form). Remember that dBASE adds the .DBF file identifier to database files. dBASE uses several different kinds of disk files, and has its own labeling system to keep them identified. The .DBF identifier is added to database filenames automatically; .FRM is added to report form filenames.

Once you've entered the filename, you will be guided through the process of describing exactly what you want included in the report and what you want the report to look like. dBASE provides a series of five screen menus to help you define your report. The first of these menus, the Options menu, is shown in Figure 2-6. The names of all five menus — Options, Groups, Columns, Locate, and Exit — are located at the top of the screen. The bottom two lines on the screen contain additional information on how to navigate through the five menus.

The name of the *active menu* and one item within the menu are highlighted in reverse video. You can change these selections with the arrow keys. The Left and Right arrow keys move the highlight that selects the menu while the Up and Down arrow keys are used to highlight an item within a menu.

To make entries or changes in any of the five menus, first highlight the desired selection using the arrow keys. Then, press Return to "enter" the selection. Make the appropriate entry, then press Return again to "exit" from the selection.

Options

The Options menu is used to enter a report title and make adjustments to the page layout. The standard values for each item in the Options menu are shown in the right-hand column of the menu. For our report, we want to set both the left and right page margins to 10 characters. Use the Down arrow key to highlight *Left margin*. Press Return to "enter" the menu selection. Type the new value over the old, then press Return to leave the menu selection.

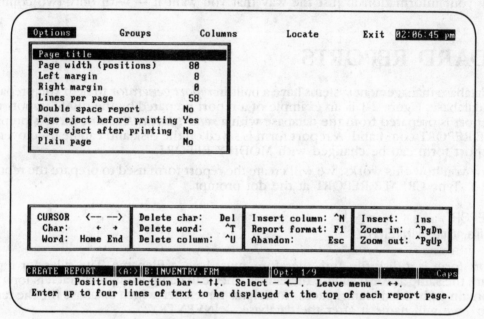

Figure 2-6: Options menu

The Report Title: To enter a title, highlight *Page title*, then press Return. A box will appear to the right of the Options menu, as shown in Figure 2-7. Enter the title into the title box. Press the Return key again. When the report is printed, the title will be centered automatically within the page margins.

Groups

For this menu to make any sense, you need to know what a *group* is. Look at the data shown in Figure 2-5. All the entries for each kind of LIQUOR are in adjacent records — these records are *grouped* by the contents of the LIQUOR field. In this little database, we have four groups — one for each kind of liquor. Keep in mind that the report does not actually rearrange data — it just formats the output when like data items are in adjacent records. Look at Figure 2-1 to see how these data items are grouped in the report.

The Groups menu is shown as Figure 2-8. Use the Up and Down arrow keys to highlight the selection *Group on expression*. Press the Return key to enter the selection, and then type in the

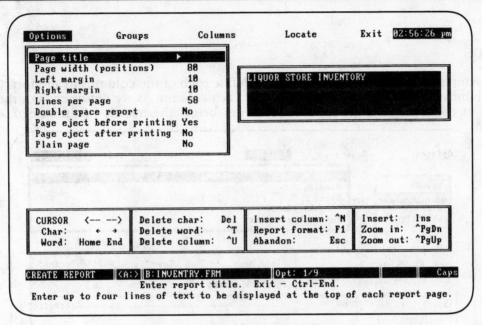

Figure 2-7 Report title menu

fieldname LIQUOR. This will cause the content of the LIQUOR field to be printed at the beginning of each liquor group. It will also cause subtotals to be printed for each kind of liquor. Numeric columns within groups will automatically be subtotalled if the column is to be totalled.

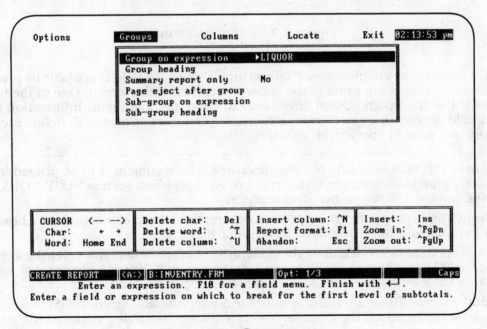

Figure 2-8: Groups menu

Simple Database Example

Columns

This menu, shown as Figure 2-9, is used to define each of the columns in a report. Our report has five columns. We will use this menu once for each column. As we define each of the columns, a mock-up of the report is built up in the box just below the middle of the screen.

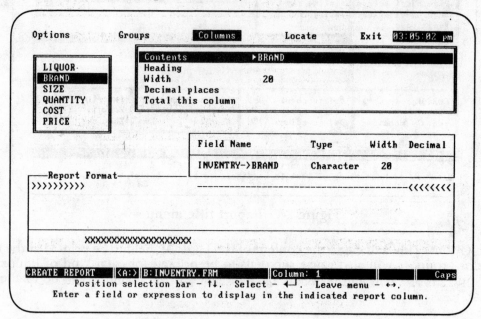

Figure 2-9: Columns menu

To make defining the columns easier, information about each field is available by pressing **F10**. The fieldnames will appear in a box in the upper left corner of the screen. One of the fieldnames is highlighted. Use the Up and Down arrow keys to move the hightlight. Information about the highlighted field appears in a box immediately below the Columns menu. To define each column in the report, we need to specify the following:

Contents: This item is usually just the fieldname whose content is to be printed in the particular column. Content can be the result of an expression, such as COST * QUANTITY as in the last column in the sample report.

Heading: This item specifies the (optional) column title. If you choose to have a heading, it can have up to 4 lines, as shown in Figure 2-10.

Width: This value is the width of the column as printed. When you enter the column content, dBASE will automatically assign a column width. You can change that assignment to a value that you might think is more appropriate.

Decimal places: These are filled in only for numeric fields. Again, dBASE will assign an initial value based on the content. You can change that value as necessary.

Chapter Two

Total this column: This value is normally NO. However, for numeric fields you can elect to have dBASE compute column totals. If you elect to have totals and the report is *grouped* as in this example, the totalled fields are automatically subtotalled by group. For our sample report, we get subtotals for each kind of liquor.

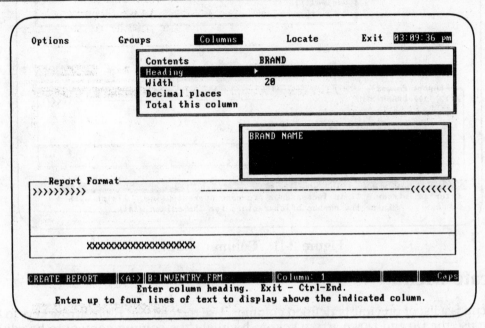

Figure 2-10: Column heading

As each column is defined, you must tell dBASE that you want to advance to the next column. To move from column to column use the PgDn key. To move back to a previous column definition, use the PgUp key.

A sample column definition for the brand name information is shown in Figures 2-9 through 2-11. These three screens set *Contents* to the field BRAND, Heading to BRAND NAME, and *Width* to 25. The complete column definitions for the report of Figure 2-1 are shown in the table below.

Contents	Heading	Width	Decimal places	Total this column
BRAND	BRAND NAME	25		
SIZE	SIZE	7		
QUANTITY	QTY	3	0	Yes
COST	COST	10	2	No
COST*QUANTITY	INVEST	10	2	Yes

Simple Database Example

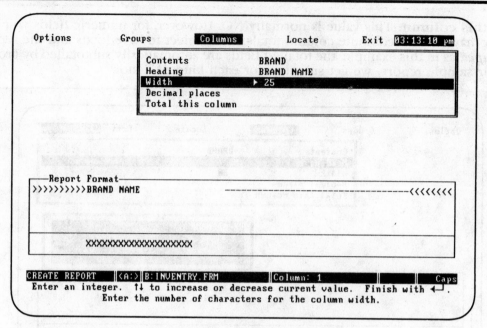

Figure 2-11: Column width

The Locate Menu

This menu is a list of previously defined columns. Use the Left and Right arrow keys to highlight *Locate*, then use the Up and Down arrow keys to highlight the column content to be edited. Press the Return key. This will take you to that column in the *Columns* option.

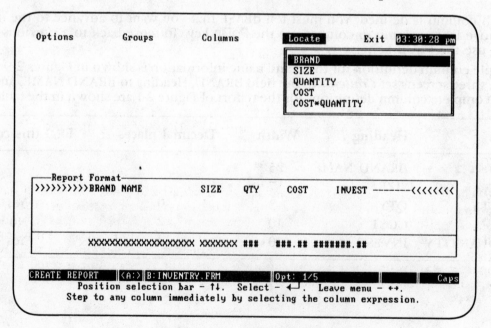

Figure 2-12: Locate menu

Chapter Two

The Exit Menu

This menu has two choices, *Save* and *Abandon*. Use the Up and Down arrows to highlight your selection — in this case *Save* — then press Return.

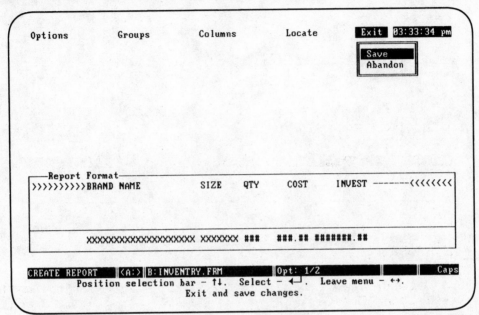

Figure 2-13: Exit menu

This step completes the preparation of the report form that will prepare the inventory report shown in Figure 2-1. This report form can be changed at any time with the MODIFY REPORT command. To run the report, use the command:

. REPORT

To obtain a printed copy of your report, add TO PRINT to the command:

. REPORT TO PRINT

If we had actually conducted an inventory with pencil and paper, we would have spent a considerable amount of time making the final calculations. When we conduct the same inventory with a database management system, the final results are available within seconds. In addition, we significantly reduce the chances for error. All this is possible without knowing anything about a computer, computer programming, or even database management. All we have to do is follow the simple steps outlined above. If you think about it, the example is remarkable: All this has come from just two basic commands, CREATE and REPORT.

CHAPTER THREE

SORTING AND INDEXING

One of the attractions of a database management system is its ability to *sort* the data records. We can easily rearrange the records so they appear in virtually any order that is convenient for us — alphabetical, chronological, or numeric. In the last chapter, the records in the liquor store inventory were entered alphabetically by the type of liquor. In effect, they were presorted by LIQUOR.

There are any number of reasons why we might want to reorganize our database. We might want to see the records grouped by COST or brand name, or we might stock the shelves by the container size. dBASE provides us with *two* commands that we can use to rearrange data: SORT and INDEX.

SORTING

In dBASE, sorting creates a completely new copy of a database. The records in the copy are arranged according to a *sort key*. To illustrate, the command to sort the inventory database by container SIZE is:

. SORT ON SIZE TO NEWNAME

As the records are sorted, they are physically copied to a new database file. The filename for this new database file can be anything you like, but it must conform to the rules for filenames. The records in the new file will be arranged by the *sort key*. When the SORT command has finished you are still using the original "unsorted" file. To use the sorted file, you must *close* the file you are using and *open* the sorted file. The USE command closes the file you are using and opens the specified file.

. USE NEWNAME

NEWNAME is a copy of INVENTRY whose records are grouped by SIZE (Figure 3-1). The *sort key* for this example is SIZE. When we sort by SIZE, we are sorting on the arrangement of characters in the SIZE field — *not* on the capacity of the container.

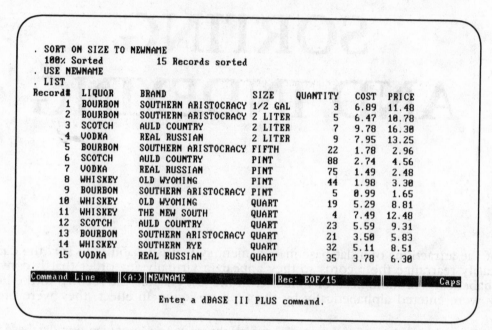

```
. SORT ON SIZE TO NEWNAME
  100% Sorted          15 Records sorted
. USE NEWNAME
. LIST
Record#  LIQUOR    BRAND                 SIZE      QUANTITY   COST    PRICE
      1  BOURBON   SOUTHERN ARISTOCRACY  1/2 GAL        3    6.89    11.48
      2  BOURBON   SOUTHERN ARISTOCRACY  2 LITER        5    6.47    10.78
      3  SCOTCH    AULD COUNTRY          2 LITER        7    9.78    16.30
      4  VODKA     REAL RUSSIAN          2 LITER        9    7.95    13.25
      5  BOURBON   SOUTHERN ARISTOCRACY  FIFTH         22    1.78     2.96
      6  SCOTCH    AULD COUNTRY          PINT          88    2.74     4.56
      7  VODKA     REAL RUSSIAN          PINT          75    1.49     2.48
      8  WHISKEY   OLD WYOMING           PINT          44    1.98     3.30
      9  BOURBON   SOUTHERN ARISTOCRACY  PINT           5    0.99     1.65
     10  WHISKEY   OLD WYOMING           QUART         19    5.29     8.81
     11  WHISKEY   THE NEW SOUTH         QUART          4    7.49    12.48
     12  SCOTCH    AULD COUNTRY          QUART         23    5.59     9.31
     13  BOURBON   SOUTHERN ARISTOCRACY  QUART         21    3.50     5.83
     14  WHISKEY   SOUTHERN RYE          QUART         32    5.11     8.51
     15  VODKA     REAL RUSSIAN          QUART         35    3.78     6.30

Command Line    <A:> NEWNAME                  Rec: EOF/15              Caps

Enter a dBASE III PLUS command.
```

Figure 3-1: Liquor store inventory — sorted by SIZE

Quite often we want to sort the database so that we have a sort within a sort. For example, we might want to group our inventory by BRAND and have the records belonging to each BRAND sorted by SIZE. We can do this by listing both *fields* as sort keys in the SORT command. This operation and its result are shown in Figure 3-2.

The *sort* order of the records is called the *logical* order. When we sort a database, we physically rearrange it so that its physical order and its logical order are the same. The order will be either alphabetical, chronological, or numeric — and will be determined automatically by the field type. Character fields are sorted alphabetically, date fields are sorted chronologically, and numeric fields are sorted numerically.

Alphabetic sorts are usually done in ASCII order, which means that the sort order of the characters is given by the table shown in Appendix D. Such a sort is sometimes called an ASCII sort to differentiate it from a dictionary sort. If you aren't conscientious about how you use uppercase and lowercase characters, your sort may not give you the results you expect. All uppercase letters come before any lowercase letters. "ZEBRA" would be after "ALPHA" but before "alpha." Numeric digits used as characters come before letters. Blank spaces come before anything else. (For

```
. SORT ON BRAND,SIZE TO NEWNAME2
  100% Sorted           15 Records sorted
. USE NEWNAME2
. LIST
Record#  LIQUOR    BRAND                 SIZE      QUANTITY    COST   PRICE
      1  SCOTCH    AULD COUNTRY          2 LITER         7    9.78   16.30
      2  SCOTCH    AULD COUNTRY          PINT           88    2.74    4.56
      3  SCOTCH    AULD COUNTRY          QUART          23    5.59    9.31
      4  WHISKEY   OLD WYOMING           PINT           44    1.98    3.30
      5  WHISKEY   OLD WYOMING           QUART          19    5.29    8.81
      6  VODKA     REAL RUSSIAN          2 LITER         9    7.95   13.25
      7  VODKA     REAL RUSSIAN          PINT           75    1.49    2.48
      8  VODKA     REAL RUSSIAN          QUART          35    3.78    6.30
      9  BOURBON   SOUTHERN ARISTOCRACY  1/2 GAL         3    6.89   11.48
     10  BOURBON   SOUTHERN ARISTOCRACY  2 LITER         5    6.47   10.78
     11  BOURBON   SOUTHERN ARISTOCRACY  FIFTH          22    1.78    2.96
     12  BOURBON   SOUTHERN ARISTOCRACY  PINT            5    0.99    1.65
     13  BOURBON   SOUTHERN ARISTOCRACY  QUART          21    3.50    5.83
     14  WHISKEY   SOUTHERN RYE          QUART          32    5.11    8.51
     15  WHISKEY   THE NEW SOUTH         QUART           4    7.49   12.48

Command Line    <A:> NEWNAME2              Rec: EOF/15              Caps

            Enter a dBASE III PLUS command.
```

Figure 3-2: Liquor store inventory — sorted by BRAND and SIZE

the value of special symbols such as commas, consult Appendix D). You can approximate a dictionary sort by using the UPPER function. This function causes dBASE to treat lowercase letters as though they were uppercase.

. SORT ON UPPER(BRAND) to NEWFILE1

The sorting arrangement, from A to Z, is called an *ascending* sort. The reverse, from Z to A, is a *descending* sort. Each sort key can be separately specified as ascending or descending by adding /A or /D to the sort key. If you do NOT specify the sort order, dBASE will assume that it is to be an ascending (normal) sort. If we want to sort the INVENTRY database by BRAND and SIZE (both in descending order), for example, we would use:

. SORT ON BRAND/D, SIZE/D TO NEWFILE2

We can *sort* the data into as many arrangements as we like. Each new sort, however, requires a separate database file. If we need to change any of the data, we must either change the records in each of the several sorted files — or we can edit the original and re-sort it into its several sorted variations. This is much the same problem that a public library has with its *card catalog*. Each library book is listed in three separate card files: author, subject, and title. When a book is added to the library, at least three identical new cards, must be added to the catalog — one for each of the three card files.

In dBASE, sorting creates a new database file. Some database managers allow you to sort records without creating a new file. This approach offers some advantage in that it can be a little faster than when creating the new file. Also, there is only one database file — which makes maintaining your database simpler and more reliable. The disadvantage is that you must sort each time you want to use the records in a particular sort order.

dBASE provides an attractive alternative to sorting. This alternative is called *indexing*.

INDEXING

Indexing creates the same effect as sorting: The data can be used in alphabetical, chronological, or numerical order. This order is created with the help of a separate *index file*. The index file is not a copy of the database, but a special file which makes the database *appear* to be sorted. It is automatically created by dBASE when you use the INDEX command. To illustrate, let's index the database INVENTRY by SIZE. This operation, shown as Figure 3-3, is similar to sorting by SIZE.

Compare Figure 3-3 with Figure 3-1. The result of the LIST commands are identical *except* that the record numbers in Figure 3-3 are not in sequential order. The record numbers are the same as in the original database shown in Figure 2-5. In the command

. INDEX ON SIZE TO SIZEINDX

SIZE is an *index key*, and SIZEINDX is the filename of the index file. The rules for index filenames are the same as for database and report filenames. dBASE automatically assigns the .NDX file identifier to index filenames.

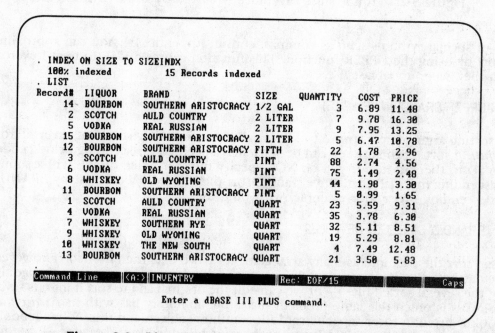

```
. INDEX ON SIZE TO SIZEINDX
  100% indexed          15 Records indexed
. LIST
Record#  LIQUOR    BRAND                 SIZE      QUANTITY   COST   PRICE
     14  BOURBON   SOUTHERN ARISTOCRACY  1/2 GAL         3   6.89   11.48
      2  SCOTCH    AULD COUNTRY          2 LITER         7   9.78   16.30
      5  VODKA     REAL RUSSIAN          2 LITER         9   7.95   13.25
     15  BOURBON   SOUTHERN ARISTOCRACY  2 LITER         5   6.47   10.78
     12  BOURBON   SOUTHERN ARISTOCRACY  FIFTH          22   1.78    2.96
      3  SCOTCH    AULD COUNTRY          PINT           88   2.74    4.56
      6  VODKA     REAL RUSSIAN          PINT           75   1.49    2.48
      8  WHISKEY   OLD WYOMING           PINT           44   1.98    3.30
     11  BOURBON   SOUTHERN ARISTOCRACY  PINT            5   0.99    1.65
      1  SCOTCH    AULD COUNTRY          QUART          23   5.59    9.31
      4  VODKA     REAL RUSSIAN          QUART          35   3.78    6.30
      7  WHISKEY   SOUTHERN RYE          QUART          32   5.11    8.51
      9  WHISKEY   OLD WYOMING           QUART          19   5.29    8.81
     10  WHISKEY   THE NEW SOUTH         QUART           4   7.49   12.48
     13  BOURBON   SOUTHERN ARISTOCRACY  QUART          21   3.50    5.83
.
Command Line    <A:> INVENTRY                 Rec: EOF/15                    Caps

          Enter a dBASE III PLUS command.
```

Figure 3-3: Liquor store inventory — indexed by SIZE

How does dBASE do this? The index file is a specially designed file that contains only the contents of the *key* field (the index key) and the corresponding record numbers. Figure 3-4 provides

Key	Data Record Numbers
1/2 GAL	14
2 LITER	2, 5, 15
FIFTH	12
PINT	3, 6, 8, 11
QUART	1, 4, 7, 9, 10, 13

Figure 3-4: Conceptual view of an index file

a conceptual view of SIZEINDX; it doesn't describe the implementation of the actual database index file.

As long as the index file is in use, it controls the order in which the database manager accesses the database records. This makes the database *appear* to be arranged according to the index key. If we *turn off* the index, the database would appear in its "unindexed" form. To turn the index off, use the command:

. CLOSE INDEX

To turn it back on, use the command:

. SET INDEX TO SIZEINDX

We can have as many index files as we might like. We still have only one copy of the database — the original. Index files can even be kept up-to-date, which adds greatly to their usefulness. If the index files are *in use* when we make changes to the database the changes are automatically incorporated into the index files. Up to seven index files can be in use with a database at any time. When we place an index file in use, it is said to be *open*. Suppose we have three index files for our database INVENTRY — LIQUOR, BRAND, and SIZEINDX. We can place all three in use (that is, open them) with the command:

. USE B:INVENTRY INDEX BRAND, LIQUOR, SIZEINDX

All three index files will be kept current if records are added, deleted, or edited. Only open index files will be updated. If the database is already open, we can open the index files with the command:

. SET INDEX TO BRAND, LIQUOR, SIZEINDX

The first index file in the list is the initial *controlling index*. The controlling index is the one that determines the order in which we can work with the data records. dBASE assigns each index file in the list an *order* number. In the example above, BRAND is number 1, LIQUOR is number 2, and SIZEINDX is number 3. BRAND is the controlling index. If we want to view records by SIZE, we could use the command:

. SET ORDER TO 3

Sorting and Indexing

which selects the third index file in the list (in this case, SIZE) as the controlling index. The other two are still open. All three will still be kept current.

Indexes within Indexes

In the second example of sorting a database, we showed how to create a sort within a sort by using multiple sort keys. An index can have only one index key. We create the equivalent of the index within an index for character fields by *concatenating* the fields together as shown in Figure 3-5.

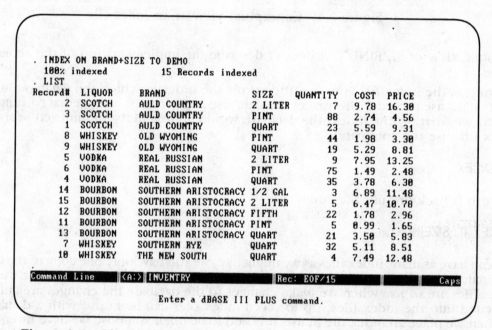

```
. INDEX ON BRAND+SIZE TO DEMO
  100% indexed          15 Records indexed
. LIST
Record#  LIQUOR   BRAND                SIZE      QUANTITY   COST   PRICE
     2   SCOTCH   AULD COUNTRY         2 LITER        7     9.78   16.30
     3   SCOTCH   AULD COUNTRY         PINT          88     2.74    4.56
     1   SCOTCH   AULD COUNTRY         QUART         23     5.59    9.31
     8   WHISKEY  OLD WYOMING          PINT          44     1.98    3.30
     9   WHISKEY  OLD WYOMING          QUART         19     5.29    8.81
     5   VODKA    REAL RUSSIAN         2 LITER        9     7.95   13.25
     6   VODKA    REAL RUSSIAN         PINT          75     1.49    2.48
     4   VODKA    REAL RUSSIAN         QUART         35     3.78    6.30
    14   BOURBON  SOUTHERN ARISTOCRACY 1/2 GAL        3     6.89   11.48
    15   BOURBON  SOUTHERN ARISTOCRACY 2 LITER        5     6.47   10.78
    12   BOURBON  SOUTHERN ARISTOCRACY FIFTH         22     1.78    2.96
    11   BOURBON  SOUTHERN ARISTOCRACY PINT           5     0.99    1.65
    13   BOURBON  SOUTHERN ARISTOCRACY QUART         21     3.50    5.83
     7   WHISKEY  SOUTHERN RYE         QUART         32     5.11    8.51
    10   WHISKEY  THE NEW SOUTH        QUART          4     7.49   12.48

Command Line     <A:> INVENTRY            Rec: EOF/15              Caps
```

Enter a dBASE III PLUS command.

Figure 3-5: Liquor store inventory — indexed by BRAND and SIZE

Indexing on something that isn't there

Although all the examples that we have used so far used fields as the index key, we can index on some other item — as long as it can be derived from the contents of the fields. For example, we can build an index on the value of each item in the inventory. Here we define value as the PRICE times the QUANTITY. An index of VALUE is shown in Figure 3-6.

Finding a Particular Record

Index files offer an additional bonus. They can be used to *find* any record almost instantly by its index key. Let's suppose that we have indexed our database by BRAND. BRAND is the index key. BRAND has also been selected as the controlling index. We want to find the first record for "SOUTHERN RYE."

Chapter Three

```
. INDEX ON PRICE * QUANTITY TO VALUE
  100% indexed            15 Records indexed
. LIST OFF LIQUOR,BRAND,SIZE,QUANTITY,PRICE,PRICE * QUANTITY
  LIQUOR      BRAND              SIZE    QUANTITY  PRICE PRICE * QUANTITY
  BOURBON     SOUTHERN ARISTOCRACY PINT       5    1.65           8.25
  BOURBON     SOUTHERN ARISTOCRACY 1/2 GAL    3   11.48          34.44
  WHISKEY     THE NEW SOUTH      QUART        4   12.48          49.92
  BOURBON     SOUTHERN ARISTOCRACY 2 LITER    5   10.78          53.90
  BOURBON     SOUTHERN ARISTOCRACY FIFTH     22    2.96          65.12
  SCOTCH      AULD COUNTRY       2 LITER      7   16.30         114.10
  VODKA       REAL RUSSIAN       2 LITER      9   13.25         119.25
  BOURBON     SOUTHERN ARISTOCRACY QUART     21    5.83         122.43
  WHISKEY     OLD WYOMING        PINT        44    3.30         145.20
  WHISKEY     OLD WYOMING        QUART       19    8.81         167.39
  VODKA       REAL RUSSIAN       PINT        75    2.48         186.00
  SCOTCH      AULD COUNTRY       QUART       23    9.31         214.13
  VODKA       REAL RUSSIAN       QUART       35    6.30         220.50
  WHISKEY     SOUTHERN RYE       QUART       32    8.51         272.32
  SCOTCH      AULD COUNTRY       PINT        88    4.56         401.28
```
```
Command Line     <A:> INVENTRY              Rec: EOF/15               Caps
```
Enter a dBASE III PLUS command.

Figure 3-6: Liquor store inventory — indexed by VALUE

```
. USE INVENTRY INDEX BRAND, LIQUOR, SIZEINDX
. FIND SOUTHERN RYE
. DISPLAY
Record#  LIQUOR    BRAND              SIZE    QUANTITY  COST   PRICE
     7   WHISKEY   SOUTHERN RYE       QUART      32     5.11    8.51
```

You need not enter an entire name. You can manually search by entering just the first few letters. If, in our above example, we had entered only the letter "S," the result would be

```
. USE INVENTRY INDEX BRAND, LIQUOR, SIZEINDX
. FIND S
. DISPLAY
Record#  LIQUOR    BRAND              SIZE    QUANTITY  COST   PRICE
     5   BOURBON   SOUTHERN ARISTOCRACY ½ GAL    3     6.89   11.48
```

This is the first record beginning with the letter "S" in the BRAND field. You may have noticed that the brand name we wanted to find was *not* enclosed in quotes. The FIND command *expects* to search for character strings.

FIND can locate a record quickly because it does not search the database itself. Instead it searches the index file for the *first occurrence* of the key — just as you would if you were searching a book index. The index file is designed so that it can be rapidly searched by the computer.

Sorting and Indexing

Sort vs. Index

There are some limitations to indexing that do not apply to sorting. Each index can have only one index key. A sort can have multiple sort keys. An index key cannot be longer than 100 characters in dBASE. An index can only be in ascending order; sorts can be in either ascending or descending order.

Some Index Terminology

Let's return to our library analogy. Imagine that the library books are data records. The card catalog comprises three index files: author, subject, and title. Each card in the card catalog represents a book that is somewhere on the shelves. Suppose that we know the title of a book. To find the book, we first find the title card in the title index. The card contains a Library of Congress number. This number *points* us to the location of the book in the library. In database terminology, the categories Author, Subject, and Title are *secondary* keys. The Library of Congress number is the *primary* key. It is also a *pointer* to the book because it translates into a physical position in the library. The books are *physical records* while the cards in the card catalog are *logical records*.

In our database example, the index keys, such as SIZE, are the *secondary* keys. The record number is the *primary key*. The record number in the index file is a *pointer* to the actual data record. The data records in INVENTRY are the *physical records*; the index records are *logical records*.

The real purpose of the card catalog is not to sort the books into some order — but to help us find particular books. The index cards are in order to make finding the card easier than finding the book. This is exactly the same with our database index files. Although they allow us to see data records in sorted order, their real use lies in helping us *find* a particular record.

Some database operations, such as LIST and REPORT, may appear to be somewhat faster with a sorted version of a database than with the equivalent indexed database. For a sorted database the DBMS (database management system) moves sequentially through adjacent records. For an indexed version the DBMS may have to jump around through the database to produce the same output.

In this chapter we've learned that we can arrange data records in alphabetical, chronological, or numeric order by either the SORT or INDEX commands. Each has its advantages and disadvantages. Sorting creates duplicates copies of the data records in the original database. Indexing creates an index file which contains the index key and pointers back to the original data records.

As far as performance goes, indexing is a clear-cut winner. In a test, sorting a 975-record (261-kilobyte) mailing list by NAME took 1 minute and 20 seconds. Indexing the same database took only 19 seconds. The NAME key was 30 characters wide and the record length was 267 bytes. In this case sorting was slower than indexing. In addition, the sorted copy took 261 kbytes of disk space while the index file required only 47 kbytes of disk space. In a second test, sorting a 975-record list of 30 character names (30 kbytes) took only 17 seconds when the list contained only the NAME field. Indexing this same file took 10 seconds. Interestingly enough, in this case the index file was larger (requiring 47 kbytes) than the database itself — because the index file must contain the key (in this case the names) *plus* the pointers back to the records in the database.

Chapter Three

CHAPTER FOUR

HELP!

Sooner or later, most of us will need some extra *help* from the computer. If you don't know quite *how* to do something or if you make a mistake, your computer should help you out. Programmers are finally beginning to get the idea that the rest of us don't want to learn about programming; we just want the computer to help us with our daily chores. dBASE provides several kinds of help — depending on your circumstances.

TYPOGRAPHICAL ERRORS

As you enter either commands or data you may, upon occasion, make a typographical error. For example, let's suppose that you are working with the liquor store inventory database. It's late, and you're tired. So, you type in the command:

. DISPAY FFIR LIKKER = 'SCOTCH'

You can be certain that dBASE isn't going to like this command as is — it won't even know what to do with it. You've got two choices: to retype the command or to *fix* it. The command line should read

. DISPLAY FOR LIQUOR = 'SCOTCH'

In order to fix the command line, you will need to use several of the special keys that are on your keyboard. The special keys are shown in Figure 4-1. Use the Left arrow to move the cursor so that it is positioned to the "A" in DISPAY. We need to *insert* an "L" between the "P" and the "A". Press the Ins (insert) key. "Ins" will appear on the top of the screen—just right of center. You're now in the insert mode. Press "L". The letter "L" will be inserted where the "A" was. The "A" and all remaining characters on the line will be moved to the right.

To change FFIR to FOR, use the Right arrow key to move the cursor to the "F". Press the Del key. Del erases the character the cursor is on. Use the Right arrow to move the cursor to the "I" in what is now FIR. Press the Ins key to turn the insert mode off. The letters "Ins" will disappear from the top line of the screen. You are now in the normal, or *overwrite*, mode. Whatever you type will now overwrite what is on the screen. Press the "O" key to replace the "I" with the "O". To change LIKKER to LIQUOR, move the cursor to the offending letters and retype. We have just *fixed* the command.

THE SPECIAL KEYS

Your computer has a number of keys that are not on an ordinary typewriter keyboard. These special keys are indicated in the drawing of Figure 4-1. The use of these keys varies according to the particular software program. It is worth your time to learn about these keys and their use in dBASE III. These keys are:

F1	NumLock	Alt	End
F2 to F10	Backspace	PrtSc	PgUp
Esc	Arrow Keys	Ins	PgDn
Ctrl	Home	Del	

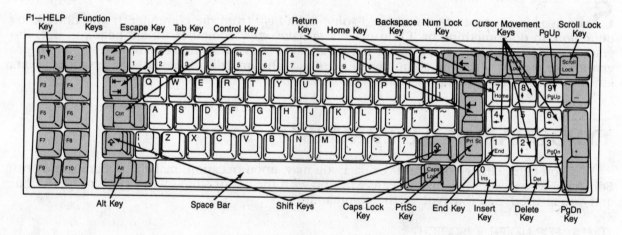

Figure 4-1: Keyboard diagram

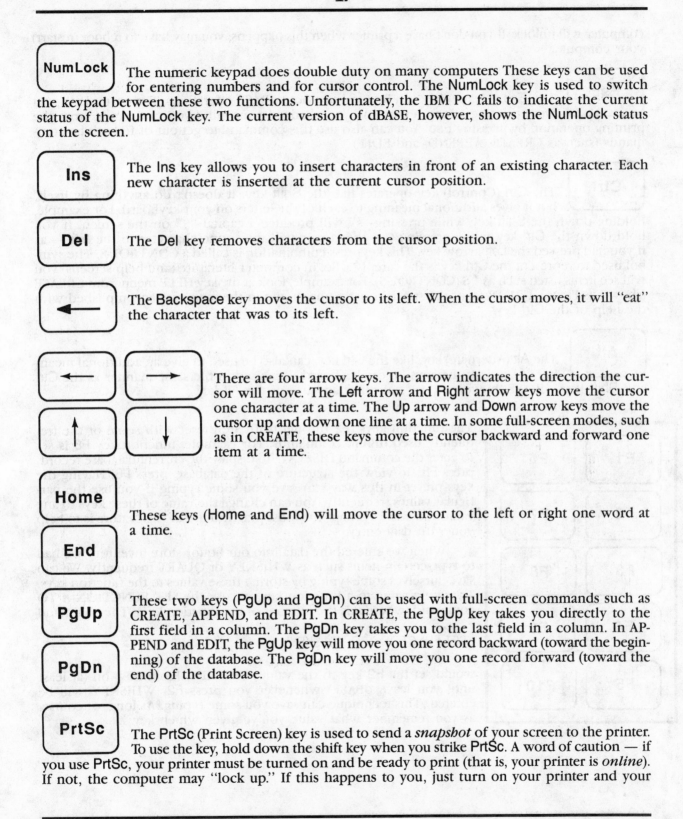

NumLock — The numeric keypad does double duty on many computers These keys can be used for entering numbers and for cursor control. The NumLock key is used to switch the keypad between these two functions. Unfortunately, the IBM PC fails to indicate the current status of the NumLock key. The current version of dBASE, however, shows the NumLock status on the screen.

Ins — The Ins key allows you to insert characters in front of an existing character. Each new character is inserted at the current cursor position.

Del — The Del key removes characters from the cursor position.

The Backspace key moves the cursor to its left. When the cursor moves, it will "eat" the character that was to its left.

There are four arrow keys. The arrow indicates the direction the cursor will move. The Left arrow and Right arrow keys move the cursor one character at a time. The Up arrow and Down arrow keys move the cursor up and down one line at a time. In some full-screen modes, such as in CREATE, these keys move the cursor backward and forward one item at a time.

Home / **End** — These keys (Home and End) will move the cursor to the left or right one word at a time.

PgUp / **PgDn** — These two keys (PgUp and PgDn) can be used with full-screen commands such as CREATE, APPEND, and EDIT. In CREATE, the PgUp key takes you directly to the first field in a column. The PgDn key takes you to the last field in a column. In AP-PEND and EDIT, the PgUp key will move you one record backward (toward the beginning) of the database. The PgDn key will move you one record forward (toward the end) of the database.

PrtSc — The PrtSc (Print Screen) key is used to send a *snapshot* of your screen to the printer. To use the key, hold down the shift key when you strike PrtSc. A word of caution — if you use PrtSc, your printer must be turned on and be ready to print (that is, your printer is *online*). If not, the computer may "lock up." If this happens to you, just turn on your printer and your computer will unlock. If you don't have a printer when this happens, you may have to reboot (restart) your computer.

Esc The Esc (Escape) key can be used to *abort* dBASE operations. For example, if you were printing a long report and you changed your mind you can escape from the printing operation by pressing Esc. You can also use this command to get out of full-screen commands (such as CREATE, APPEND, and EDIT).

Ctrl The Ctrl (Control) key operates like the Shift key; it doesn't do anything by itself, but it gives additional meaning to each of the letters on your keyboard. For example, holding down the Shift key while pressing "s" will produce a capital "S" on the screen. If you hold down the Ctrl key while pressing "s", the cursor will move one character to the left — as if you had pressed the Left arrow key. This keypress combination is called a CONTROL-S. The symbol used to represent the Ctrl key is the caret (^). So, in computer literature (and help screens) you will see items listed such as ^S (CONTROL-S). For example, look at the key HELP menu from CREATE (shown as Figure 4-2). Many of the special operations shown in the menu are accomplished with the help of the Ctrl key.

Alt The Alt (Alternate) key, like the Ctrl key, can also be used to give an additional meaning of some of the keys on the keyboard. It is used in the same manner as the Ctrl and Shift keys. dBASE, however, does not make any use of the Alt key.

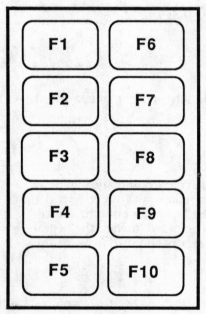

The function keys (F2 through F10) are preset with some of the frequently used dBASE commands. For example, function key F8 is set to enter the command DISPLAY. To display the current database record, press F8. To view the structure of the database, press F6. Having the keys preset in this way can save you some typing if you use the particular values frequently. You can change the value of these keys to any value you wish. Perhaps the most practical use of this feature is to help you with data entry.

When we entered the data into our liquor store inventory we had to type certain items such as WHISKEY or QUART frequently. We can save ourselves some typing by storing these values to the function keys. To store a value to a function key, we use the SET FUNCTION *n* TO command (where *n* is the number of the function key). The command

. SET FUNCTION 2 TO 'WHISKEY'

would set the F2 key to the value WHISKEY. From now on (at least until you leave dBASE) whenever you press F2, WHISKEY will be entered. This technique can save you some typing. As long, of course, as you remember what value you've given which key.

Chapter Four

F1   The value in function key F1 cannot be reassigned in dBASE, at least not by us mortals. F1 is reserved as the dBASE HELP key. The HELP you get depends on what you are doing. If you are working with one of the full-screen commands, such as CREATE or AP-PEND, pressing F1 will fetch a HELP menu (such as the one shown in Figure 4-2). Pressing F1 again will send the HELP menu away and leave more of the screen free.

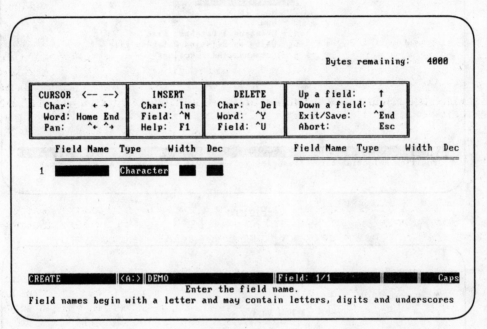

Figure 4-2

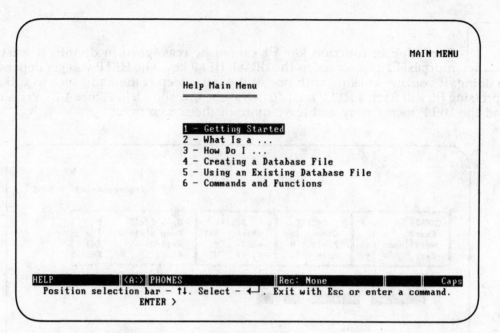

Figure 4-3

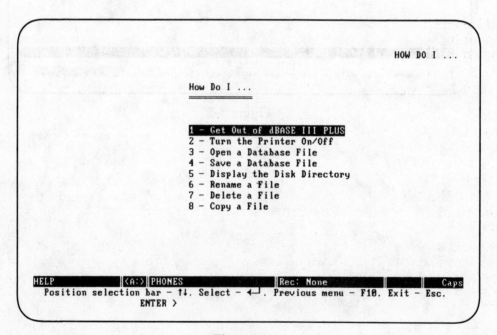

Figure 4-4

Chapter Four

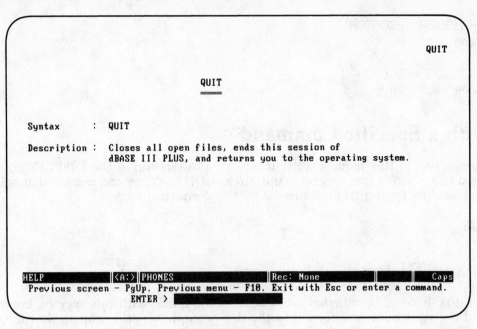

QUIT

QUIT

Syntax : QUIT

Description : Closes all open files, ends this session of
              dBASE III PLUS, and returns you to the operating system.

HELP   <A:> PHONES   Rec: None   Caps
Previous screen - PgUp. Previous menu - F10. Exit with Esc or enter a command.
                   ENTER >

Figure 4-5

If you are entering commands from the dot prompt, you can get help by pressing F1 at the dot prompt or by typing the word HELP and pressing the Return key, which provides the screen display shown in Figure 4-3. This HELP screen is designed for the newcomer to dBASE III. There is, however, a specific menu option for the more experienced user, *New Features*, which discusses the major new additions since the last release. Experienced users can also profit from HELP selection 7, which discusses the dBASE commands.

To illustrate the way the HELP system works, let's examine selection 3, *How Do I …*, from the MAIN HELP MENU shown in Figure 4-3. To select a menu option, use the Up or Down arrow key to highlight an option. When the option that you want is highlighted, press the Return key. You will be presented with the HELP screen shown in Figure 4-4.

This HELP menu, however, contains a list of specific items for beginners. Let's select menu option 1, *Get Out of dBASE III*. Select this option by using the Up arrow and Down arrow keys to highlight the option and then press Return — which brings up a brief discussion of the QUIT command (Figure 4-5).

In these HELP screens, the bottom three lines on the screen are intended to guide you through the HELP system. Software designers sometimes refer to these messages as *navigational aids*. The second line from the bottom provides you with specific information about how to select an option, how to return to the previous screen and how to *escape* from HELP. Incidentally, press Esc to leave HELP.

Error Messages

If you make a mistake while typing in a command, dBASE will respond to your command by displaying an *error message* and redisplaying the command with a question mark to the right of the suspected error.

Help!

```
. DISPLAY FER LIQUOR = 'SCOTCH'
Variable not found
          ?
DISPLAY FER LIQUOR = 'SCOTCH'
Do you want some help? (Y/N)
```

HELP with a Specific Command

If we answer yes to this request we will receive a discussion of the DISPLAY command. If we had wanted HELP with a specific command, such as DISPLAY, we can request that help directly from the keyboard by typing HELP followed by the command name.

```
. HELP DISPLAY
```

A Command History

If, when dBASE asked us whether we wanted some HELP with this specific command, we had answered no, we would be returned to the dot prompt. We still want to do the command. Of course we can retype it but dBASE offers us a better way. Press the **Up** arrow from the dot prompt and dBASE will retrieve this last command. We can then make corrections to this command and press **Return** to execute it.

In fact, we can *back up* to any of the last twenty commands. Each time you press the **Up** arrow, you'll move back one command. You can re-execute that command by pressing **Return**. These previous commands are the command history. Use the **Up** arrow and **Down** arrow to move about within the command history. You can view the command history by using either

```
. DISPLAY HISTORY
```

or

```
. LIST HISTORY
```

To change the number of commands that are retained in the command HISTORY, use

```
. SET HISTORY TO n
```

where *n* is the number of commands that you wish to retain.

dBASE provides help in four specific ways. You can use special keys on your keyboard to correct entry errors. You can use the function keys to store specific items to help with either command entry or data entry. The HELP system guides the beginner as well as giving specific help to the more experienced user. Finally, a command history is maintained that you can use for a variety of purposes.

Most current database management software will have at least some variation of these dBASE III HELP features. Software designers have come to recognize that they must provide a product that is easy to learn and use as well as powerful.

Chapter Four

SECTION TWO
BEGINNING USAGE

In Section Two we will look at database planning and database use. We begin with a discussion of the importance of simplicity and good planning. Then, we proceed to build, modify, maintain, and work with databases.

CHAPTER FIVE

PLANNING A DATABASE

Planning is often considered a nuisance, particularly by the beginner — not just the database beginner. But if you do not plan well, you may be unhappy with the result, and of course, you might have to begin all over again.

Take the example of constructing a paper database with a typewriter. If the typist does not plan the layout of the columns properly the database will, most likely, "fall off" the right margin of the paper, and it will have to be done over.

The same is true of a computer database. It is not going to fall off the paper but, if it's not properly planned, you may have to go back and start over. But with a computer, this isn't all bad. In fact, one good approach to planning a database is to take a shot at it *expecting* to have to redo it once or twice (we can call this process *iterative enhancement*). One of the benefits of working with a computer database (as opposed to a paper one) is that you can make major changes to the database without having to reenter the data. The computer can recover most, if not all, of the data stored in the database before the change was made.

The first step in planning your database is to know what you want to accomplish with it. The next step is to make a list of the items (data) that must be included. Don't be concerned about perfection. Nearly any shortcoming or omission can be easily repaired or overcome.

As an example, let's take another look at the liquor store database. This inventory database is intended to tell us the stock on hand and how much it is worth. When we created this database, we used the column headings to establish the record structure. But to plan this database, we make a list of the items to be included:

Brand of liquor
Size of container
Kind of liquor
Retail price
Wholesale price
Quantity on hand

This list describes what was included in our liquor store inventory. Since we created the database, we have thought of an additional item that should be included:

Location of the item

Such an oversight is easily remedied; in this case, all we have to do is add another field to our database. Let's go through the necessary process step by step; you'll see how easy it is to change the database — which should set your mind at ease. You already have a database, B:INVENTRY, and it has a lot of data in it. What do you do? You can add a field without losing any of the data that you have already entered.

MODIFY THE STRUCTURE

dBASE allows you to change the structure of the database with the command MODIFY STRUCTURE. When the structure of a database is changed, the data belonging to that structure can be destroyed or damaged. To prevent any loss of data, dBASE automatically makes a backup copy of the database during the MODIFY COMMAND process. The backup copy will have the same name as the database, but will have .BAK as its file identifier.

After the structure is modified, data from the backup copy is automatically copied to the new database structure. There must be enough space on the disk to contain both the database and the backup copy.

You must be USEing the database that you want to change. To start the process we use the commands

. USE B:INVENTRY
. MODIFY STRUCTURE

This takes us to the screen display shown as Figure 5-1, which is identical to that used to CREATE the original database.

In this example we will insert a new field between QUANTITY and COST. Press the Down arrow key four times. This positions the cursor to the beginning of the fieldname COST. Then,

• Press Ctrl-N to insert a blank at field 5.
• Enter the new field definition. The display will resemble Figure 5-2.

Press Ctrl-End to save the modified database. The database B:INVENTRY now has the new field that you wanted to add. The existing data from the backup file B:INVENTRY.BAK will be added automatically.

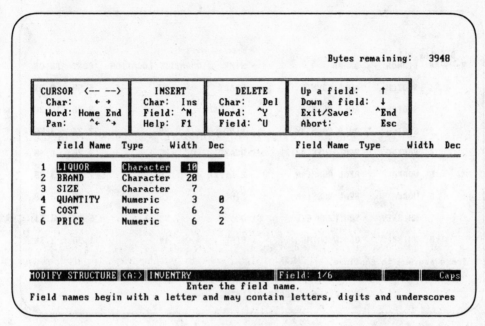

Figure 5-1

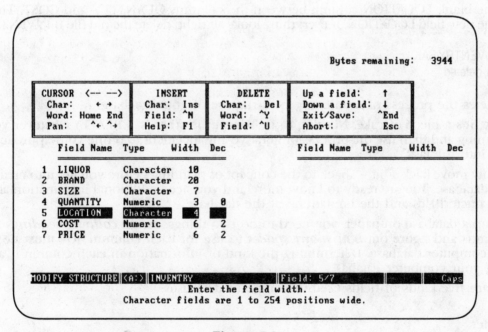

Figure 5-2

At this point you have both the new and the old versions of your database. Check the new database to make sure that everything is okay before deleting the old version. Type DISPLAY ALL at the dot prompt. The contents of the database should look like Figure 5-3.

Planning a Database

```
. DISPLAY ALL
Record#   LIQUOR     BRAND          SIZE       QUANTITY LOCATION   COST   PRICE
       1  SCOTCH     AULD COUNTRY   QUART         23             5.59   9.31
       2  SCOTCH     AULD COUNTRY   2 LITER        7             9.78  16.30
       3  SCOTCH     AULD COUNTRY   PINT          88             2.74   4.56
       4  VODKA      REAL RUSSIAN   QUART         35             3.78   6.30
       5  VODKA      REAL RUSSIAN   2 LITER        9             7.95  13.25
       6  VODKA      REAL RUSSIAN   PINT          75             1.49   2.48
       7  WHISKEY    SOUTHERN RYE   QUART         32             5.11   8.51
       8  WHISKEY    OLD WYOMING    PINT          44             1.98   3.30
Press any key to continue...
Command Line       <A:> INVENTRY            Rec: 9/15              Caps
```
Enter a dBASE III PLUS command.

Figure 5-3

Note the blank LOCATION column between the columns QUANTITY and COST. This blank column is the new field LOCATION. If everything looks all right, delete the old file B:INVENTRY.BAK.

. ERASE B:INVENTRY.BAK
File has been deleted

This completes the process of modifying the structure of your database.

You see, it's a piece of cake. Nothing to it. You put in (that is, CREATE) whatever you want in the beginning and then use the process of iterative enhancement to refine your approach as you get further into the task.

Let's now move back a bit — back to the concept of planning before you get into creating and using your database. You are ready to know more and you need additional information about the working characteristics and the limitations of the database.

To set up a database on paper, you need to do two things: assign *column headings* for each of the columns and figure out *how many spaces* to use for each column. You must do both of these for a computer database. Determining the kind of information in each column is also part of planning your computer database.

There are five kinds of fields used in computer databases:

Character
Numeric
Logical
Date
Memo

Chapter Five

Character fields: These fields are used for short textual data items such as names, addresses, and phone numbers. They can be up to 255 characters long, and can contain anything that can be entered from your keyboard. This includes letters (both uppercase and lowercase), numbers, and special symbols, such as ?, &, <, "space," and so on. Normally a character field can be used for any purpose. In fact, we can make every field in the database a character field.

The size (width) of a character field is the number of "typewriter" spaces that would be required to contain the longest entry for that field. Each letter, number, special symbol, and space counts as one character. Each character takes one byte of memory. Each time we relate the field width to space on a typewritten page, we can use that as an analogy to the space in the computer's memory. To summarize, field width is always represented in bytes, and the number of bytes is the same as the number of spaces required to put the field on a typewritten page.

Numeric fields: These fields can contain only numbers. They are used when the numbers they contain are to be used for arithmetic calculations. They can contain either whole numbers (called integers) or decimal numbers. In addition to the digits, they can contain one decimal point (.) and a negative sign (-). In most database systems the positive (+) sign is understood and does not need to be entered. The negative sign and the decimal point each occupy a space and must be counted when determining the field width. A negative number such as -281.65 takes seven spaces (bytes) and has two decimal places.

Numeric fields are right-justified by the computer; character fields are left-justified by the computer. Examples of number columns that are right- and left-justified are shown in Figure 5-4.

Logical fields: These fields are used when there are only two possibilities for the data (Yes/No, True/False). For example, bills are either paid or they are not. Students either attended a class or they did not. You are either reading this or you are not. Logical fields are automatically assigned a width of one byte (space).

Date fields: These fields, as you may have guessed, are used to store dates. They are automatically assigned a field width of 8 bytes. Date fields will only accept valid dates, which are normally entered and displayed as *mm/dd/yy*. The special characteristics of date fields are discussed in Chapter Sixteen.

Memo fields: These are special variable-length fields and are normally used to store large blocks of text such as memos and short documents. Memo field data is not stored in the database file, but is actually stored in a separate auxiliary file — called a database text file. This file has the same name as the database file and is automatically assigned a .DBT file identifier. The maximum size of a memo field is 4,096 bytes. As data is entered into a memo field, space is automatically allocated in 512-byte increments. No space is required in the text file until data is entered into this field. A ten-byte field in the database file is used to keep track of the memo field data. Memo fields, and their special characteristics, are discussed in more detail in Chapter Sixteen.

Unless you really need the special characteristics of logical or memo fields, it is a good idea to limit your field selection to character, date, and numeric fields.

Planning a Database

LEFT JUSTIFIED	RIGHT JUSTIFIED
1	1
10	10
100	100

Figure 5-4

Close on the heels of determining what type of field you want is assigning that field a fieldname. We know that the fieldname must contain ten or fewer characters. Choose fieldnames that are descriptive — but keep them as short as possible. You will be using the fieldnames in commands, and long names require more typing than short ones. Suppose that you need one field for each month of the year. You could name the fields JANUARY, FEBRUARY, and so forth, or you could use the shorter, and equally descriptive, JAN, FEB, and so forth.

The other decision option is relevant only to numeric fields. Will the data in the field require decimal numbers? If so, how many decimal places will be needed? This decision depends entirely upon the data.

We are going to work through the plan — a database plan — for the inventory database created in Chapter Two. This is currently B:INVENTRY, amended to add the item's location. We will use the same fieldnames, fieldtypes, and widths that we used in the example. The new field containing the item's location will be a character field called LOCATION. We'll arbitrarily assign a width of ten to this field.

A plan for the database B:INVENTRY looks something like that shown in Figure 5-5. Notice that it resembles a database itself. If you have several databases, it is often wise to have a database which contains the database plans. We can call this database of plans a *data dictionary*. (Data dictionaries are discussed in Chapter Twenty-One.)

This database has seven fields and requires 62 bytes of memory for each record. Before you say, "Big deal, why should I go through this whole process for something that I can do in my head?", remember: If you could do it in your head, you wouldn't need a computer. Each database file can contain as many as 128 fields and 4,096 bytes. Your database could well require several dozen fields with hundreds of bytes for each record. If so, then you must compare your plan with the resources available to you.

Each database management system, as well as your computer, has limitations that must be taken into account if your application is large. Computer limitations primarily concern the capacity of the disk drive(s). The disk drive must have enough capacity to store your database file. The size of the database file will be approximately the size of a record times the total number of records. It is advisable to have a disk drive with enough capacity to store the database itself plus a backup copy.

The operating system can also limit your database size. PC/MS-DOS, for example, limits file sizes to not more than 32 million bytes — that's pretty big.

The limitations imposed by the database management system are more interesting. Database system "limitations" could easily lead you off on a quest for some new and wonderful database management system that will be a panacea for all your problems. The alternative to this potentially costly approach is to use your head. The resource limitations imposed by the database system are typically:

Chapter Five

Number of Fields
Field Width
Number of Bytes in a Record
Number of Records in a File (database)

FIELD DESCRIPTION	FIELDNAME	TYPE	WIDTH	DECIMALS
Kind of Liquor	LIQUOR	C	10	
Brand of Liquor	BRAND	C	20	
Size of Container	SIZE	C	7	
Retail Price	PRICE	N	6	2
Wholesale Price	COST	N	6	2
Quantity on Hand	QUANTITY	N	3	
Location of the Item	LOCATION	C	10	
TOTAL NUMBER OF BYTES			62	
EXPECTED NUMBER OF RECORDS			1000	

Figure 5-5

In dBASE, 128 fields are allowed in *each* database file. Each field is limited to 254 bytes and each record to 4,000 bytes. The number of records is limited to one billion. The maximum size for each dBASE III database file is two billion bytes. That's pretty big. It's so big that you are unlikely to encounter the limits.

To give you an idea of just how big this is, consider the following. Using a standard typewriter paper (8½ by 11), standard one-inch margins, and pica type, a paper database of this size contains more than 569,000 pages. A microcomputer with a hard disk can read the database at about 22,000 characters a second. This means that it takes the computer more than twenty-four hours just to read the database. When you encounter databases that are this large, you are likely to encounter limitations in either the computer hardware or the operating system — and you probably shouldn't be using a microcomputer.

One of the most common problems in database planning is that a plan requires more than the maximum number of fields in a file. The solution to this is easy. Simply split the plan into two or more databases. When this happens, each database becomes a file within a larger database, and perhaps you should refer to each of the databases as a file. All of the files taken together become the database. When you split your plan into two or more files you must find a way to link the databases together. One way to do this is to have one or more common fields in each database file. As an example, let's look at a database for an elementary school. Our hypothetical database plan might have 130 fields and might resemble Figure 5-6.

This is a good example of a moderately large database. It requires mass storage of a little over 200,000 bytes (characters). It's been estimated that more than 90% of all databases have fewer than 100,000 bytes. All of which illustrates an important and often overlooked point: You should understand your application before you buy your hardware and software.

Planning a Database

FIELD	FIELD DESCRIPTION	FIELDNAME	TYPE	WIDTH	DECIMALS
1	Student's Name	NAME	C	30	
2	Room Assignment	ROOM	C	3	
3	Grade	GRADE	C	1	
4	Teacher's Name	TEACHER	C	15	
5	Retained last year Y/N	RETAINED	L	1	
—	—	—	—	—	
—	—	—	—	—	
127	Home Address	ADDRESS	C	30	
128	Home Telephone Number	PHONE	C	8	
129	Emergency Notification	ENAME	C	30	
130	Emergency Telephone	EMERGENCY	C	8	

TOTAL NUMBER OF BYTES   341

EXPECTED NUMBER OF RECORDS   600

Figure 5-6

For the application illustrated in Figure 5-6, the minimum hardware configuration should include two disk drives where at least one of the drives is capable of storing 500,000 bytes. You can get by with less, but you may be constrained within the range of your plans. For example, if you should want to add a field to a database, you will need 400,000 bytes to store the two databases at the point where you have appended all of the records from one database to the other.

The only database software limitation (for dBASE) in this example involves the number of necessary fields: There are more fields than one database file can support (128). The solution is to break the database into two or more files. When databases are broken and occupy two or more files, we must link the files together.

Linking is done using a common element — some piece of data that appears consistently across the whole database, such as a student's name. Think about old-fashioned paper files. It is quite likely that each student's file (for paper files) is on more than one piece of paper. In a paper file, the student's name would commonly appear on each piece of paper. In our database, each file has a NAME field which contains the student's name. The total number of fields is now 131 and the total number of characters is 371. There are 131 fields because we have added NAME again in field 129 to identify the information in fields 129–130. This installs the necessary common element after 128. 130 is split off from the first database.

The only problem arises when there are two students in the school with the same name, not unlikely. We minimize this problem by making three fields — NAME, ROOM and GRADE — common to both files. The plan now requires 133 fields with 375 bytes per record. With dBASE, two files can fulfill the plan and form the complete database.

Another possible solution is to assign each student an identification number. This solution has some merit. It requires fewer bytes than the recommended solution and requires only two additional fields instead of three. On the negative side, it will require additional effort on someone's

Chapter Five

part to make sure that the identification number is unique for each student.

Let's take a look at the fields ROOM, GRADE, and TEACHER. In an elementary school, Mr. Jones is usually assigned to room 201 and grade six. If this is the case, it is reasonable and efficient to establish a third database file which contains information regarding the teachers. Because it is likely that the school has a file of personnel information, this allows the elimination of a field from the student file. In this particular case, that saves approximately 9,000 bytes of disk space (600 records times 15 bytes) — plus the bother of typing the 600 names in the first place and changing it all when a teacher is replaced.

This school database now has three related files. This demonstrates, by the way, the definition of a *relational* database system. Files may be related to each other and needless duplication minimized. As a matter of fact, the technical term for a database file is *relation*. It is usually wise to group information that is used together into a single relation. It is simpler to work with one database than with two or more.

In our example, the three database files (relations) are linked as shown in Figure 5-7. This figure illustrates the way in which the files can be tied together.

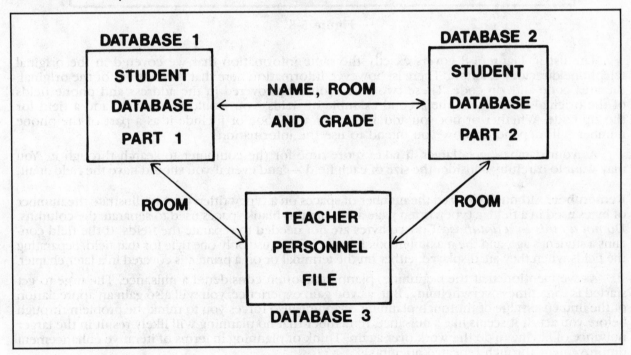

Figure 5-7

Figure 5-8 demonstrates another item to consider in planning: An item can cover a lot of ground. In one case, we have three fields, in the second, eleven. Your application will likely be somewhere in the middle. However, deciding whether to combine data items into a single field or not requires an understanding of how the data will be used. One rule of thumb is that if the items are rarely (if ever) used separately, then they may be combined. Grouping items such as last name, first name, and middle initial into a single name field often allows for more efficient use of space. And it's certainly simpler to do so.

Planning a Database

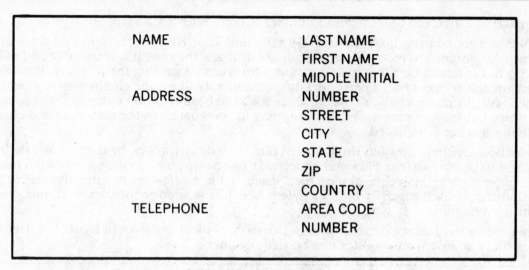

Figure 5-8

The list in Figure 5-8 covers exactly the same information that we covered in the original telephone directory example. There is, however, information here that was left out of the original: the area code and zip code. These two items could be covered in the address and phone fields of the original example. In the second example of fields, you would most likely add a field for the zip code. Whether or not you add a field for area code or include it as a part of the phone number will depend on how you intend to use the information.

As your database gets larger, it takes more time for the computer to search through it. You may want to carefully consider the size of each field — and even if you should have the field at all.

Remember: Although we used the number of spaces on a typewritten page to illustrate the number of bytes used in a field, a typewritten page also contains blank spaces used to separate the columns. *Do not do this in a database.* Unused bytes are not needed to separate the fields. If the field contains a student's age, and the maximum possible age is nine, use only one byte for that field. Separating the fields when they are displayed, either on the terminal or on a printer, is covered in a later chapter.

As we mentioned at the beginning, planning is often considered a nuisance. The urge to get started is sometimes overwhelming. But, as you gain experience, you will also gain an appreciation of the immense value of thorough planning. Planning also forces you to think the problem through before you act. If it seems like a nuisance, remember that no planning will likely result in the larger nuisance of having to do the work over again. Think of planning in terms of iterative enhancement (improvement through repeated attempts):

- Begin with a workable skeleton of a plan.

- Build on this workable framework until you have the system ready to put on the computer.

The most serious trap you can get caught in is to seek perfection. This can cost you time, money, and energy. Remember, you may be unfamiliar with computer database management systems, but the concept, construction, and use of computer databases is not difficult or unfamiliar. Relax and make the necessary connections from your experience. A computer database is an easy step to take into your future — not trivial, just easy.

Chapter Five

CHAPTER SIX

BUILDING
YOUR DATABASE

When you have finished the planning process, you are ready to begin construction of your database. First, you plan the structure of the database that we discussed in depth in Chapter Five. The construction phase is then completed by entering all of the data — a record at a time — into this structure. The most serious problem you are likely to encounter during this data entry period is to keep from being bored to death.

Prior to the development of microcomputers and database management systems, the process of creating a database wasn't easy. It was a lengthy and expensive process involving costly hardware and the use of professional programmers. Though you could have learned to program yourself, until recently there wasn't any way to avoid the use of expensive hardware. Today, with one of the available database management systems and inexpensive microcomputer hardware you can easily do everything yourself. And, unless you are a very slow typist, it can be done quickly.

SOME REVIEW FROM CHAPTER ONE

The process of data entry was illustrated with the construction of two sample databases, B:FONEBOOK and B:INVENTRY. In these examples, we learned that the mechanical process of creating the database structure has two parts: *first*, selecting a filename (title) for the database; *second*, defining each of the fields (columns) in the database. The rules for selecting a filename are determined by the computer's operating system.

A filename may have eight or fewer letters and numbers. It must begin with a letter. It may not contain blank spaces. Some examples of valid filenames are:

```
CHAPTER1
SCHOOL
FONEBOOK
```

Examples of *invalid* filenames are:

```
CHAPTER 1        Too long and contains a blank space
GOBBLEDEGOOK     Too long
8CHAPT           Starts with a number
```

The purpose of the filename is to identify to the computer which file you want to work with. If the computer has more than one disk drive, you usually must add a disk-drive identifier to the filename. PC/MS-DOS disk drives are identified by a letter followed by a colon (for example, A:). Here are some examples of the valid filenames with disk-drive identifiers:

```
A:CHAPTER1         File is on the A drive
C:SCHOOL           File is on the C drive
B:FONEBOOK         File is on the B drive
```

The disk-drive identifier is not a permanent part of the filename. It varies according to the drive in which the disk currently resides. For example, if we remove the disk containing the file CHAPTER1 from drive A and insert it into drive B, the file will then be identified as B:CHAPTER1.

You may have more than one database file with the same name as long as the files are not on the same disk. The system will not permit you to have two database files with the same name on a disk.

A database is a particular kind of file, a .DBF file. There are other kinds of files. In Chapter Two, we worked briefly with another kind of file called a report form file (.FRM file), which we used to prepare the liquor store inventory report. A database file and a report form file may be on the same disk, and have the same filename. When a database file is created, dBASE automatically appends .DBF to the filename. When a report is created, .FRM is automatically added to the filename. .DBF and .FRM are examples of filetypes. The filename is chosen by the user. In dBASE, the filetype is determined by the system because it uses the filetype information in the performance of tasks.

Once you have selected a filename for your database, you are ready to define the database structure. The DBMS needs to know:

- the number of fields (columns)
- the name of each column
- the width of each column, that is, the number of characters or digits
- the type of information in each column (whether numeric, character, date, memo, or logical)

The DBMS prompts you to provide the information it needs. dBASE prompts you with the full-screen form shown in the creation of the FONEBOOK and INVENTRY databases in Chapters One and Two. For your convenience, the screens that created the database B:INVENTRY are shown again as Figures 6-1 and 6-2. B:INVENTRY is a database with the filename INVENTRY that is located on disk drive B.

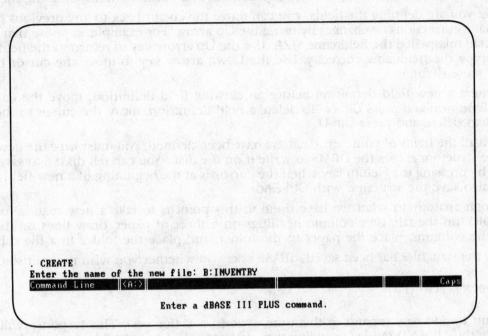

Figure 6-1

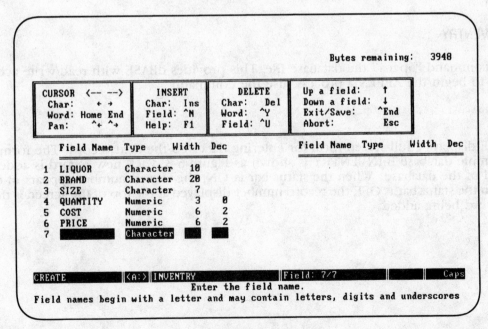

Figure 6-2

Building Your Database

The CREATE command starts a process that guides you through the mechanics of naming the database and defining each field (the structure). Each field is defined by: typing a fieldname into the ten-character space provided by the screen form, pressing a key corresponding to the first character of the desired field type, and (for character and numeric fields) entering the field size.

While you are defining the fields, you can move the cursor back to any previous field definition to make corrections or changes by using the Up arrow. For example, suppose that you notice that you had misspelled the fieldname SIZE. Use the Up arrow key to return to the field definition and to retype the fieldname correctly. Use the Down arrow key to move the cursor back to the field you were defining.

To insert a new field definition before an existing field definition, move the cursor to the existing definition and press Ctrl-N. To delete a field definition, move the cursor to the field that you want to delete and press Ctrl-U.

When all the fields of your new database have been defined, you must *save* the new structure. Saving the structure causes the DBMS to write it on the disk. You can tell dBASE to save your new structure by pressing the Return key when the cursor is at the beginning of a new field definition. You can also save the structure with Ctrl-End.

A rough analogy to what we have done to this point is to take a new manila folder, write INVENTORY on the tab, type column headings on a sheet of paper, draw lines on the paper to separate the columns, place the paper in the folder, and place the folder in a file cabinet.

Once the structure has been saved, dBASE asks you whether you wish to input some records:

Input data records now? (Y/N)

If you want to add new records at this time, type in a Y (for yes). This response will place the database in the APPEND mode for adding new data records. You can add new records at *any* time. To add new records to an existing database you must first place the database in use with the USE command.

. USE B:INVENTRY

The USE command "opens" the database file. This provides dBASE with read/write access to the database. To begin the APPEND process, use the command

. APPEND

and dBASE displays a full-screen form for entering data into the next record. The form provided for the sample database B:INVENTRY is shown as Figure 6-3. Each new record is added directly to the end of the database. When the status bar is ON, the record number appears in the fourth box. When the status bar is OFF, the record number displayed at the top of the screen is the number of the record being added.

Chapter Six

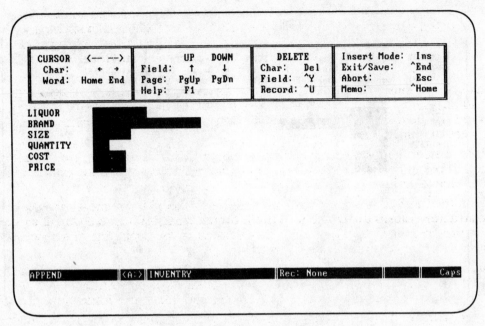

Figure 6-3

The standard screen form used by dBASE displays the fieldnames in a single column down the left side of the screen. The fields are displayed in reverse video, with the cursor initially positioned at the beginning of the first field (in this case, LIQUOR). You can move the cursor to any screen position displayed in reverse video by either typing in characters or by using the arrow keys. Fill out the form as you would when using an electric typewriter.

When you have entered the data for a complete record (see Figure 6-4), dBASE automatically presents a new screen form for the next record. The process continues until you tell it to stop. You can stop appending records by pressing the Return key when a new blank record is presented on the screen. Press the Esc key and the new record about to be added is discarded and the APPEND process stops.

ON ENTERING DATA

The value of a database depends in large part upon the quality of its data. You won't get far if you tell the tax auditor, "I know there are some errors, but it was really fast!" Because data entry is often dull and repetitive work, it is common practice to turn data entry over to the lowest-paid help available. This is a *bad* idea.

In many cases, there will be an enormous amount of data to enter into the new database. Most real liquor stores, for example, have far more than fifteen items in stock. Data entry will be, far and away, the most time-consuming part of most database usage. Entry is done at human speed; retrieval is done at computer speed.

Data entry is the part of the process most prone to error. Although entering several records may be accomplished without error, error-free input for hundreds, perhaps thousands, of records is unlikely.

Building Your Database

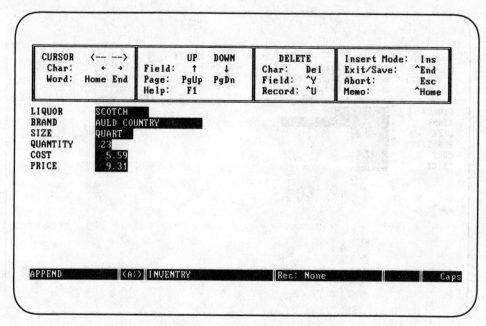

Figure 6-4

DATA-ENTRY ERRORS

When you are adding a large number of new records to a database, such as during the initial construction, you may lose track of where you are. Or, as you are busily working, you may realize suddenly that you made an error during data entry on the last record. To correct an error or find your place, you can back up to the previous record. This is accomplished by pressing PgUp. Each time you press PgUp, you will move back one record in the database. To return to the APPEND mode, press PgDn to move forward (toward the end) of the database.

Errors in a record can be easily corrected by moving the cursor back to the error and typing in the correct information. On most terminals, the arrow keys on the cursor keypad allow you to move the cursor while entering data into the database. The Up arrow and Down arrow move the cursor a field backward and forward in the record. The Right arrow and Left arrow move the cursor one character space to the right and to the left.

Let's try some sample corrections. Suppose that you type in TESSTT and you want TEST. The final T can be removed by placing the cursor on the last T and striking the space bar. The surplus S can be removed by placing the cursor on the second S and pressing the Del key. Del eliminates the character that the cursor is on. You could have just typed over the word TEST and used the space bar to clean up the extra two characters at the end.

Suppose that you typed TET when you wanted TEST. You want to insert the letter S between the E and the T. Use the Ins key. Place the cursor on the last T. To insert the letter S, press the Ins key, type S, and then press Ins again. Ins toggles insert mode on and off. When the insert mode is on, "Ins" is displayed on the screen.

Perhaps you have available only part of the information necessary to complete a record, but you still want to enter what you have. Enter the information you have and then press PgDn. This

Chapter Six

will advance you to the next record without having to step through each of the remaining fields.

To this point, the process of constructing a database has been purely mechanical. You create a file structure according to simple rules and then you enter data. Data entry continues until all the data have been entered. At this point the database is ready to be used to fulfill some purpose — such as providing you with the information needed to help manage a business.

If the data-entry job is small, the simple mechanical approach described above is probably the best way to get the job done. It is straightforward and simple. If there is a lot of data to enter, it might be a good idea to find ways that the computer system can actually help with the entry process.

DATA-ENTRY ASSISTANCE

There are some built-in data entry aids as well as some simple procedures that you can write which enable the computer to assist with or perform some of your data entry tasks for you. In the remaining pages of this chapter, we'll look at custom screen forms, SET CARRY ON/OFF, and menu systems.

SET CARRY ON/OFF is a built-in aid and is initiated with a simple command. Custom screen forms and menu systems are developed by simple procedures that you will learn to write to suit your needs. A *procedure* is an easy way of getting the computer to perform special things for you. The details of "teaching" the computer a procedure will be discussed in Section Six, which begins with Chapter Twenty-Four. The use of procedure-generated end products — that is, custom prompts and menu systems — is included here because of their added value to the data-entry process.

Custom Forms

Custom screen forms illustrate one kind of assistance the computer can provide. We'll show you how to create and use custom forms later on. In the liquor store example, the fieldnames are reasonably descriptive of the field contents. This is often, but not always, the case. When it is not the case, it's nice to be able to include more information. For example, we could make the prompt read something like:

ENTER THE KIND OF LIQUOR (SCOTCH, WHISKEY, ETC.):

This gives much more information than simply displaying the word LIQUOR. In general, such help from the computer is useful, particularly if the filenames are not descriptive or if you have a quantity of data that you want someone else to enter. Custom prompts such as this one can be provided with relative ease via format files. Format files, like databases, have filenames. The same filename rules that apply to other files apply to format files. You must also identify which disk drive the format file is stored on.

To show you how a CUSTOM FORM might work, we will assume that a format file to create the custom form — provide descriptive prompts — has been written. We will call our sample format file B:ENTRY. To have the computer use this format file, following a dot prompt, you enter:

. SET FORMAT TO B:ENTRY

SET FORMAT TO B:ENTRY produces Figure 6-5. From this point on, the custom form B:EN-TRY will be used whenever the EDIT or APPEND commands are used. (Incidentally, writing procedures for database management systems is not at all hard. In fact, it can be fun as well as rewarding.)

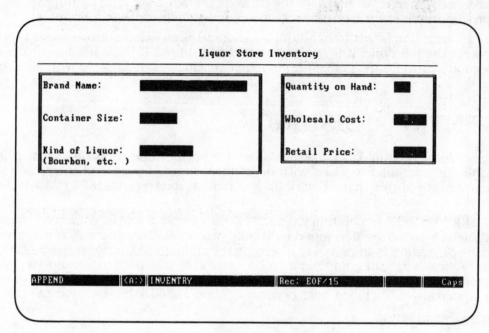

Figure 6-5

SET CARRY ON/OFF

We'll take a short break from what you can teach the computer to do and talk about another capability. In many databases, much redundant data must be entered. In a school for example, there are far more children than there are rooms and teachers, so many teacher names and room numbers are repeated. In the liquor store example, there are several brand names for each kind of liquor. The stock on the shelves is grouped by kind of liquor — vodka, bourbon, and so forth — for the convenience of the customer. The various sizes for a given brand are usually grouped within the brand.

In many cases, the data may be grouped in such a way as to reduce the amount of data that must be typed in. When redundancy is grouped, as in these two examples, the computer can reduce the amount of typing required by "carrying" the data forward from record to record. In dBASE, the command SET CARRY ON allows data to be carried forward. It is turned off by SET CARRY OFF.

Let's consider how data entry would progress for our example if CARRY were SET ON. First, with APPEND, we get an initial screen display and enter the data for Record 1.

With SET CARRY OFF (dBASE's default setting), the display for Record 2 would appear blank. With CARRY ON, the display is exactly like Figure 6-6 with the record counter advanced by one. All we need do is change those fields which are different from Record 1. When we advance, the Record 3 display will be exactly as Record 2 at the time of the advance. This particular assistance can reduce both the amount of typing the number of errors owing to typing mistakes.

Chapter Six

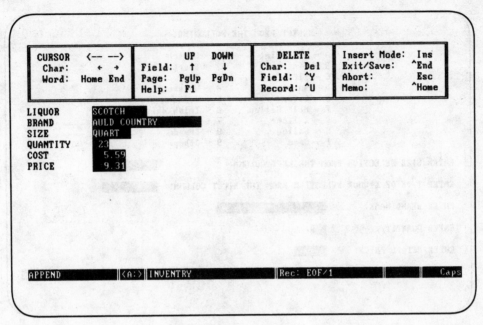

Figure 6-6

A Menu System

Now back to another technique you can teach the computer to do. With this technique, a procedure is written that provides the data entry person with a set of multiple choices from which to select. Such a technique is called a MENU SYSTEM. It also minimizes the possibility of typing error. Unfortunately, it increases the possibility of absolute error. It is profitably used where the data to be input is so different that carrying forward data is not helpful.

Let's suppose that we have written a procedure to do a liquor store inventory using the menu technique. In our hypothetical example, the terminal might provide the display shown in Figure 6-7.

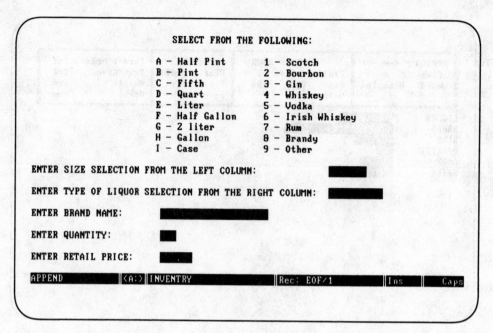

Figure 6-7

This particular example uses some of the helpful aspects of our earlier discussion of custom prompts, as well as the menu selection idea. The information "gallon of gin" is entered as H3. In this example, the entire data entry and menu process is accomplished with one screen display.

If the data to be entered is more extensive, we might require more than one screen display. For example, if there are thirty or forty choices for each of the liquor and size selections, we might want to use one screen display for each of the two selection columns. For this example, three successive screen displays would be required.

Menu procedures, as well as other elaborate prompt systems, can be profitably used when you need a lot of data entered and don't want to have to explain either the nature of the data or anything about the database system — that is, cases where everything that needs to be entered can be selected for a menu.

Conditional Replacement

In addition to these three rather straightforward data-entry aids, there is another, somewhat sneakier, method available for entering certain kinds of conditional information.

The example appropriate to this CONDITIONAL REPLACEMENT method comes from a student database built for an elementary school. The database contains the NAME, ROOM, GRADE, and TEACHER for each student. When the database is built, only the NAME, ROOM, and GRADE need to be entered. When this is completed for each child, the TEACHER information can be added with the dBASE command REPLACE.

```
.REPLACE TEACHER WITH 'MR. JOHNSON' FOR ROOM='101'
.REPLACE TEACHER WITH 'MRS. ADAMS' FOR ROOM='201'
```

Chapter Six

and so on. The best thing about the process of building a database is that usually it is a one-time operation. This process — entering the data — is sometimes called *loading* the database. The build process is critical to all future use of the database. If the information is not complete or if it is entered with errors, the ultimate result will be incomplete and erroneous. And you will be unhappy. If the data has been correctly entered, however, you can begin to make profitable use of it — which is what this is all about.

Moving Data From Other Programs

Many readers may already have stored data using an applications program such as Lotus 1-2-3, WordStar, or SuperCalc. If you've already entered data into the computer for another program you may be able to avoid having to reenter it for dBASE. More and more programs are providing you with tools that let you move information from program to program. For a complete discussion of how to move data into dBASE from another program, see the chapter on "Importing and Exporting Data."

To summarize, the options you have when "building" the original database range from the simple and straightforward APPEND to elaborate procedures for more descriptive prompts. These aids can help minimize your effort:

- custom forms
- data carry forward
- menus
- conditional replacement

These aids reduce the amount of typing required. The larger and more complicated your database, the more helpful these procedures will be.

CHAPTER SEVEN

MODIFYING A DATABASE

Once the database has been built, it will inevitably be changed. In addition to changing the contents of fields like QUANTITY and PRICE, some records will have to be added and some deleted. Evolving government regulations may require new fields to be added to the database. This everyday activity — changing the database — is called *updating*.

Updating a database takes time because it is a manual operation. Routine reports and other output products are usually accomplished automatically at computer speeds and require relatively little time.

The frequency with which the database is updated will depend, in large part, on your needs. Some updating tasks must be done daily. Others can be done weekly or even monthly. Still others are done only as necessary.

The Little Liquor Store, for example, might update an inventory database as each new shipment is received. Employee hours might be updated either daily or weekly. The magnitude of the updating tasks will depend upon the particular application.

Changes to a database usually fall into one or more of these four categories:

• Changing the database structure
• Adding records
• Removing records
• Changing the contents of records

CHANGING THE STRUCTURE OF A DATABASE

The structure of a database is not changed very often. Structural changes are usually in response to some change in the business environment — such as a new government regulation. Changing the structure should be undertaken with some care because there is always a chance, however slight, of losing data.

In many systems the content of the database is destroyed whenever the structure is changed. Users tend to find this more than annoying. DBMS designers have responded with ways to guard against the loss of data. dBASE, for example, automatically makes a backup copy of a database when a change is made to its structure. After the structure has been changed data from the backup copy is automatically moved back to the modified database. The backup copy has the same name as the database, but has the filetype .BAK. Remember also that there *must* be enough space on the disk to hold this backup copy. The dBASE command to change the structure of a database is

. MODIFY STRUCTURE

and it can be used to:

- add fields
- delete fields
- change a fieldname
- change a fieldwidth
- change a fieldtype

In dBASE, the process for modifying the structure looks just like the process for creating the structure. Suppose that we want to make changes to the inventory database B:INVENTRY. First, we must place the database in use. Then we can modify its structure:

. USE B:INVENTRY
. MODIFY STRUCTURE

The dBASE response to the command is shown as Figure 7-1. This is the same screen we used to CREATE the database. At the top of the screen is *key help* menu that shows you which special keys can be used within MODIFY STRUCTURE. F1 toggles this menu on and off.

Adding a Field

To add a field, move the cursor to where you want the new field and press Ctrl-N. A blank field definition will be inserted. For example, to insert a new field between the current fields BRAND and SIZE, use the arrow keys to move the cursor to the SIZE field. The SIZE field definition will be highlighted. Press Ctrl-N. A blank field space for a new field definition will be inserted between BRAND and SIZE as shown in Figure 7-2. The cursor will be automatically positioned to begin entering the new field name.

Chapter Seven

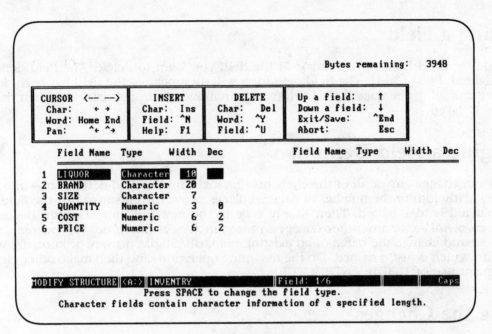

Figure 7-1

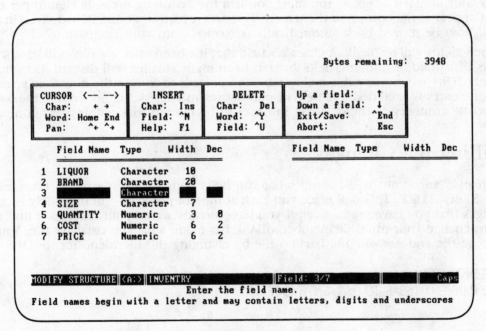

Figure 7-2

Modifying a Database

Deleting a Field

To delete a field, move the cursor to the field you want to delete. The field definition will be highlighted. Press **Ctrl-U**. The field definition will disappear — the field has been deleted. The fieldname and all of the data in that field will be removed from the database when the modified structure is saved.

Changing a Field Definition

You can change any or all of the elements that make up the field definition — the fieldname, fieldtype, fieldwidth or the number of decimal places. Move the cursor so that the field definition to be changed is highlighted. Then simply type in the new field information. If you change a fieldname do *not* make any other change to the structure at that time. For example, if you add a new field and change the name of an existing field, dBASE has no way of knowing which field is new and which is just renamed. Do the renaming operation, and then make other changes with a subsequent use of MODIFY STRUCTURE.

Saving the Changes

To exit from MODIFY structure and save any changes you have made, press **Ctrl-End**. The **End** key is on your numeric keypad. You must confirm the action by pressing **Return** per the instructions that appear at the bottom of the screen. The data records that dBASE had saved in the backup copy will now be moved back automatically (reloaded) into your database.

All new fields will be blank. A character field that has been made smaller will have its rightmost characters discarded. A numeric field that has been made smaller will discard its rightmost (least significant) digits whenever a decimal number is too large to fit into the new field space. If an entire numeric entry is excluded, the field display shows an asterisk. Before erasing the backup copy, look over the contents of the database in order to be certain that nothing has gone awry.

Cancelling the Changes

You can change your mind about what you have done — up to a point. Press **Esc** to abort MODIFY STRUCTURE. This will place you back at the dot prompt — immediately — and discard any changes that you have made. Even if you have already *saved* your changes it may still not be too late to change your mind. Remember, dBASE has made a backup database file. You can *erase* the database file and *rename* the backup file by changing the file identifier to .DBF.

```
. ERASE B:INVENTRY.DBF
. RENAME B:INVENTRY.BAK TO B:INVENTRY.DBF
```

ADDING RECORDS

New records can be added to a database at any time. To add records you must be using the database that you want to add records to. The commands to add new records are APPEND and INSERT.

Chapter Seven

Appending Records

The most commonly used command to add new records is APPEND. This command is identical to the way data records are added when the database is created and has already been described in Chapters One, Two, and Six. When records are appended they are added at the end of the database. That is to say the end of the physical database. If index files are in use the new record will still be added to the end of the physical database. However, it will appear to be inserted into its correct place in the *index order*.

APPEND uses a standard screen form (Figure 7-3) for entering data. Data is entered just as though you were filling out the form with an ordinary typewriter. As you enter the data for each record, dBASE will automatically file it away and present a new screen form for the next record. This process will continue automatically until you tell it to stop. The append process will stop if you press the Return key when a new blank record is presented on the screen. Press the Esc key and the new record being added will be discarded and the APPEND process will stop.

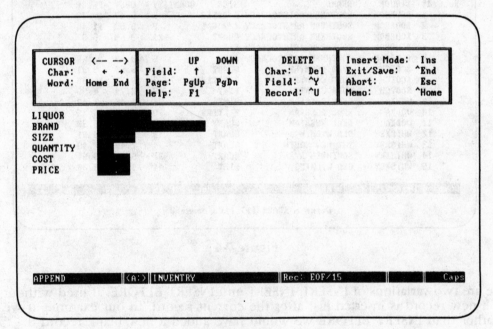

Figure 7-3

Inserting Records

Occasionally, it is desirable to insert a record directly into the middle of a database. This is most commonly done with a sorted database in order to maintain the sorted order. For example, suppose we want to add a new record to the inventory database (Figure 7-4). This database is already sorted by LIQUOR. We can keep it sorted by inserting the new record where it should go. Let's suppose that the new record is for a pint of Southern Rye whiskey. The record should go just in front of the current record 7. Use the command sequence:

Modifying a Database

. GO 7
. INSERT BEFORE

to make the insertion. GO 7 positions the inventory database to the current record 7. INSERT BEFORE inserts a new blank record into this slot — just like sticking a new index card into a card file. The existing record 7 becomes record 8, record 8 becomes record 9, and so on. Once the reordering is completed, dBASE presents a new blank record 7. The data-entry screen is a blank version of Figure 7-3. Once we have entered the data for record 7 the insert process terminates. INSERT allows us to insert only *one* record at a time.

```
. LIST
Record#  LIQUOR    BRAND                SIZE      QUANTITY    COST   PRICE
      1  BOURBON   SOUTHERN ARISTOCRACY 2 LITER          5    6.47   10.78
      2  BOURBON   SOUTHERN ARISTOCRACY 1/2 GAL          3    6.89   11.48
      3  BOURBON   SOUTHERN ARISTOCRACY QUART           21    3.50    5.83
      4  BOURBON   SOUTHERN ARISTOCRACY FIFTH           22    1.78    2.96
      5  BOURBON   SOUTHERN ARISTOCRACY PINT             5    0.99    1.65
      6  SCOTCH    AULD COUNTRY         QUART           23    5.59    9.31
      7  SCOTCH    AULD COUNTRY         2 LITER          7    9.78   16.30
      8  SCOTCH    AULD COUNTRY         PINT            88    2.74    4.56
      9  VODKA     REAL RUSSIAN         PINT            75    1.49    2.48
     10  VODKA     REAL RUSSIAN         2 LITER          9    7.95   13.25
     11  VODKA     REAL RUSSIAN         QUART           35    3.78    6.30
     12  WHISKEY   OLD WYOMING          QUART           19    5.29    8.81
     13  WHISKEY   THE NEW SOUTH        QUART            4    7.49   12.48
     14  WHISKEY   SOUTHERN RYE         QUART           32    5.11    8.51
     15  WHISKEY   OLD WYOMING          PINT            44    1.98    3.30
.
Command Line    <A:> LIKRSORT               Rec: EOF/15              Caps
                  Enter a dBASE III PLUS command.
```

Figure 7-4

There are two variations of INSERT: INSERT and INSERT BEFORE. If used without the word BEFORE, a new record is inserted just after the current record. In our example, if we had used INSERT rather than INSERT BEFORE we would have added a new blank record 8.

REMOVING RECORDS

The other side of the coin from adding new records is removing records. The dBASE commands associated with removing records from a database are:

DELETE
RECALL
PACK

Records are removed by a two-step process. First, a record is *marked* for removal with the DELETE command. Then we remove all records that have been marked for removal with the PACK command. The deletion mark can be removed with the RECALL command — if we RECALL *before* we PACK.

To illustrate the process, let's remove the record having the BRAND name *The New South* from the sample database shown in Figure 7-3. Figure 7-5 shows the transaction. Figure 7-6 shows the resulting database.

The DELETE command marks a record for deletion by placing an asterisk (*) at the beginning of the records that we want to remove. It also tells us how many records were marked by that particular DELETE command. In the example, we expected that only a single record would be marked — any other message tells us that something unexpected has occurred. It is important to realize that many other records could already be marked for removal by earlier DELETE commands.

DISPLAY FOR DELETED( ) shows us *all* of the records that are marked for removal. In this case we have only the one record — the one that was just marked for elimination. The deletion symbol (the *) appears between the record number and the beginning of the record. DELETED( ) is a special dBASE term (a function) which allows us to specify deleted records.

PACK actually removes the deleted records. Once the database is packed those records are *gone*. There is NO unpack command. When we look at Figure 7-6 we see that the record that was marked for deletion is gone. There are now only 14 records. Record 11 is now record 10, Record 12 is now Record 11, and so forth.

As long as we haven't PACKed the database, we can change our minds about records that have been marked for deletion. The command to "undelete" (remove a deletion mark) is RECALL. Here are some examples of RECALL:

```
. RECALL
. RECALL ALL
. RECALL RECORD 14
. RECALL FOR NAME = 'BRONCO, BILLY'
. RECALL FOR BRAND = 'KILARNY GREEN' .AND. LIQUOR = 'IRISH MALT'
```

There are times when you will want to get rid of everything in a database and start over again. One example is a daily sales register. At the end of each day we print out the transactions, clean out the database, and we're ready for the next day. One way to erase all of the records is

```
. DELETE ALL
. PACK
```

Another command that you can use is

```
. ZAP
```

When you use ZAP, dBASE will ask you verify that you really mean it. If you confirm that you do, your records are *gone*. There is no way to get them back.

Modifying a Database

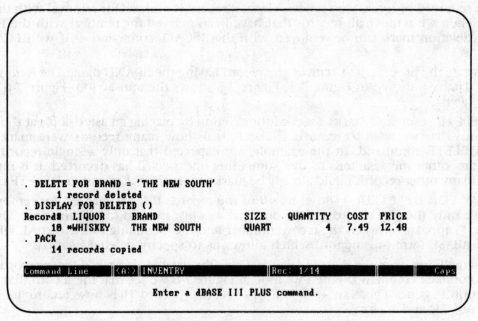

```
. DELETE FOR BRAND = 'THE NEW SOUTH'
      1 record deleted
. DISPLAY FOR DELETED ()
Record# LIQUOR       BRAND           SIZE    QUANTITY   COST   PRICE
     10 *WHISKEY     THE NEW SOUTH    QUART          4   7.49   12.48
. PACK
     14 records copied
.
```

| Command Line | ⟨A:⟩ INVENTRY | Rec: 1/14 | | Caps |

Enter a dBASE III PLUS command.

Figure 7-5: Example of deleting a record

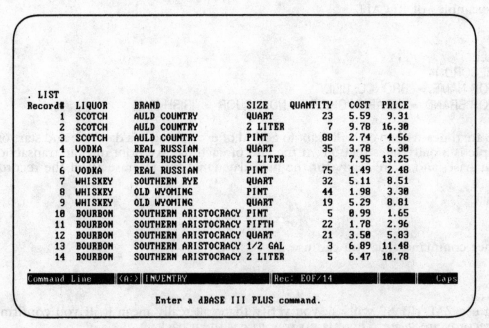

```
. LIST
Record# LIQUOR    BRAND                   SIZE      QUANTITY    COST    PRICE
      1 SCOTCH    AULD COUNTRY            QUART           23    5.59     9.31
      2 SCOTCH    AULD COUNTRY            2 LITER          7    9.78    16.30
      3 SCOTCH    AULD COUNTRY            PINT            88    2.74     4.56
      4 VODKA     REAL RUSSIAN            QUART           35    3.78     6.30
      5 VODKA     REAL RUSSIAN            2 LITER          9    7.95    13.25
      6 VODKA     REAL RUSSIAN            PINT            75    1.49     2.48
      7 WHISKEY   SOUTHERN RYE            QUART           32    5.11     8.51
      8 WHISKEY   OLD WYOMING             PINT            44    1.98     3.30
      9 WHISKEY   OLD WYOMING             QUART           19    5.29     8.81
     10 BOURBON   SOUTHERN ARISTOCRACY    PINT             5    0.99     1.65
     11 BOURBON   SOUTHERN ARISTOCRACY    FIFTH           22    1.78     2.96
     12 BOURBON   SOUTHERN ARISTOCRACY    QUART           21    3.50     5.83
     13 BOURBON   SOUTHERN ARISTOCRACY    1/2 GAL          3    6.89    11.48
     14 BOURBON   SOUTHERN ARISTOCRACY    2 LITER          5    6.47    10.78
```

| Command Line | ⟨A:⟩ INVENTRY | Rec: EOF/14 | | Caps |

Enter a dBASE III PLUS command.

Figure 7-6: Inventory database after removing the record

Chapter Seven

CHANGING THE CONTENTS OF RECORDS

Now let's suppose we want to make changes to the content of the inventory database. This time we want to revise the prices and recount the quantity on hand. This gives us the opportunity to demonstrate the commands for changing record contents:

    EDIT
    BROWSE
    REPLACE

EDIT

EDIT allows us to display and edit a single record at a time. EDIT uses the same screen "form" as APPEND and INSERT. We can select a single record, a group of records, or all of the records for editing. Records can be specified by either record number or content.

To illustrate the use of the command, let's EDIT record 6 in the liquor store inventory (Figure 7-6). Select this record with either

. EDIT RECORD 6

or

. EDIT FOR LIQUOR = 'VODKA' .AND. SIZE = 'PINT'

and the screen in Figure 7-7 is displayed. To change the QUANTITY to 81 and the PRICE to 2.27, use either the Down arrow key or the Return key to position the cursor to the QUANTITY field. Type 81 and press Return. The value stored in QUANTITY will change to 81 and the cursor will advance to the next field. Move the cursor to the PRICE field and type in 2.27. This changes the PRICE to 2.27, advances to the next record — in this case, Record 7 — and returns to the dot prompt.

We can also use EDIT to display records one at a time. For example, if we use

. EDIT FOR LIQUOR = 'VODKA'

we can *leaf* through the VODKA records one at a time. Each time you press the PgDn key you will move one record toward the end of the database. Each time you press PgUp you will move one record toward the beginning of the database. If you try to move out of the three record VODKA group, you will automatically exit from EDIT.

When you edit a record, any changes made are automatically saved when you exit from *that* record. You can abort changes to a record by pressing the Esc key before you leave that record. Once changes are saved, you cannot *undo* them with the Esc key.

Modifying a Database

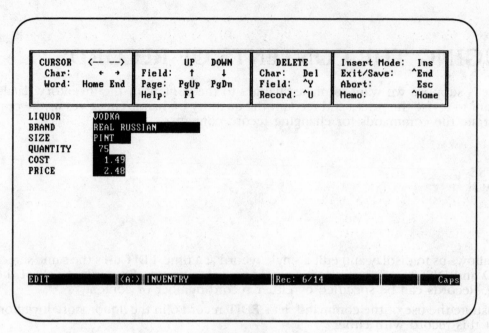

Figure 7-7

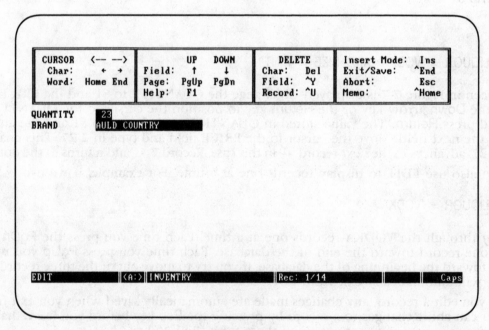

Figure 7-8

Chapter Seven

You can select which fields are to be presented for editing and the order in which they appear on the screen. To edit the fields QUANTITY and BRAND, use

. EDIT FIELDS QUANTITY, BRAND

and the screen shows the display in Figure 7-8.

BROWSE

Another full-screen editing command that allows us to view and change database contents is BROWSE. A graphic description of BROWSE is provided by cutting a section from a piece of paper. Now place the paper with the hole in it over this page. By moving this "window" about, you can view the entire contents of the page — a portion at a time. BROWSE provides a window onto your database. It allows you to view a part of the database at a time and to make changes wherever you wish. A BROWSE view of our liquor store inventory is shown as Figure 7-9. To use the BROWSE command, simply type

. BROWSE

BROWSE displays each record as a single row. If the record is too long to fit on the screen (it is longer than 80 characters) only as much as *will* fit is displayed. To move the window and view the off screen part of a long record, press **Ctrl-Right** arrow or **Ctrl-Left** arrow. This *pans* the database one field at a time in the direction of the arrow.

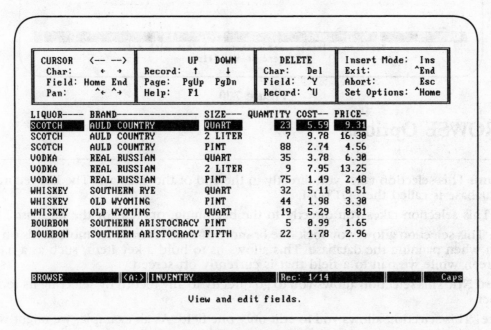

Figure 7-9

Modifying a Database

The currently selected record is highlighted. The Up and Down arrow keys can be used to change the record selection one arrow at a time. The PgUp and PgDn keys let you *scroll* through the database a screenful at a time. More records can be viewed at a time if the *key help* menu is off. Pressing F1 toggles the menu on and off. You can edit the highlighted record by simply typing in new information.

Additional features of BROWSE can be invoked by pressing Ctrl-Home. This presents a five-option menu at the top of the screen (Figure 7-10). This menu is initially presented with the option *Bottom* highlighted. A menu option is selected by using the arrow keys to highlight the desired menu option and then pressing Return.

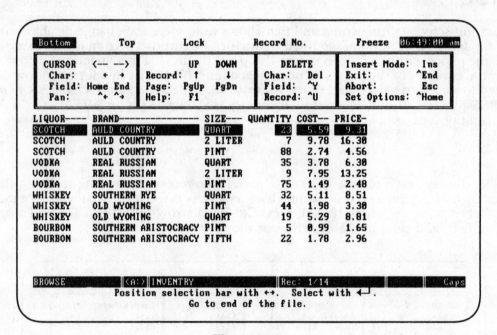

Figure 7-10

The BROWSE Options

Bottom: This selection takes you directly to the end of the database. The last record in the database is called the BOTTOM.

Top: This selection takes you directly to the beginning, or TOP, of the database.

Lock: This selection allows you lock one or more of the currently leftmost fields on the screen when panning the database. This allows us to hold a key item, such as a name, on screen while we pan to a field that is currently off screen.

Record No: This selection allows you to go directly to any record by selecting its record number.

Freeze: This selection allows you to edit only one field. As an example, we might want to edit only the quantity on hand when we conduct an inventory.

You can also select which fields are to be browsed and the order in which they are to be used by adding a field list to the BROWSE command.

. BROWSE FIELDS BRAND, SIZE, QUANTITY

REPLACE

The REPLACE command is used to replace the contents of specified fields with new data. This command is most useful when you want to change several records at a time. For example, suppose that our cost for SCOTCH has increased by 10%. We want to pass on this increased cost to our customers so, we need to increase the values of both COST and PRICE by 10%. REPLACE does it easily:

. REPLACE COST WITH COST * 1.1 FOR LIQUOR = 'SCOTCH'
        3 Records replaced
. REPLACE PRICE WITH PRICE * 1.1 FOR LIQUOR = 'SCOTCH'
        3 Records replaced

Similarly, to increase *all* prices by 10%, use the command:

. REPLACE ALL PRICE with PRICE * 1.1
        15 Records replaced

When REPLACE is used with a condition, *every* record that meets the condition will be changed. The number of records that were changed is displayed on the line following the command.

If you are working with an indexed file, do *not* use REPLACE to change more than one record at a time in a key field. The result depends on a number of factors and may not be at all what you expected. When making multiple changes to a key field, it is best to *turn off* the index, make your changes and then reindex.

Changing Record Contents with Indexed Databases

If your database is used in conjunction with tables such as INDEX files, the database *may* require reindexing whenever records are added, removed, or changed. Most modern database managers provide for automatic updating of indexes — provided that the INDEX files were active (open) when you made the changes. If you were not using the INDEX files you can either reindex or you can use the REINDEX command. This command can be used to reindex up to seven indexes at a time. For example:

. USE INVENTRY INDEX BRAND, SIZE, VALUE
. REINDEX

Database applications that require frequent changing can benefit from the kinds of procedures illustrated in the last chapter: descriptive prompts and menus. The use of procedures can be an effective substitute for your memory. Procedures also allow a database to be manipulated by less skilled (hence less costly) help. The two techniques can be combined to provide very powerful and versatile aids to changing a database.

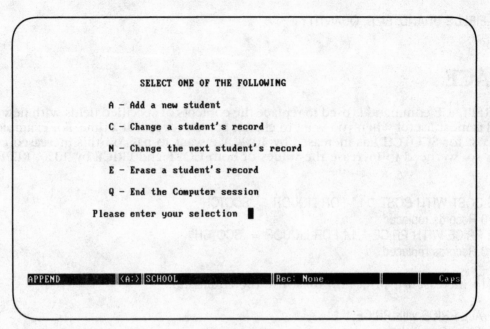

Figure 7-11

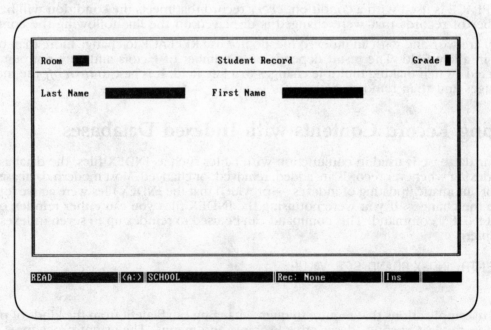

Figure 7-12

Chapter Seven

Figure 7-11 illustrates changing an elementary school database using a combination of descriptive prompts and menus to help the person entering the data. This particular example will add records, delete records, and provide the capability of changing records. The records contain the NAME, ROOM, GRADE, TEACHER, and fields containing other information about each student.

If selection C is chosen, the computer can be set up to provide a new display (Figure 7-12).

When the information above has been provided to the computer, there is a short delay while the computer locates the student of interest. The computer then displays the student's record as in Figure 7-13.

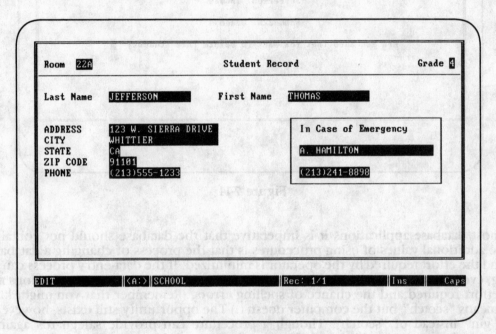

Figure 7-13

An operator can select information to be changed by moving the cursor to the field to be changed and typing in the new information. When the changes have been completed, the operator is returned to the first (main) menu. A new change operation is selected and the process is repeated. The menu option A would go directly to the last student record. The new record displayed would, of course, be all blank. Menu option S provides a means of moving from record to record, as when entering test scores, without the necessity of entering unnecessary information. Menu option D would display the screen in Figure 7-11 to request information about the student. If the delete option is selected, the procedure should always provide the operator a display like that in Figure 7-14.

This example shows how the use of menus and descriptive prompts can aid the person who must enter new information into the computer. It is somewhat analogous to the use of paper forms by clerical help wherein a written procedure tells the clerk which form to use. In the case of the computer, a procedure tells the computer which "form" to use. If the operator using the computer is not familiar with the computer, the procedure should contain at least one menu selection for operator assistance or HELP.

Modifying a Database

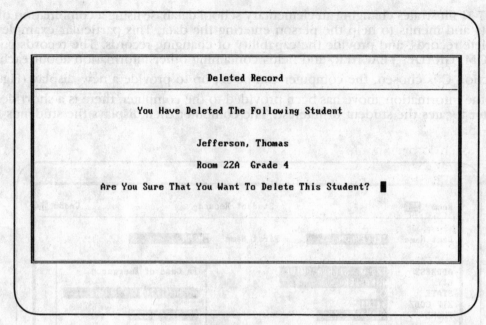

```
                    Deleted Record


     You Have Deleted The Following Student


                 Jefferson, Thomas

               Room 22A   Grade 4

     Are You Sure That You Want To Delete This Student?  ▮
```

Figure 7-14

For most database applications it is imperative that the database should not contain errors. One of the additional values of using procedures is that the process of changing a database is formalized and the effort required by the operator is minimized. If the data-entry process can be made interesting, even entertaining, the likelihood of error is reduced. Some menu operations minimize both the effort required and the chance of spelling errors. (Remember that you might know that ''scocth'' means ''scotch'', but the computer doesn't.) The opportunity still exists, however, for the entry of ''gin'' instead of ''scotch''. Though a procedure can provide safeguards against these possibilities, it does require additional effort on the part of the person writing the procedure.

MAINTAINING A DATABASE

Maintaining can be viewed as *safeguarding* a database. If you have a database that consists of records on paper, there are some problems to safeguarding those paper records: a coffee spill can obscure part of a record; a piece of paper can be inadvertently thrown away. However, few things short of absolute calamity (fire, flood, or hurricane) are catastrophic to the database. This is not true with a computer database. Accidentally placing your finger on the floppy disk surface can damage your database. A cigarette can destroy it completely. A floppy disk is more vulnerable than a filing cabinet full of paper. All the things that work to make the database convenient to use also work to make it susceptible to damage.

Much of the foregoing gloom can be avoided by strictly adhering to some simple procedures. One or two backup copies of the database should be maintained and protected. This is one very good reason for having at least two disk drives on your computer system. If this is the case, you can easily copy your database file onto a floppy disk using the PC/MS-DOS command COPY. If your database file is too large to fit onto a floppy disk, you can use the PC/MS-DOS command BACKUP. This command will backup your database file onto several floppy disks.

Let's demonstrate the use of the DOS COPY command by making a backup copy of our IN-VENTRY database, which is located on the B disk drive. Exit from dBASE by using the dBASE command QUIT. When you leave dBASE, you are in the operating system — and you will see an operating system prompt. If you are using a computer with two floppy disks — and no hard disk, you should remove the dBASE disk from the A disk drive. Insert a fresh, formatted disk into the A disk drive. Then type in the COPY command as shown below

```
A> COPY B:INVENTRY.DBF A:INVENTRY.DBF
```

One approach to backing up your files is to have two copies and to use them on alternate days. Properly used, two copies protect against loss of all except, perhaps, one day's work. If you can limit the liability to this value (barring fire, flood, or war), you have done about as well as you can do.

It's actually possible to protect against major disasters to a higher degree than is possible with paper records. Although it is not reasonable to maintain two complete sets of paper records in two separate locations, you can easily do so with computer databases. Since you can copy the database onto floppy disks or tape, copies can be dispersed and stored at remote locations — providing some reasonable protection for disasters short of nuclear war.

Modifying a Database

CHAPTER EIGHT

USING
A DATABASE

There are really two parts to using a database. The first, keeping it current (that is, updating) was covered in the last chapter. The second, getting it to do something for you, is the subject of this chapter.

BASIC USES OF THE DATABASE

There are two basic uses for a database:

- To perform routine tasks such as payroll, tax reports, and inventory management
- To obtain specific information whenever necessary

Most database management systems, like dBASE, have a report writer that is suitable for producing a variety of standard reports. If the report writer isn't up to a task, you can prepare procedures that will enable you to produce specialized custom reports. You can also obtain ad hoc data directly from your keyboard with the help of the *query language*.

The database provides a "central pool" of information that you can use for any purpose. You can obtain specific information on an ad hoc basis and you can use the data to prepare standard reports on a regular basis.

For example, suppose that your company is considering a new union contract. Management needs to know the impact of the contract before agreeing to the terms. If, as is often the case even in large, professionally designed and managed systems, the personnel and payroll systems are separate, it might take a considerable effort to determine the impact of the proposed contract. With separate systems there is much duplication of effort and information. For example, a computer system for payroll needs a certain amount of information about each employee — name, employee number, number of dependents, and so on. The personnel system needs that same information, plus some additional data. When the systems are separate, the data stored in one cannot always be used by the other.

The separation (and duplication) of related information by applications programs is one of the factors that led to the development of database management. In a database system, the data is independent of the application. It is up to the user to decide what to do with the data. If the personnel and payroll systems use a common database, the information is directly available to each and can also be available directly from the keyboard with simple queries.

EXTRACTING INFORMATION

Database systems respond to user requests for information. These requests are called *queries*. The part of the DBMS that does this is usually called its *Query Language Processor* (QLP). The dBASE QLP is just one part of its Applications Development Language (ADL), which is usually referred to as simply dBASE.

There are a number of ways to extract information from your database. The REPORT command offers one straightforward method of retrieving data. Another technique is offered by the QUERY file. Both REPORT and the QUERY file are discussed in detail in Section 5. In this chapter we want to discuss what we usually refer to as the query language. In dBASE, the specific commands that we think of as the query commands are:

DISPLAY	AVERAGE	LOCATE
LIST	SUM	FIND
COUNT	?	

The query language allows you to tell the computer what you want it to do. Most contemporary query languages resemble ordinary English. In some systems, the *only* function of the QLP is to extract ad hoc information from the database.

We will use the query commands to show you how to extract information from your database. In addition, we will cover the general structure of dBASE commands — the command terminology, what the parts are called, and how to make sense out of the manual. The terminology in this chapter is just for your information — don't bother with trying to memorize it. Use it to impress your boss.

Query Languages

There are two types of query languages: procedural and nonprocedural.

Procedural query languages are much like traditional computer languages, such as BASIC, FORTRAN, PL/1, and COBOL. With a procedural language you tell the computer *how* to do what you want it to — step by step. In such languages you tell the computer how to solve the problem — not what the problem is.

Nonprocedural languages allow you to tell the computer *what* you want it to do. The system figures out how to get the answer.

For example, if we have a telephone directory database and want to know how many entries are from Glendale, the command

. COUNT FOR 'Glendale' $ ADDRESS

will give us the result. This is an example of a nonprocedural command. We've told the machine *what* we want it to do — not *how* to do it.

Some query languages have both procedural and nonprocedural features. dBASE has features of both. There are specific terms that are used to describe these aspects of a relational database query language. Procedural features of the language are called the *relational algebra*. Nonprocedural features are called the *relational calculus*. These terms have value for the database specialist; for the average user they can be a source of intimidation and confusion.

Specific information can be obtained directly from the keyboard via the query language. To make effective use of the query commands, you need to know the fieldnames, and have some idea as to what is contained in the fields.

The Query Commands

Here are some examples of dBASE query commands:

. SUM QUANTITY FOR LIQUOR = 'BOURBON'
. COUNT FOR 'Robert' $ NAME
. DISPLAY QUANTITY FOR LIQUOR = 'SCOTCH' .AND. SIZE = 'PINT'
. DISPLAY NEXT 5 FOR LIQUOR = 'VODKA'

There are typically four parts to a command:

- the command name
- the object
- the scope
- the condition

The command *usually* begins with a verb whose dBASE meaning is close to the ordinary English meaning. SUM, COUNT, DISPLAY, and LOCATE are examples of dBASE command names.

The *object* specifies the fields to which the command applies. The *scope* is the physical section of the database to which the command applies. It doesn't depend on content. The *condition* is the logical part of the database to which the command applies. It does depend on content. Let's look at an example command:

. SUM QUANTITY FOR LIQUOR = 'BOURBON'

In ordinary English, this command would read: "How many bottles of bourbon are in the inventory?" The command name is SUM. The object is the field QUANTITY. The condition is LIQUOR = 'BOURBON'. There is no stated scope; so, the scope takes on its *default* value.

Scope is a troublesome term for beginners; scope simply defines the *physical* part of the database that the command applies to — one record, all records, the next 30 records. Most commands have a scope. If we don't explicitly state a scope, dBASE supplies one. If dBASE supplies a scope, it is called the *default* scope. The default scope is either the current record — or all records — depending on the particular command. Probably 95% of your commands make use of the built-in, or default, scope. The specific values that you can use for scope are:

record *n*	use only a specific record
next *n*	use only the next *n* records for the command
rest	to the end of the database
all	the entire database

Similarly, there is usually an object (a what). The object is usually a list of the fields you want included in the command. If you don't specify an object, dBASE selects one. The default object is usually the entire record. If we had not explicitly specified the field QUANTITY in SUM example above, all the numeric fields would be summed.

Let's look at the example DISPLAY command:

. DISPLAY NEXT 5 FOR LIQUOR = 'VODKA'

The command verb is DISPLAY. The unstated object is the entire record (all fields). The scope is the next 5 records. The condition is LIQUOR = 'VODKA'.

Command Syntax

The structure of a command is called its *syntax*. No matter what language you are using you *must* adhere to the proper syntax for that language. The manual for the language you are using will define the syntax of each command, including all the options, in detail. Let's look at the command syntax for the DISPLAY command as it appears in the dBASE manual.

DISPLAY [OFF][<scope>][<expression list>][FOR <condition>]
[WHILE <condition>][TO PRINT]

The parts of the command that appear in square brackets ([ ]) are optional. Don't type in the square brackets — they simply identify which parts are optional. The angle brackets (< >) identify the parts that are selected by the user. Again, as before, don't enter the angle brackets. The terms OFF and TO PRINT are special options for the DISPLAY command. OFF keeps the record number from being displayed.

The manual defines the default scope for each command as well as the default object. For DISPLAY the built-in scope is the current record. If you use a FOR or WHILE condition in the command, the scope automatically switches to ALL — unless you explicitly restrict the scope with either NEXT N or REST.

The default object is the complete record. The object — what is to be displayed — is an *expression list*. What's an expression? One example of an expression is PRICE * QUANTITY, which asks that two fields be multiplied. We don't want to display the contents of the two fields, we want to display the result of the calculation. An expression can be just a field or it can be an operation involving one or more fields, variables, and constants. Some of our examples have used expression lists. In the simplest form, an expression list is just a list of fieldnames (expressions) separated by commas:

QUANTITY, PRICE, COST, BRAND, QUANTITY * PRICE

Chapter Eight

This list is called a *comma delimited* list because the items (expressions) are separated by commas. dBASE expects items in a list to be comma delimited.

How we put the pieces of the command together doesn't matter — as long as the verb comes first. It's probably a good idea to put the command into something resembling an English statement. The following commands will produce identical results, but the first command is much easier to read and understand:

```
. DISPLAY NEXT 5 QUANTITY * PRICE FOR LIQUOR = 'VODKA'
. DISPLAY FOR LIQUOR = 'VODKA' QUANTITY * PRICE NEXT 5
```

Conditions

When we are extracting information from the database we will, most often, attach some condition to the command because we want to obtain information based on content. For example, we might want to see which inventory items represent an investment of more than $100.00:

```
. DISPLAY FOR COST * QUANTITY > 100.00
```

A condition, such as the one above, usually involves a comparison between two items. If the comparison holds, the condition is *True*. Otherwise, it is *False*. The command is applicable only when the condition is True. In the above example, the condition is evaluated as True whenever the contents of COST multiplied by the contents of QUANTITY are greater than 100.00.

You can use the content of a *logical* field as a condition. In that case, no comparison is made. For example, suppose that we have a check register database which contains the Logical field CANCELLED. This field indicates whether or not a check has cleared the bank. When we use this field in a FOR clause we do NOT make a comparison. Logical fields have a built in comparison — they are always True or False.

```
. DISPLAY FOR CANCELLED
```

Comparison Operators

Character, date, and numeric fields, when used in conditions, are always compared with something. Comparisons are made with the help of comparison or *relational* operators. These are:

<	Less Than	< =	Less Than or Equal
>	Greater Than	> =	Greater Than or Equal
=	Equal	#	Not Equal
$	Contained in	< >	Not Equal

The $ (contained in) operator can be used only with character comparisons. The remaining seven can be used for comparisons involving any of the three data types. Comparisons are always made from left to right. For example, A < B means: Is A less than B? If we turn the symbol around, A > B means: Is A greater than B?

Here is an example of a numeric comparison:

```
. DISPLAY FOR COST * QUANTITY > 87.50
```

We can compare date fields directly. Suppose that our database has two date fields: PURCHASED and PAIDON. The command:

. DISPLAY FOR PURCHASED = PAIDON

will compare the two. If we want to compare the purchase date with an explicit date such as 8/15/85, we must make the comparison with the help of the CTOD function.

. DISPLAY FOR PURCHASED = ctod('8/15/85')

Why all of this? We can make comparisons only between items of the same data type. We need to have a way of telling dBASE the data type of the value we are comparing the field to. The dBASE programmers decided that this was the way to make direct date comparisons. (The CTOD( ) function is discussed in Chapter Sixteen.)

Now let's take a look at comparing character data. You can use *all* the comparison operators with character data. Making character comparisons, however, isn't quite as straightforward as comparing numbers and dates. The following command illustrates a simple character comparison. This command compares the contents of the LIQUOR field with the *constant* SCOTCH

. DISPLAY FOR LIQUOR = 'SCOTCH'

to display all the scotch records in the database. Note that the compared value was enclosed in single quotes. These quotes are called *delimiters*. Delimiters can be single quotes, double quotes, or square brackets. *When using single quotes, make sure to use closing quote for both opening and closing the character string.* The following are equivalent commands:

. DISPLAY FOR LIQUOR = 'SCOTCH'
. DISPLAY FOR LIQUOR = "SCOTCH"
. DISPLAY FOR LIQUOR = [SCOTCH]

In the liquor store inventory, SCOTCH is the only LIQUOR that begins with an S. We would obtain exactly the same display with

. DISPLAY FOR LIQUOR = "S"

In character comparisons, the equal sign does *not* usually mean equality; it means BEGINS WITH. For this reason, the comparison does not work the other way around. For example

. DISPLAY FOR 'SCOTCH' = LIQUOR

results in no output at all. There are more characters — albeit blanks — in LIQUOR than in our comparison word. We are really comparing character strings. A character string is a sequence of characters. LIQUOR represents a sequence of characters that is *always* ten characters long — that is its fieldwidth.

The $ (contained in) operator works similarly. The command

. DISPLAY FOR 'Glendale' $ ADDRESS

Chapter Eight

will display every record where the word 'Glendale' is contained anywhere within the ADDRESS field. On the other hand

. DISPLAY FOR ADDRESS $ 'Glendale'

results in no display at all. ADDRESS is larger than *Glendale*. As such, it can never be contained within the word.

There are no such problems associated with the use of *greater than* or *less than* operators. When you use these operators, think about the comparison as if you were putting words in alphabetical order. SMITH comes after SAMUELS. This means that SMITH is *greater than* SAMUELS. These comparisons use the ASCII ordering of letters and numbers. If you are unsure of the relative value of characters, consult the ASCII Chart in Appendix D.

We can become more specific with our requests for information by combining conditions. Suppose, in our liquor store inventory, we want to see only quarts of whiskey. We can do this like

. DISPLAY FOR LIQUOR = 'WHISKEY' .AND. SIZE = 'QUART'

The .AND. is used in just about the same way as you would use it in ordinary English. Be sure to add the periods to both ends of the word — they *must* be there. When we use the .AND. *both* conditions must be satisfied. Sometimes this requires some thought. For example, the command

. DISPLAY FOR LIQUOR = 'WHISKEY' .AND. LIQUOR = 'SCOTCH'

results in the dot prompt. No records are displayed. How can this be? We've asked the computer for both the WHISKEY and SCOTCH records. We know we have both. What's wrong? We tend to think in terms of the whole database. The computer must deal with a record at a time. There are no records where the content of the LIQUOR field is both WHISKEY and SCOTCH. Remember, all the conditions must be satisfied. In this case, whenever one is satisfied the other cannot be satisfied. This would read "Display all the records where the LIQUOR field contains both WHISKEY and SCOTCH" in ordinary English. Let's rewrite this command:

. DISPLAY FOR LIQUOR = 'WHISKEY' .OR. LIQUOR = 'SCOTCH'

This command translate to the ordinary English request "Display all of the records where the LIQUOR field contains either WHISKEY *or* SCOTCH." Now the command will be honored whenever *either* condition is satisfied. This is what we want — at least in this case. You can connect as many conditions as are necessary together in this way. By doing this (connecting conditions), your requests become increasingly specific. The only limitation is that the maximum command length is 254 characters.

Boolean Operators

The .AND. and .OR. in the above examples are *Boolean* operators. They were named after George Boole, the 19th-century mathematician who is credited with the development of mathematical logic. The Boolean operators are also called *logical* operators. As we have seen, .AND. and .OR. are almost the same as *and* and *or* in everyday English. The operators are written with periods at each end to make sure that we think of them and use them as operators — to distinguish them from their ordinary English counterparts. You must take some care when using the logical operators or you can get an unexpected result. The result will *always* be technically correct — you get what you ask for. Although technically correct, it may well give you the "wrong" answer. This is an example of where the computer does exactly what you tell it to do — not what you want it to do. The Boolean operators are described in more detail in the chapter "A Little Logic."

Some Query Examples

Queries are appropriate to a wide range of user needs. We might want — for one reason or another — to manipulate data contained in a database, but not actually change it. This can allow us to play *what if* games with our data. One way to do this is to copy all or part of the database and play games with the copy.

You can copy selected records and fields to another database file. For example, let's copy the fields BRAND, SIZE, and PRICE from INVENTRY to a new file that we'll name WHATIF. To make it more interesting, we'll copy only the SCOTCH records. We can do all this with the single command:

. COPY FIELD BRAND,SIZE,PRICE TO WHATIF FOR LIQUOR = 'SCOTCH'

This new file WHATIF is a database file just like INVENTRY. The difference is that it has only three fields — BRAND, SIZE, and PRICE and three records. Technically this is the *projection of the relation INVENTRY onto WHATIF as restricted by the predicate LIQUOR = 'SCOTCH'.* For that matter, all of the display operations are also *projections*. Who would recognize that as a description of COPY or DISPLAY — and who cares?

DISPLAY and LIST

The DISPLAY and LIST commands do *almost* the same thing. They are both used to display data. DISPLAY, however, is primarily intended to send data to your video monitor. LIST is primarily intended to send data to your printer. DISPLAY, when used alone, will display all of a single record. LIST, by itself, will display the entire database. DISPLAY ALL is roughly equivalent to LIST. The difference is that DISPLAY ALL will pause after every screenful. You must press a key (any key) to see the next screenful. LIST displays the entire database without pause. In order to see the difference, you must have a database that takes more than a single screenful.

You can print the output of either command by adding the phrase TO PRINT. This automatically directs the command output to *both* the screen and the printer.

The Math Queries

There are three commands that can you can use to obtain numeric values regarding the contents of a database. These commands are COUNT, SUM, and AVERAGE. COUNT is used to count the records that meet a specified criteria. COUNT used alone counts all of the records in the database. If you need to know the number of records, it is a lot faster to use DISPLAY STRUCTURE — the number of records is part of the information contained in the structure.

COUNT is best used in conjuction with a condition. For example, if you want to know how many database records there are for the brand Real Russian, you would use

. COUNT FOR BRAND = 'REAL RUSSIAN'
    3 Records

Chapter Eight

The answer is returned on the next line: Three records satisfied the condition BRAND = 'REAL RUSSIAN' in this example.

You learned about the SUM command in Chapter Two. This command returns the arithmetic sum of an expression for a number of records. Unless otherwise specified, all numeric fields in the database will be summed for all records. To obtain the sum of QUANTITY, QUANTITY * COST for all SCOTCH records, use

```
. SUM QUANTITY, QUANTITY * COST FOR LIQUOR = 'SCOTCH'
    3 records summed
    QUANTITY      QUANTITY * COST
       118             438.15
```

The AVERAGE command gives you the arithmetic value of the specified items over a number of records. An average is just the sum divided by the number of records involved in the calculation. Unless otherwise specified, all numeric fields in the database will be averaged for all records. To obtain the AVERAGE cost of pints, use

```
. AVERAGE COST FOR SIZE = 'PINT'
    4 records averaged
COST
1.80
```

Finding Records

There are any number of reasons that you might want to find a particular record. The commands that find records are usually called *positioning* commands since they position the database. The dBASE positioning commands are LOCATE, CONTINUE, and FIND.

LOCATE is the most general of these two commands. It can be used just like any of the query commands. That is to say, you can specify a scope and/or conditions for the search. Suppose that we want to locate a record with the brand Real Russian where the container size is a pint. The command is

```
. LOCATE FOR BRAND = 'REAL RUSSIAN' .AND. SIZE = 'PINT'
Record =      6
```

If a record that matches the search criteria is found, the database is positioned to the record and the record number is displayed on the line below the command, as shown above. If there is no matching record, the database will be positioned to the first record following the search scope. LOCATE searches the entire database unless the scope is somehow restricted. In any event, if the LOCATE fails the message is

End of LOCATE scope

LOCATE gives us an excellent opportunity to demonstrate the use of WHILE and FOR conditions together in the same command. Now of course the use of any positioning is silly in a 15-record database, still the principals are the same as in a 15,000-record database. Suppose we are positioned to the first BOURBON record in the liquor store inventory. To locate a pint of Bourbon, use

. LOCATE FOR SIZE = 'PINT' WHILE LIQUOR = 'BOURBON'

LOCATE will get us the first occurrence of a record. Let's suppose that we are searching for bourbon records.

. LOCATE FOR LIQUOR = 'BOURBON'

Our first try — assuming that the search began with the database positioned in front of the first bourbon record — will give us the first bourbon record. We can continue the search by using the command

. CONTINUE

This command will resume the search even if we issue other dBASE commands between it and the original LOCATE. We can even reposition the database and resume the search with CONTINUE.

FIND can only be used with an indexed database. We first discussed this command in the chapter on indexing and sorting. FIND will search an index file for the desired record content. The advantage to FIND is that it is much faster than LOCATE. It is also much less flexible and you can find a record only by its index key. In addition, you cannot use logical operators in a FIND (index) search.

Although indexing is not usually thought of as a query operation, you can make effective use of this technique to obtain needed information. Let's suppose that our liquor store owner wants desperately to know which item the store has the most of and which item the store has the least of. An index will provide a list of the inventory items ordered by quantity.

. INDEX ON QUANTITY TO QTY
    15 records indexed

The index will always be in ascending order (from least to most); so, the first database record will be the one with the smallest quantity, and the last will be the one with the largest quantity. To go to the beginning of the database use the command GO TOP. To go to the end of the indexed database use the command GO BOTTOM. The beginning of the database is the TOP. The end of the database is the BOTTOM.

```
. GO TOP
. DISPLAY OFF BRAND, SIZE, QUANTITY
BRAND                  SIZE                QUANTITY
SOUTHERN ARISTOCRACY 1/2 GAL                   3

. GO BOTTOM
. DISPLAY OFF BRAND, SIZE, QUANTITY
BRAND                  SIZE                QUANTITY
AULD COUNTRY           PINT                     88
```

From the keyboard we have directly answered the question. The item we have the least of is half gallons of Southern Aristocracy. The one we have the most of is pints of Auld Country.

Another way to obtain information by indexing is to SET UNIQUE ON. With this in place we can find the unique occurrences of data items with the database. In the liquor store inventory we

Chapter Eight

can immediately see that we have four kinds of liquor. That might not be so apparent in a real inventory. Let's go through this operation so that you can see the result. Don't forget to turn UNIQUE back off when you are finished.

```
. SET UNIQUE OFF
. INDEX ON LIQUOR TO UNIQUE
    4 records indexed

. LIST LIQUOR
Record #    LIQUOR
      1     BOURBON
      2     SCOTCH
      9     VODKA
     12     WHISKEY

. SET UNIQUE OFF
```

These query examples are only a tiny sampling of the kinds of things you can ask a database for. The possibilities are really unlimited. The important point is that you must understand enough about the process to make query use sensible and useable in light of your own needs.

YOUR OWN ELECTRONIC SCRATCHPAD

There is another very useful tool available to you, an accessory to all the larger things possible with your database and computer. You can temporarily store data items such as the content of a field or the result of a calculation into a temporary location in your computer's memory. This is often convenient when performing operations from the keyboard and vital when preparing procedures for automatic operations. It's much like having an electronic scratchpad. To store an item into the scratchpad all you have to do is assign the item a name and a value:

```
. MYNAME = 'Robert'
. ANUMBER = 5
```

You can retrieve these items from your scratchpad at any time by simply typing a question mark followed by the name of the item

```
. ? MYNAME, ANUMBER
Robert 5
```

Each item stored in memory is a *memory variable*. The examples above are both memory variables. You can have up to 256 separate items, memory variables, at any one time as long as total memory used by these variables is less than 6,000 bytes. How does dBASE know these are memory variables? When you request an item as in the above example, dBASE searches the current database for a field name. If the name doesn't belong to a field, dBASE searches a special table for the name of the memory variable.

The process of squirrelling an item away in memory is actually called *assignment*. In the example above we assigned the value *Robert* to the variable *MYNAME*. Each variable has a data type just like each field has a field type. Memory variables can be one of *four* data types — *character, date, logical*, or *numeric*. Unlike fields, however, you don't explicitly state the data type when you create the variable. The datatype is automatically determined by the kind of data that you store in the variable. In the examples above, MYNAME is a character variable because we stored character data in it. ANUMBER is a numeric variable because we stored a number in it. You can change the data type of a memory variable at any time by simply storing a new datatype in it.

A memory variable also has a *size*, just as a field has a field width. The size is automatically established by whatever you put in it. If you store something new in a variable the variable size will automatically become larger or smaller to accommodate the new contents.

A variable also has a name. The name can be anything that you want it to be — within certain limits. The name can be up to ten characters long. It *must* begin with a letter. It cannot contain embedded blank spaces. It can contain letters, numbers, and underscores. Another caution, it should not be the same as an *active* fieldname or a dBASE command verb. Nothing catastrophic will happen if it is, but the result will not be what you expect. Let's suppose that we create a variable with the same name as a field. What happens? Let's see

```
. USE INVENTRY
. ? COST
6.89
. COST = 'Robert'
. ? COST
6.89
```

Our inventory database has a field named COST. This is a numeric field where the value of the field for the current record is 6.89. We have assigned the value *Robert* to a memory variable with the same name. When we try to look at the variable we get the field value. What's happened? The variable is really there, but we now have two items with the same name: COST. dBASE must choose between them, and it will always choose the field. Fields have *precedence* over memory variables. We can see the content of the memory variable by telling dBASE what we want.

```
. ? M -> COST
Robert
```

The M (for memory) followed by a minus sign (–) and the greater than symbol (>) is used to identify a memory variable when there is an active field with the same name. If the database in use does not have a field with that name, we need not use the pointer.

If you try to assign a value to a dBASE key word (command verb) you may be surprised. If try to assign the value 6 to a memory variable named DISPLAY, we will get

```
. DISPLAY = 6
syntax error
        ?
DISPLAY = 6
Do you want some help? (Y/N)
```

There is, incidentally, a way that you can create a memory variable named DISPLAY and store a value in it. You can also get it back — anytime that you want. An alternative to variable assigment is the dBASE command STORE. You can create and assign a value to a memory variable with this command:

Chapter Eight

```
. STORE 6 TO DISPLAY
. ? DISPLAY
        6
```

Another feature of the STORE command, as opposed to the direct assignment is that you can create several memory variables at a time. For example,

```
. STORE 0 TO A,B,C,D,E,F,G,H,I,J
```

This command has created 10 memory variables named A through J. Each contains the value 0.

To store character data to a memory variable, place the character data in quotes. The maximum size for character data is 254 bytes.

```
. MYNAME = 'Robert'
. ROOMNO = '12'
```

To store numeric data, just enter the number — without quotes. Remember that the item being stored goes last.

```
. NUMBER1 = 12
. NUMBER2 = 79.88342
```

To store a logical value (true or false) you must enter periods on either side of the logic value.

```
. TRUEVALUE = .T.
. NOT_TRUE = .F.
```

To store a date, you would use the CTOD( ) function in conjunction with the date.

```
. THEDATE = ctod('8/27/85')
```

To store the *contents of a field* to a variable, use the fieldname in the assignment. The data type of the variable will automatically be the same as the fieldtype. The content of the variable will be the field content for the current record. You can assign expressions with fields.

```
. MCOST      = COST
. LIQTYPE    = LIQUOR
. BRANDNAME  = BRAND
. VALUE      = QUANTITY * COST
```

Once you have created a variable, you can use the variable by name instead of the content. As an example, the database contains the cost of an item. The sales tax is 6% in this state. It doesn't make sense to have a field for tax rate — it's always the same. We can create a variable, TAXRATE, that contains the tax rate and use it wherever we need to compute taxes.

Using a Database

```
. TAXRATE = 0.06
. ? COST
. 6.89

. ? COST * 0.06
     0.4134

.? COST * TAXRATE
     0.4134
```

As you can see from the above examples, you can use memory variables to perform arithmetic functions. You can also store the results in a new variable.

```
. AMOUNTDUE = COST * (1 + TAXRATE)
```

You can also use the commands SUM, AVERAGE, and COUNT in conjunction with memory variables.

```
. SUM QUANTITY * COST, QUANTITY * PRICE TO TOTALCOST, TOTALVALUE
. AVERAGE COST, PRICE TO AVECOST,AVEPRICE
```

The values of the operations are assigned to the variables in the order that they occur. For example in the AVERAGE above, COST is stored in AVECOST, while PRICE goes to AVEPRICE. If memory variables are used in these commands, the number of variables must match the number of operations.

To give you another view of the use of memory variables, suppose that we have a computerized checkbook. This particular checkbook has the standard checkbook entries as fields: CHECKNO, PAIDTO, DATE, CHECKAMT, DEPOSIT, CANCELLED. To determine the balance of the account, we might use the commands:

```
. SUM CHECKAMT, DEPOSIT TO SPENT, SAVED
     15997.18     17454.53

. BALANCE = SAVED - SPENT
     1437.35
```

Here, with only two instructions, we have obtained the current account balance. We have also obtained this result without the opportunity for error (unless of course the data is bad). Had we attempted the same operation with paper and pencil, or even a hand calculator we would have had a significantly greater chance for error. As long as the data in the database is valid, our result will always be accurate.

Displaying Memory Variables: You can view the content of all memory variables at once with the command

```
. DISPLAY MEMORY
```

Chapter Eight

Erasing Memory Variables: You can "erase" a memory variable at any time with the RELEASE command. To release the memory variables A, B, and C, the command

. RELEASE A,B,C

Saving Memory Variables: Memory variables are automatically discarded when you leave dBASE. If you have a number of variables that you create and use regularly, you can save those variables to a special file.

. SAVE TO MEMFILE

MEMFILE can have any valid filename. The same rules apply to memory files as to any other disk filename. dBASE will automatically assign the file identifier .MEM to this file.

If you don't want to save all variables, you can save all of them that have some common characteristic in their names. For example, to save only those whose names begin with the letter A

. SAVE ALL LIKE A* TO MEMFILE

Or, to save all except those with a common characteristic, use

. SAVE ALL EXCEPT A* TO MEMFILE

Restoring Memory Variables: To get the variables back from your memory file, you use the RESTORE command.

. RESTORE FROM MEMFILE
. RESTORE FROM MEMFILE ADDITIVE

The RESTORE command *overwrites* any existing memory variables unless the word ADDITIVE is included in the command.

If you are beginning to get the feeling that this is just too easy — that you must be overlooking something vital, rest assured: it really is easy. Much of the literature in textbooks contributes substantially to the notion that computers are difficult. Textbooks usually address the subject from a technical person's frame of reference. In a standard textbook, the discussion of the use of the .OR. operator might be substantially different from the discussion in this book. A textbook would also discuss the *third normal form* which is of interest only if you are designing database systems. A condition such as LIQUOR = 'SCOTCH' .OR. LIQUOR = 'BOURBON' might be called a *predicate*, and a predicate would be defined as a *relationship among the values of the domains*.

There is nothing wrong with this specialized jargon. Although there are times it when seems that computer professionals use jargon to justify their positions and salaries, it isn't really true. Jargon allows the specialists to communicate better among themselves — which will result in better database systems for us to use.

But we don't need the jargon. It gets in our way. The barrier that technical language creates for those of us who are not yet familiar with computers, creates the illusion that these machines

---

Using a Database

are strange, inaccessible, and difficult to use. It gives the beginner the feeling that "it just can't be this easy." In reality, most of the difficulty lies in nothing other than unfamiliarity. Computers aren't just for computer professionals. They have incredible capabilities that are available to *anyone* with a need to store, retrieve, and manipulate information.

The database stores data. The database management allows you to extract information from that data. If we have a liquor store, we can learn that we are dangerously low on tequila and scandalously overstocked on scotch. If we combine this simple inventory with a database that keeps track of the stock as we receive it, we can determine annual sales of each kind and size of liquor. Over time, we can learn to manage our stock more efficiently. This, in turn, results in a more efficient use of our money and provides a better return on investment. There are, of course, many other uses for database management systems in business, education, and government. The point is that a DBMS is easy to use. It can provide real support for whatever your endeavor. It can be fun. It can release you to do more interesting kinds of activities. It can certainly broaden your perspective about your business operation — giving you a better view of that operation.

Chapter Eight

CHAPTER NINE

WORKING WITH MULTIPLE DATABASES

Up to this point, we have been working with just a single database file at a time. A database management system that can work with *only* one file at a time is called a *file manager*. A true *database manager* can work with several database files at one time. The database itself consists of all the database files. Up to this point we have created and used two database files: INVENTRY and FONEBOOK. Our database consists of these two files. As we create additional files, they automatically become a part of our database.

When a database has more than a single file the individual database files are usually called *relations*. This allows us to distinguish between the individual files that make a database and the database itself. This is an important distinction in some systems; it is relatively unimportant in dBASE.

In dBASE, your database can consist of *any* number of database files. You are limited only by the number of files you can pack onto your disks. The files that are on disks that are actually connected to your computer are said to be *online*. All other database files are said to be *offline*.

You may want to be able to use some of your database files at the same time. To demonstrate the use of two files at the same time let's suppose we have two new database files, STUDENTS and TEACHERS, that we would like to use together. We won't have to go through the process of creating these files — but you can do so if you like. The information needed to create these files is shown in Figures 9-1 through 9-3. Figure 9-1 shows the database structure for the files, Figures 9-2 and 9-3 list their contents.

STUDENTS			TEACHERS		
NAME	Character	20	NAME	Character	20
ROOM	Character	2	ROOM	Character	2
GRADE	Character	1	GRADE	Character	1

Figure 9-1: Database plans for TEACHERS and STUDENTS

Record#	NAME	ROOM	GRADE
1	Chips, Mr.	11	1
2	Brooks, Miss	12	1
3	Crane, Ichabod	22	2
4	Stern, Emma	24	2

Figure 9-2: TEACHERS database

Record#	NAME	ROOM	GRADE
1	Aardvark, Anthony	11	1
2	Bear, Cuddly	11	1
3	Beaver, Eager	12	1
4	Cowlick, Calvin	12	1
5	Frog, Frederick	22	2
6	Goose, Mother	22	2
7	Kangaroo, Captain	24	2
8	Tiger, Timothy	24	2

Figure 9-3: STUDENTS database

dBASE III allows you to use *up to* ten database files at the same time. In order to do this, dBASE divides into ten independent *work areas*. One database file can be in use in each of these ten work areas. The work areas are *initially* identified by the numbers 1 through 10. To use files together, we first select a work area for the file and then place the file in use. To demonstrate the process, let's place STUDENTS in work area 1, and TEACHERS in work area 5. You can put the files in any work areas that you wish — it's your choice.

```
. SELECT 1
. USE STUDENTS
. SELECT 5
. USE TEACHERS
```

When we USE (open) a database file in a work area, any file that is already in use in that work area is automatically closed. You can only have one database file in a particular work area at a time. Similarly, a particular database file can only be in use in one work area at a time. For example, we cannot have STUDENTS in both work area 1 and work area 9 at the same time.

Chapter Nine

The SELECT command is used to tell dBASE which work area we want to use. When a database file is open in a work area, we can select *that* work area by either the name of that database file, or by the work area number. For example, now that STUDENTS is in use in work area 1 we can select work area 1 by either

```
. SELECT STUDENTS
. SELECT 1
```

The select command differs from the USE command in that it does not open a file, it merely switches between work areas. When we specify a work area by the name of the file in that work area we are using its *alias*. We can give the work area a different name by specifiying an alias when we open the database file. The alias is just an alternative name that we can use for the work area that contains the file. Suppose that we want to use a file whose name is H26B19 in work area 9. We can give the file a more descriptive name — SUPPLIERS — by specifying an alias in this way:

```
. SELECT 9
. USE H26B19 ALIAS SUPPLIERS
```

The alias SUPPLIERS has more than eight characters. An alias can have up to ten characters. The *default* alias of any database is the name of the database file.

Now, suppose that we want to know the name of MOTHER GOOSE's teacher. How do we do it? The very same way we would without a computer. We note that both STUDENTS and TEACHERS are identified by room and grade. There are two teachers for each grade, but there is only one teacher for each room. The contents of the ROOM field tell us which teacher belongs to a student.

If we were to determine MOTHER GOOSE's teacher without the help of the computer we first find MOTHER GOOSE in the STUDENT list and note the ROOM number. Then we look up the ROOM number in the TEACHERS list. This gives us the teacher's NAME. We can do exactly the same way in dBASE:

```
. SELECT STUDENTS
. LOCATE FOR NAME = 'GOOSE, MOTHER'
Record 6
. ? ROOM
22
. SELECT TEACHERS
. LOCATE FOR ROOM = '22'
. ? NAME
Crane, Ichabod
```

ROOM was used as a *pointer*. Its contents point to the desired teacher record. If the content of ROOM was a record number in the TEACHER file, we would say that ROOM was a *physical* pointer. However, ROOM is a common field, and we make the connection between these two files by the *content* of both fields. ROOM is a *logical* pointer. In this example, we used the ROOM pointer indirectly. We can make more direct use of the ROOM connection. The following example does exactly the same as the above — but is more direct:

```
. SELECT STUDENTS
. LOCATE FOR NAME = 'GOOSE, MOTHER'
Record 6
. SELECT TEACHERS
. LOCATE FOR ROOM = STUDENTS->ROOM
. ? NAME
Crane, Ichabod
```

Let's examine the condition for the LOCATE command above. We wanted to compare the contents of the ROOM field in TEACHERS with the contents of the ROOM field in STUDENTS. To specify a field in the *selected* work area, use just the fieldname. To specify a field from another work area, you must use the alias of the work area followed by a minus sign (–), a greater than symbol (>), and the name of the field. The hyphen and the > form an *arrow* that points from the work area alias to the fieldname.

In the last example, we were able to conduct our search without bothering to find out what the room number was. We don't really care what it is — only that it leads us to the correct teacher. Up to this point, we're still doing part of the work ourselves. Now let's let the computer do it all — automatically.

We can link two files together by the contents of a common field. In this example, we will link the TEACHERS database file to the STUDENTS database file by the contents of the ROOM field. To do this, the file being linked must be indexed on the field we're using to connect them.

```
. SELECT TEACHERS
. INDEX ON ROOM TO T_ROOM
      4 records indexed
```

The STUDENTS and TEACHERS files are connected (linked) with the SET RELATION command.

```
. SELECT STUDENTS
. SET RELATION TO ROOM INTO TEACHERS
```

The relation is set from the selected file. The file being linked is identified with the phrase INTO. The connection from the selected file is specified by the TO phrase. In this case, we are linking the files by ROOM. The ROOM identified in the command is the fieldname in the selected file STUDENTS. Perhaps we can make this a little clearer if we rewrite the last command:

```
. SET RELATION TO STUDENTS->ROOM INTO TEACHERS
```

We can specify a field, by its alias, the pointing symbol consisting of a minus sign (–) and a greater than symbol (>), and the fieldname. We can omit everything but the fieldname for fields in the selected file. We must specify the alias for fields in other active files. Active files are those files that are currently in use. With this background, we can identify the teacher directly.

Chapter Nine

```
. SELECT STUDENTS
. LOCATE FOR NAME = 'GOOSE, MOTHER'
Record 6
. ? TEACHERS->NAME
Crane, Ichabod
```

We can make the teacher's name *appear* to be in the STUDENTS file — provided that we work from the STUDENTS file.

```
. SELECT STUDENTS
. LIST NAME, TEACHERS->NAME
Record#   NAME                    TEACHERS->NAME
     1    Aardvark, Anthony       Chips, Mr.
     2    Bear, Cuddly            Chips, Mr.
     3    Beaver, Eager           Brooks, Miss
     4    Cowlick, Calvin         Brooks, Miss
     5    Frog, Frederick         Crane, Ichabod
     6    Goose, Mother           Crane, Ichabod
     7    Kangaroo, Captain       Stern, Emma
     8    Tiger, Timothy          Stern, Emma
```

Again, an alternative command will make the output a little clearer:

```
. SELECT STUDENTS
. LIST STUDENTS->NAME, TEACHERS->NAME
Record#   STUDENTS->NAME          TEACHERS->NAME
     1    Aardvark, Anthony       Chips, Mr.
     2    Bear, Cuddly            Chips, Mr.
     3    Beaver, Eager           Brooks, Miss
     4    Cowlick, Calvin         Brooks, Miss
     5    Frog, Frederick         Crane, Ichabod
     6    oose, Mother            Crane, Ichabod
     7    Kangaroo, Captain       Stern, Emma
     8    Tiger, Timothy          Stern, Emma
```

This operation, since we're into terminology, can be called a *virtual JOIN*. Now there's a term to drop around the office. Virtual means that the image is displayed only to screen or the printer. Speaking of JOIN, this is one of the standard operations for a relational database. To be a relational database, the system must be able to PROJECT, RESTRICT, and JOIN.

JOIN produces a third database from two existing databases. The operation is conceptually the same as producing the list above, except that the two fields would become the fields in a new database. The fields *cannot* have the same fieldname. If we restructure our databases so that the field for student names becomes STUDENT and that for the teacher's name becomes TEACHER we can use the JOIN command to produce a new file that has the fields STUDENT and TEACHER. The command would look like

Working With Multiple Databases

```
. SELECT STUDENTS
. JOIN WITH TEACHER TO JOINFILE FOR ROOM = TEACHER->ROOM ;
     FIELDS STUDENT, TEACHER->TEACHER
```

Now let's see how this works. Both of the files that will be used in the JOIN must be active — they must both be in use. The target file (JOINFILE) must not be in use. The name of the target can be any name you want as long as it is a valid database name. If a file with that name exists it will be overwritten with this new file. The condition ROOM = TEACHER->ROOM tells the command the criteria for creating the new records. Finally, the fields list specifies the fields in the current files that are to become part of the new file (they are still in the old files).

JOIN *rewinds* both databases. All this means is that both are initially set to their first record. Then *all* the records in the file being *joined* (TEACHER) are read. Every time a TEACHER record matches the criteria in the FOR condition a new record with the specified fields is created in the output file. The STUDENT database is then advanced one record and the TEACHER database is rewound to its beginning. Then all of the records in TEACHER are scanned for records meeting the join criteria. This process continues until the selected database (STUDENTS) is exhausted. Every record in the TEACHER file is read for each record in the student database. The total number of records processed is the product of the records in the two files. If there are 1,000 students and 100 teachers, JOIN must process 100,000 records.

The kind of JOIN is a *general* join. It is simple, thorough, and *slow*. There is another, far superior, kind of join. It's the one we would choose if we had a choice. Unfortunately, we rarely do. This is the *natural* join. For this JOIN, both databases must be either indexed or sorted. As before, the files are rewound, but the join operation works its way down the two files in a ladder-like manner. The natural join processes only the sum of the number of records in the two files. As before, if there are 1,000 students and 100 teachers, the natural JOIN processes only 1,100 records — a substantial improvement. dBASE uses the SET RELATION process to create a *virtual* equivalent to the natural join — a *virtual*, *natural* join.

Another command, UPDATE, can be used to make changes in the contents of one database file based on the contents in another. For this to work the way we want it to, the database *must* have a field that *uniquely* identifies each record. This is an important point that we have glossed over up to now. Our FONEBOOK can easily contain several identical names. It's not that unlikely that we might know four or five Vladimar Koshycalizs. We rely on their different addresses to discriminate between them in the FONEBOOK. The entire *record* is unique. The liquor store inventory has the same characteristic. There are several entries for each kind of LIQUOR, several entries for each BRAND, and several entries for each SIZE. But, there is *only* one entry for a particular LIQUOR of a particular BRAND of a particular SIZE. If we look at enough fields, each inventory record is unique. To specify a particular record we must use LIQUOR and BRAND and SIZE. What a bother.

This hasn't been a problem because our databases have been small. We can just look at it to see what we want to do and fetch a record by its record number. But, if databases are small, who needs a computer? As the database grows larger and we want to make these processes more automatic, we may have to change some of our ways — depending on what we are trying to do.

Have you ever wondered why you are identified by all of those numbers in your life. You have a social security number, a driver's license number, and employee number, and heaven knows what else. When you purchase something large, like a car, it has an identification number, and is made up of lots of smaller pieces that each have part numbers. *Everything* seems to have a number these days. All these numbers are attempts to provide *concise and unique identification*.

Now, after all that let's see how the UPDATE command works. Suppose we have an inventory

Chapter Nine

database of CARPARTS. CARPARTS has several fields: PARTNO, PARTNAME, QUANTITY, COST, PRICE and so on. CARPARTS has been indexed on PARTNO. When we receive new shipments of parts, we need to update the QUANTITY field. *One* way to do this is with the UPDATE command.

To use this command, we create a database NEWSTOCK that has two fields: PARTNO and QUANTITY. For each part that we receive in the shipment we add a record to NEWSTOCK. NEWSTOCK now has one record for each part number received. The records contain the part number and the QUANTITY received. The operation to update your CARPARTS database would look something like:

```
. SELECT 2
. USE NEWSTOCK
. SELECT 1
. USE CARPARTS INDEX PARTNO
. UPDATE RANDOM FROM NEWSTOCK ON PARTNO ;
    REPLACE QUANTITY WITH QUANTITY + NEWSTOCK -> QUANTITY
```

In the UPDATE command, the phrase beginning with REPLACE is part of the command. The semicolon in the command is used to indicate that the command takes more than one line and is continued on the following line. The file that is being updated must be selected. RANDOM is used when the file being updated is indexed on the update field as in this case. FROM is used to identify the update source file — the file containing the update information. The REPLACE clause is used in exactly the same manner as the REPLACE command.

In the above example, NEWSTOCK is automatically rewound to its beginning. CARPARTS is searched for a record with a PARTNO matching the PARTNO in NEWSTOCK. If a matching record is found, the QUANTITY is increased by the QUANTITY in NEWSTOCK. Then NEWSTOCK is advanced to the next record and the process is repeated until every record in NEWSTOCK has been used.

This example has taken advantage of the fact that the target file — CARPARTS is indexed on the *update key* PARTNO. If that was not the case the UPDATE command could be used only if *both* files were sorted by the update key. In that event, the word RANDOM would be omitted from the command.

Both JOIN and UPDATE can be useful commands, each in its own way. Nevertheless, SET RELATION, the command that we use to link database files together is the key to using multiple files within dBASE. You can relate the contents of two files *logically* as we did in the STUDENTS/TEACHERS example above, or you can relate two files *physically*. In the chapter on "Planning Your Database" we discussed splitting a database in two when the number of fields exceeded the maximum value of 128. You can use SET RELATION to link the two files together by their record numbers so that the two files can be used as one. Suppose that we have two database files PART1 and PART2. Each record in PART2 is really just a continuation of the record in PART1. To link the two files by their record numbers, we would use the command sequence:

```
. SELECT 2
. USE PART2
. SELECT 1
. USE PART1
. SET RELATION TO RECNO( ) INTO PART2
```

RECNO( ) is the dBASE III function meaning *record number*. In this example we have linked the two files together *physically*. You can connect multiple files together. Suppose we have four open files: A, B, C, and D. We can link A to B, B to C, and C to D. In fact we can link any one of these to any of the others. We cannot, at least for now, create a simultaneous link from one to more than one of the others. We also cannot create a *circular* relation. An example of a circular relation would be: A to B and B to A.

dBASE allows you to work with up to ten database files at once. However, before you can do so, you must tell your operating system that you want to do this. This is done with the help of a file named *CONFIG.SYS*.

CONFIG.SYS

This is a special configuration file that you need on the *root directory* of the disk that you use to *boot* your computer. This is the disk that contains your operating system — PC/MS-DOS. If you have a floppy disk computer, this is the disk that you place in the A disk drive when you turn on your computer. If you have a hard disk, your operating system is usually on the hard disk on disk drive C. If you have any doubts, consult your dealer.

Boot (or turn on) your computer. If you have a floppy disk system, the screen will show you an A prompt

A>

If you have a hard disk system, your computer will probably show you a C prompt

C>

In the following discussion, we've used the C> to indicate the operating system prompt. If you have a floppy disk system, mentally substitute an A> for the C>. To be sure that you are in the root directory, type in the following after the prompt

C>CD \

The backslash is the symbol used for the *root directory*. The *cd* is the operating system command for *change directory*. What we have told the computer is *go to the root directory*. Next, we want to find out if there is already a configuration file. We can find out by using the *dir* (directory) command.

C> DIR CONFIG.SYS

If the file is present, the operating system (DOS) will display the file name and information about the file. Otherwise, it will display the message *file not found*. If the file isn't there, the next step is to create the file CONFIG.SYS. If it is, we want to edit the file.

Creating CONFIG.SYS: You can create the file, and add the appropriate statements by simply typing the following after a operating system prompt.

```
C> COPY CON:CONFIG.SYS
FILES = 20
BUFFERS = 15
```

Chapter Nine

Once your screen looks like the above, press function key F6. This will place a mark (^Z) on your screen. The ^Z is called the end-of-file mark. Next, press the Return key. That's all there is to it, your computer now has the needed file CONFIG.SYS on its root directory.

Editing CONFIG.SYS: If you already have a CONFIG.SYS on your root directory, we want to be sure that it contains the following two statements. If it does not, we want to add these two statements to the file.

```
FILES = 20
BUFFERS = 15
```

(You can edit the file and add the above if necessary with the help of the DOS EDLIN command. Consult your DOS manual.)

Why did we have to go through this? Your operating system is normally set up to handle eight files. But it immediately takes four back: your keyboard, your screen, your printer, and communications. dBASE will take one more, which leaves only three files. By placing the above statements into CONFIG.SYS you can use a total of fifteen files of all types from within dBASE III — and ten of them can be database files.

Once you have created or modified CONFIG.SYS, you should reboot your computer, forcing it to *read* the configuration file. Whenever the computer is booted, the operating system looks for this configuration file on the root directory. If it's there, then the operating system will read it and follow the configuration instructions.

Working With Multiple Databases

SECTION THREE
GENERAL INFORMATION

Section Three provides some general information. Hardware is discussed in Chapter Ten. Chapter Eleven discusses various types of databases, examining the nature of each system and recognizing the differences among them. Chapter Twelve looks at hierarchical and network systems.

Although technical and complex terminology may sometimes make computers seem mysterious or difficult, this impression is inaccurate and misleading. Computers are quite understandable and a lot of fun besides. Section Three attempts to fill in some of the gaps and answer some common questions people ask about computers. Doing so will increase our understanding of the computer world and help us make further progress with our computer databases.

CHAPTER TEN

HARDWARE SYSTEMS

In this chapter we will introduce computer hardware systems. Although you don't need to know much about the hardware, it can be helpful to have a basic understanding of the computer, and what makes it "go." In case you are not familiar with computers, this brief discussion will cover the basic elements of computer systems and indicate what is needed to use a database system. As you will see, your database needs have a significant effect on the computer hardware you select — and conversely, your computer hardware can have a significant effect on how well your database management system (or other software) performs. A typical computer system is diagrammed in Figure 10-1.

The diagram describes any computer system: a microcomputer that can be carried in a briefcase or a mainframe computer that fills an entire room. The computer itself consists of what is inside the box labeled computer: the central processing unit, the main memory, and the I/O (input/output). The other four boxes — monitor, mass memory, printer, and keyboard — are called peripherals.

THE COMPUTER

The computer, consists of the central processing unit, main memory, and I/O (input/output). The Central Processing Unit (CPU) is the device that actually does the "computing". For the CPU to function, however, it must have main memory. Main memory is used directly by the CPU.

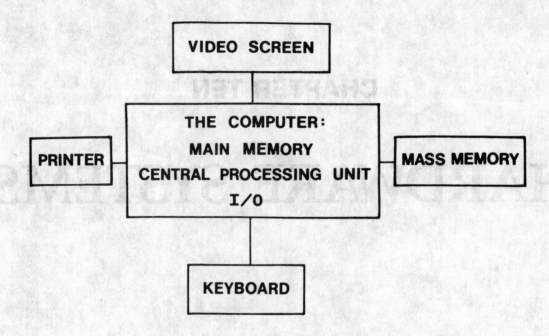

Figure 10-1: A typical computer

Advertisements for microcomputers usually say something like

BUY A 256K Cucumber IV

The 256K refers to the amount of main memory in bytes. A byte is the amount of memory needed to store a typewriter character such as "m" or "$." K (for kilobyte) stands for 1,000. In a computer system, K actually means 1,024. Thus, a 256K computer system actually has 262,144 bytes of memory.

Main memory is made up of integrated circuits, popularly called *chips*. These electronic devices are relatively expensive when compared to mass memory — although the price of both has dropped substantially over the past few years. We can expect the cost of memory to continue to decline — at least for some time.

The amount of memory your computer has can determine which software packages you can use. Today's software packages tend to do a great deal — and take a lot of memory. Each software package (such as a database management system) will require some minimum amount of main memory. *You will need to acquire at least that amount of main memory for your computer.* Purchase as much main memory as you can comfortably afford. But don't get too carried away. Having too much memory is a little like having a car that can go 180 miles per hour.

I/O stands for input/output. This is what connects the computer to the outside world. In this case the outside world consists of the peripherals. You might reasonably assume the I/O is a standard feature like tires on a car. This is not always true — computer I/O often costs extra. For microcomputer owners, however, cost is a *relative* consideration.

THE PERIPHERALS

For most database uses, all but one of the peripherals shown in Figure 10-1 are required. That is, mass memory, video screen, and keyboard are mandatory. For some uses, the printer is also a must; for others it can be optional. A printer is always useful.

Keyboards, Monitors, Terminals

The keyboard is similar to a typewriter keyboard; it is used to communicate with the computer. The computer, in turn, communicates with you by means of the video screen. The keyboard and video screen may be separate devices. When they are separate, video is supplied by a television-like device called a monitor. The keyboard and video screen are often incorporated into a single device called a computer terminal, a video terminal, or CRT (for cathode ray tube).

Whether you have a terminal or keyboard and monitor usually depends upon the brand of microcomputer system you own. There is no practical difference between a video terminal and a keyboard with separate monitor, and in this book we refer to it as terminal for convenience sake. Typical video screens can display 24 lines of 80 characters at a time; some display less and others more. The keyboard and video screen are extremely important from a subjective point of view: These devices are your means of interaction with the computer. You "talk" to the computer via the keyboard; the computer "talks" to you via the video screen.

Mass Memory

Mass memory stores your information for future use. Mass memory is significantly less expensive than main memory, and it is also significantly slower (more than a thousand times). When power is turned off, main memory is erased while mass memory is not. Finally, mass memory must be deliberately changed.

Mass memory is used to store the information you want to save, much the same as an audio tape is used to save "memories" of sounds. Mass storage systems are designed so the computer can easily find the information it wants. There are two kinds of mass storage commonly used by microcomputers: tape and disk.

Tape systems usually employ cassettes similar to those used for audio storage. These systems are relatively slow and, except for particular applications, are not suitable for use with database systems other than for *backing up* data.

Disk systems, technically referred to as direct access storage devices (DASD), are like magnetic phonographs. The information is magnetically stored on a rotating disk (hence the name) on tracks like a record. A device which is similar in concept to a tone arm (except that it has a magnetic head like those used on tape recorders) is used to "read" and "write" on the disk. The information is on magnetic tracks that, unlike a phonograph record, are invisible to the eye.

A disk drive is the mechanism which turns the disk and transfers information to and from the disk. The computer knows the location of each piece of information on each disk drive. It knows this by reading the disk directory for each disk. The disk directory is similar in concept to the label on a long-playing record — it tells you which musical piece is located on each band on that record.

Hardware Systems

The disk drive must be controlled by a disk controller which connects to the I/O of the computer. As instructed by the CPU, the disk controller directs the magnetic disk. The disk controller provides a path for information flowing between the CPU and the disk. It also keeps the CPU informed about conditions on the disk.

For microcomputers there are two kinds of disk systems commonly used: floppy-disk systems and hard-disk systems.

Floppy-Disk Systems

Floppy disks are often called floppies or diskettes. They were developed by IBM for use on the IBM 370 computer system; they are the most common mass storage medium for microcomputer systems. The cost of a floppy disk is about the same as the cost of a tape cassette; the cost of the floppy disk drive is usually much greater than the cost of a cassette recorder.

Most microcomputer systems for business or professional applications are equipped with from one to four disk drives. Most of these will have at least one *floppy* disk drive. The floppy disk provides a convenient way to introduce new software to the computer and to transfer data or software to other computers.

The floppy disk is made from an oxide-coated mylar film and resembles a 45-rpm phonograph record. The disk is packaged into a protective square plastic or paper envelope. The envelope has holes to allow the disk to be mounted to the disk drive hub and to provide the read/write heads access to the oxide surface. Another hole in the disk envelope allows index mark sensing. When the floppy disk is inserted into the disk drive, the envelope remains stationary while the mylar disk turns within it. Care must be taken to keep the mylar film clean: The mylar film must *not* be touched. Touching the film or exposing it to grease or dirt can cause severe damage to your data.

Floppy disks come in three primary sizes: 8-inch, 5 1/4-inch, and 3-inch. Currently, the 5 1/4-inch floppy is the most widely used, although the 3-inch floppies are gaining in popularity. Disks may be either single- or double-sided. Double-sided disks have information stored on both surfaces and can be used only in disk drives designed for their use. You cannot usually turn a double-sided disk over and play the second side in a single-sided drive.

Each disk contains a number of *tracks* which are divided into *sectors*. A sector forms a pie shaped wedge as illustrated by the diagram in Figure 10-2. The specific layout of tracks and sectors is called the disk *format*. The IBM Personal Computer uses a format consisting of 40 tracks divided into 9 sectors. Each sector contains 512 bytes. The number of bytes stored in a sector is usually independent of track position. This particular arrangement allows the data transfer rate to be independent of track — the outer tracks move faster than the inner tracks. The total amount of data that can be stored on a disk is given by

$$total\ data\ =\ sides\ x\ tracks\ x\ sectors\ x\ bytes/sector$$

There are as yet no official standards for floppy disk systems, although the 5 1/4-inch floppy used on the IBM PC has become a de facto standard. Floppy disks can be exchanged only between *compatible* systems. Compatibility includes *both* size and format. This is why disks cannot normally be exchanged between IBM and Apple microcomputers — even though the disks are the same physical size and look alike.

SECTOR   TRACKS

Figure 10-2: Diagram of a disk

Hard-Disk Systems

Many computers use a *hard disk* in addition to one or more floppy disks. Hard disks offer substantially higher performance than floppy disks — they store more data and they are "faster". The most commonly used hard disks store about 10 megabytes (10 million bytes), while hard disks with capacities of up to 100 megabytes are readily available.

A hard disk is a rigid disk made from a machined-metal plate. Some hard disks can be removed from the computer system somewhat like a floppy. Most hard disks, however, are not removeable. Nonremovable hard disks are usually called fixed disks or winchesters.

Other performance characteristics of disk systems that you may see in advertisements for microcomputers are track-to-track speed, average access speed, and data transfer rate. These are measures of the performance of the particular disk system. Track-to-track signifies the time required by the disk drive to move the head from one track to an adjacent track. Advertised values for this capability are usually a few milliseconds (1/1000 of a second). Average access speed is the average time required to reposition the head. Specifically, it is the time required to move the head from track 1 to the last track divided by two. It is normally several milliseconds for hard-disk systems and is almost never advertised for floppy disk drives (100 to 500 milliseconds). It is a performance specification that can be very misleading in advertising and should ordinarily be ignored by you. Data transfer rate is another specification that vendors like and that you should ignore. Data transfer rates are normally specified in hundreds of thousands to millions of bytes per second.

Of far more interest to you is whether the disk drive device is compatible with your computer — that is, what has to be done to connect the device and make it work properly with your computer. For your information, connecting the device and making it work properly is called *integration*.

Because our topic is databases, mass memory is of particular importance. Databases are stored on disks of one type or another, and *no* database management approach can be satisfactory if you don't have adequate disk storage. Currently available microcomputers can hold only a relatively small database in main memory. Very large databases usually require a hard disk. Databases of moderate size may be contained on floppy disks of one type or another. Even large databases that are contained on hard disks may be backed up on floppy disks (*backing up* means making a duplicate copy of the data). This extra copy protects against disk failures and provides an economical means of transferring the database from one microcomputer to another.

The Printer

A printer is useful — although not absolutely required. The two most common types of printers are the dot-matrix and the daisywheel.

- A daisywheel printer produces fully formed characters and is usually used when letter-quality printing is needed.
- A dot-matrix printer forms characters from a quantity of small dots.

There is considerable variation in the print quality of dot-matrix printers. Dot matrix printers are usually less expensive and of lower print quality than daisywheel printers. They are usually significantly faster. Typical print speeds for daisywheel printers are 20 to 35 characters per second. Print speeds for dot-matrix printers are often in excess of 100 characters per second. Dot-matrix printing sometimes does not reproduce well on copy machines.

The Operating System

When most computers are turned on, the main memory is blank: the machine has no purpose and cannot process information. You need an *operating system* to make the computer peform its functions. Most microcomputer systems that are suitable for use with a database management system use a disk operating system (DOS). When the computer is turned on, the operating system is loaded into main memory from a disk. This may be done automatically, or you may have to press a key or keys on the computer. Loading the operating system is called *booting*. Don't fret — you will not need to know much about the operating system, now or ever, to use a database system.

The discussion in this book assumes that the operating system used is PC-DOS or MS-DOS. PC-DOS is the operating system used on the IBM personal computer. MS-DOS is the operating system used on IBM compatible computers such as the COMPAQ. A different operating system *may* have different rules for addressing disk drives and/or naming files.

A FEW LAST WORDS ON HARDWARE

To get properly started, you will need to have an adequate set of computer hardware. The most critical hardware item for a microcomputer database system is the disk drive system. If you own a computer and desire to use it for a database application you will want to carefully evaluate your disk capability. Remember that you need sufficient storage space to store the entire database on a single disk. In addition, the CPU can use only the data contained on the disk drives that are connected to it. That data is said to be *online*. If you have floppy disk drives, only the floppy disks that are actually inserted into the disk drives are online.

If you have not yet selected a computer, the most effective process for you (and your bankbook) is to select the database system, determine your storage requirements, and select a computer that is compatible with your database software system and that supports your storage requirements and offers a reasonable way of adding additional mass storage if necessary.

CHAPTER ELEVEN

DATA BASICS

In this chapter, we'll attempt to answer some of the most common questions about microcomputer database systems, such as: What is an assembly language system? What is a hierarchical database? What is a network database? What is CODASYL?

Machine language is the computer's "native" language. It is the language the computer uses internally. *Assembly language* uses a system of mnemonic commands that are directly related to machine language instructions. It is often mistakenly called "machine language." Assembly Language is a "low-level" language. Beyond assembly language are higher-order languages such as FORTRAN, COBOL, Pascal, and BASIC.

Programs written in assembly language are usually more efficient than those written in high-level languages. This is because each command or instruction in these languages is built out of many assembly-language instructions. An instruction in BASIC, for example, might use 50 to 100 assembly language instructions. An assembly-language program can only be used on one kind of computer, and must usually be completely rewritten to be used on another kind of computer.

Many commercial software packages are written in a high-level language such as Pascal or BASIC. It is usually easier to write software in a high-level language. The software is often more *maintainable*, which means that it can be more easily corrected or changed. It is also more *portable*, which means that the same package can be easily adapted for use on different kinds of computers.

dBASE III and many of the newer software packages are written in the C language. C is an intermediate-to-low-level language that provides an excellent compromise between the execution speed of assembly language and the portability of a high-level language.

It is often assumed that an assembly-language program is "better" than a program written in a high-level language such as BASIC. This may be true if the programs are equally well-written. It is difficult to judge whether or not two programs are equally well-written, but this shouldn't be a consideration in selecting software. There are advantages to each approach in developing software. Since you will never see vendors advertising their systems as "mediocre" or "average to good"; so, you should probably discount how well-written a program might be as a factor in your selection. Whether or not it can do your job is the really important important question when choosing a program.

SEQUENTIAL AND RANDOM ACCESS

Sequential access and *random access* are two terms that are frequently encountered in articles on database management. These terms describe how the computer "finds" individual database records. Sequential access means that the computer searches the database record by record to find desired records. Random access means that the computer can go *directly* to any record.

The telephone directory provides an example of a paper database that is designed for random (direct) access. The telephone directory is printed in alphabetical order. When you look for a particular person's telephone number, you make use of the alphabetical order to find the person's name and, hence the number you desire. To find the name belonging to a particular phone number, you would have to examine every listing in the phone book, one by one. This is an example of sequential access.

. DISPLAY FOR NAME='BYERS,ROBERT'

. LOCATE FOR NAME='BYERS,ROBERT'

Query commands such as DISPLAY and LOCATE use the sequential approach. The DISPLAY command searches the entire database — starting at the first record — and examines each record, in turn, DISPLAYing only the specified records. The LOCATE command also searches the database sequentially. The search continues only until the specified record is found.

Sequential acess is simple, reliable, and relatively slow. The time it takes to find a particular record depends on the size of the database and the position of the record in the database. If the database is large and the desired record is near the end, it could take some time for the computer to find the record. The *average access time* is half the time required for the computer to read the entire database. For example, if the computer takes 1 minute to read the database, the average access time for records in that database is 30 seconds.

The term *random access* is somewhat misleading. It does not mean that the computer leafs through the database in a haphazard manner until it finds the desired record. It really means that the computer has direct access to every record in the database. The expression "random access" comes from the idea that if you choose any record at random, the computer can get to *that* record as quickly as to any other.

PRIMARY AND SECONDARY KEYS

In order for the computer to provide random ("direct") access to a particular record, it needs a little help. The specific 'help' is usually a special *primary key* tacked onto the front of the record when the record is created. The primary key must be unique for each record. The computer uses this key to go directly to a record, by either keeping track of or calculating exactly where the record is on the disk. When the record is requested, the computer goes directly to the record's physical location and reads it into main memory.

In dBASE III, the *record number* is the primary key. If you know a record number, you can go directly to that record. For example, to go directly to Record 254 you would use

. GO 254

Locating a record by the primary key is very fast, but you must first know the key. In dBASE III, this means that you must know the record number, which isn't too practical. It is not likely that you can remember the primary key for each record in a database. That may be possible if the database is very small. However, if it is that small, direct access isn't necessary.

A *secondary key* is used to make the primary key useful. These fare data items such as NAMES and PART NUMBERS that are of interest to us. A database can have one or more secondary keys. Unlike primary keys, these secondary keys are not directly useable by the computer. They are used to provide a transition between an item of interest to us, such as a name, and an item that can be used by the computer, like the record number.

Secondary keys do not provide true direct access, but they come close. Access is much faster than the average access time for the sequential approach. Tables provide *translation* between primary and secondary keys.

An ordinary cookbook provides a good example of the use of primary and secondary keys. The primary key is the page number. The secondary key(s) are the names of the dishes and the ingredients. The index is the table that translates the name of the food into a page number. To find a particular recipe, we search the index for the item that we want. This gives us the page number which takes us to the recipe. Of course, if we knew the recipe was on page 123, we wouldn't use the index. But, using the index is a lot quicker than leafing through the cookbook a page at a time.

If you look at the index of a real cookbook, or this book, for that matter, you'll observe that some items have more than one page number listed. These items are examples of *non-unique* keys. Secondary keys do not need to be unique.

Let's suppose that we have a database of students. Each record has the student's name, address, telephone number, room, and grade. We would like to be able to access student records by name or grade or room number. To do this, we identify these three fields as secondary keys. We have three tables, one for each of the three keys. When we want a particular student's record, we use the name key and request the student by name. The computer finds the name in the table, takes the record number and uses the record number to get the record from the database.

In dBASE, these tables are called *index files*. These index files give us nearly direct access to the desired data records. Since the tables are read only by the computer, they can be constructed so that they can be searched very quickly. dBASE uses a technique called a B-Tree. Using this technique, even the largest database can be searched in only a second or two. dBASE builds these index files for you with the INDEX command.

. USE B:SCHOOL
. INDEX ON NAME TO B:NAME
. INDEX ON ROOM TO B:ROOM
. INDEX ON GRADE TO B:GRADE

These commands have built three tables which allow you to use the three fields—NAME, ROOM, and GRADE—as secondary keys. The three tables have these filenames: B:NAME, B:ROOM, and B:GRADE. The database system adds .NDX to the end of the filename to tell the computer this is an INDEX FILE to be used for record access by the secondary key. If you need to find records

Data Basics

according to the student's name, just use the database file with the name index.

. USE B:SCHOOL INDEX B:NAME

You can now go directly to any student record by following the command FIND with the student's name.

. FIND Aardvark, Anthony

If Anthony were the only student in the school whose last name began with Aa, we could have used the command

. FIND Aa

and gotten the same result. The FIND command positions the database to the *first* occurance of the key item. In these two examples we have found the first Anthony Aardvark record. To view the record, use the DISPLAY command.

If you are interested in the sixth grade, you would

. USE B:SCHOOL INDEX B:GRADE
. FIND 6

These two commands take you directly to the first sixth-grade student record. The index file causes all of the sixth-grade student records to be grouped together. Within this group the records appear in record number order. Because they are grouped together, you can use the WHILE clause to display all sixth graders.

. DISPLAY WHILE GRADE='6'

This will appear to be much faster than using the FOR clause within the command. When the FOR clause is used, dBASE must first locate the first sixth-grade record using a sequential search. Sequential operations on indexed files will usually be slower than the same operation on the same database without an index. Why? With an index, all operations are accomplished through the index. This makes the process a little slower on a record-to-record basis. Overall, the process can be a lot faster since you won't have to process all the records.

Index files make the records appear to be sorted by the secondary key. This provides a double use for these files: direct access to individual records and as an alternative to sorting.

A secondary key can consist of several fields. For example, you can arrange the student records so that they are grouped by class (room and grade) and are alphabetical within each class. To do this, you would use:

. USE B:SCHOOL
. INDEX ON GRADE+ROOM+NAME TO B:CLASS

The plus signs (+) link the three fields together to form a single secondary key. The student records are now in grade order, by room within the grade, and alphabetically within the room.

The index files are saved on the disk where they can be used on demand. They can be kept current by placing them in use whenever records are added, edited, or removed. Let's suppose that we have four index files that are used with the database SCHOOL. We can keep these indexes up

Chapter Eleven

to date by putting them all in use, as shown in the following command.

. USE B:SCHOOL INDEX B:CLASS,B:NAME,B:ROOM,B:GRADE

• This will cause the index files B:CLASS, B:NAME, B:ROOM, *and* B:GRADE to be updated each time a record is added, one of the key fields is changed, or records are removed with the DELETE and PACK commands.

There are disadvantages to maintaining and updating multiple index files (multiple secondary keys). It's slow. Updating multiple secondary key tables in any database management system is time-consuming. For this reason it is usually recommended that multiple keys (multiple index files) be avoided if at all possible. A related disadvantage is that a change made to the database without incorporating the change into an index file can invalidate the table and any computer processing done with the use of that table.

Secondary key tables (index files), of course, require space on a disk. If you have more than one disk drive, you may place an index table on a different disk drive than the database. Though indexes don't have to be on the same disk as the database, they must be online. This means that the computer must have simultaneous access to the database and all of the index file that you are using. An index file, like a database, must be entirely contained on a single disk. Keep this in mind when planning your database system and when selecting computer hardware to support your database system.

PHYSICAL AND LOGICAL RECORDS

In Chapter One, we used the operation of an automotive parts store as an analogy to explain the concepts database management. The clerk, the parts catalogs, and the storage bins used to hold the auto parts are analogous to the database management system while the auto parts are analogous to the data items stored in a database. stored in the database. In computer literature, you will find references to *physical records* and *logical records*. Physical records are the actual data records—they correspond to the auto parts in the example. Logical records are the entries in the secondary key tables (index files) that tell the computer where the data is stored on the disk. These records correspond to the entries in the clerk's catalogs that tell where the auto parts are located.

In Chapter One we also used a library as another example of a database management system. In a library, the physical records correspond to the books. The logical records are the cards in the card catalog.

Each time you add a new record to a database, this is a physical record. Its physical position in the database is given by the record number. The physical order of the records is usually just the order in which they were added, as reflected by the record numbers. In any case, physical order and record number order are the same. When you index the database, you are creating a table of *logical records*. Each entry in the index table is a logical record. The records are arranged (sorted) by a secondary key such as NAME or PARTNUMBER. The records in the database will now appear to be arranged by this same key. This is the *logical order* of the database. A database can have one physical order but many logical orders (one for each index).

ASCII

ASCII is an acronym for American Standard Code for Information Interchange. Each character on your keyboard, such as an a, or an l or a $ is assigned a code value. A table showing the ASCII symbol codes is included as Appendix D. The computer uses the code value in its operations, *not* the symbol. The value of the ASCII codes is that different computers and programs can "understand" data that was prepared on a different computer or computer program. This may seem obvious, but it isn't. At one time each computer used its own set of codes and the data it produced wasn't directly useable by other computers. Even today there are other character code standards.

ASCII Files

ASCII files contain only the 128 ASCII characters. (See Appendix D for the table of the ASCII codes.) The first 32 ASCII characters are called the control codes. They are used to initiate actions on the computer or the printer. They are "not printable" which means that you cannot see them — only their result. These codes represent actions such as *line feed*, which advances the printer or monitor to the next line, and *form feed*, which advances to the next sheet of paper in a printer.

Most files and programs that are used on your computer are not ASCII files. Most of the program files will have filenames ending in .EXE or .COM. These files can be used only on certain kinds of computers. Some of these programs such as word processors, spreadsheets, and dBASE create other files. These files may or may not be ASCII files. Word processors, for example, usually have two modes — one for creating ASCII files, the other for preparing documents. dBASE database files are not ASCII files — although they normally contain only ASCII data values.

CHAPTER TWELVE

HIERARCHICAL AND NETWORK SYSTEMS

There are three basic kinds of database systems: *relational*, *hierarchical*, and *network*. Data organized in tables of rows and columns is a model for a relational system. The stacking hierarchy of a corporate organization chart is the picture we see in a hierarchical system. When trying to visualize a network system, think of the organization charts of two companies which have just merged. Most new database management systems are either RELATIONAL or a version of the NETWORK system called CODASYL. This NETWORK database, by the way, is based on a model of the data structure — it is not a database to be used on a network of computers.

THE RELATIONAL DATABASE

This book focuses on the relational database system because it relates easily to everyday experience and because most database management systems are variations on the relational model. The relational database system is exactly what it appears to be. Data is handled and stored in what, to most people, is a natural way. When using a relational system, a person inexperienced and unfamiliar with computer systems can produce useful work with relative ease.

An example of a simple relational database (taken from our liquor store inventory in Chapter 2) is shown as Figure 12-1.

This relational database looks just as it would if you were to take inventory using pencil and paper. Each record in a relational database has a fixed length, and each field within the record is always the same size.

LIQUOR	BRAND	SIZE	QTY	COST	PRICE
SCOTCH	AULD COUNTRY	QUART	23	5.59	9.31
SCOTCH	AULD COUNTRY	2 LITER	7	9.78	16.30
SCOTCH	AULD COUNTRY	PINT	88	2.74	4.56
VODKA	REAL RUSSIAN	QUART	35	3.78	6.30
VODKA	REAL RUSSIAN	2 LITER	9	7.95	13.25
VODKA	REAL RUSSIAN	PINT	75	1.49	2.48
WHISKEY	SOUTHERN RYE	QUART	32	5.11	8.51
WHISKEY	OLD WYOMING	PINT	44	1.98	3.30
WHISKEY	OLD WYOMING	QUART	19	5.29	8.81
WHISKEY	THE NEW SOUTH	QUART	4	7.49	12.48
BOURBON	SOUTHERN ARISTOCRACY	PINT	5	0.99	1.65
BOURBON	SOUTHERN ARISTOCRACY	FIFTH	22	1.78	2.96
BOURBON	SOUTHERN ARISTOCRACY	QUART	21	3.50	5.83
BOURBON	SOUTHERN ARISTOCRACY	1/2 GAL	3	6.89	11.48
BOURBON	SOUTHERN ARISTOCRACY	2 LITER	5	6.47	10.78

Figure 12-1: A relational database

THE HIERARCHICAL DATABASE

Hierarchical database systems require you to think of the data as being arranged in a hierarchy. A diagram of a hierarchical database resembles an organizational chart. Since it also resembles an upside-down tree, hierarchical structures are often called tree structures. Figure 12-2 shows the liquor store inventory as a hierarchical database.

When represented in this way, the hierarchical structure becomes apparent. Each data item is subordinate to another data item (except of course for the item in the topmost box). Instead of being a simple collection of fields, the *record* is a collection of subrecords or *segments*. Each box in the example is a segment or piece of the record. A segment may contain more than one field. The bottom three boxes, for example, might be grouped together to form a single segment.

The use of the term "record" is unfortunate because it is difficult to separate one use of the term from another in our thinking. In this particular version of our liquor store database, we have four records: one for each of the four different kinds of liquor represented in the relational database B:INVENTRY (scotch, vodka, whiskey, and bourbon). The hierarchical whiskey record, corresponding to the whiskey entries in the relational database version, is shown in Figure 12-3.

In these systems, each segment must belong to another segment, and no segment may belong to more than one segment. However, a segment may "own" more than one subsegment. Owners are called parents and subordinate segments are called children. In the example (Figure 12-3), whiskey is the parent of Old Wyoming, Southern Rye, and The New South. Each of these, in turn, is the parent (or owner) of various SIZE segments, they are also the children of whiskey.

Let's look at how this might work. Each segment has an identification code attached to it. That code is unique for each segment or primary key. It identifies the kind of segment and the

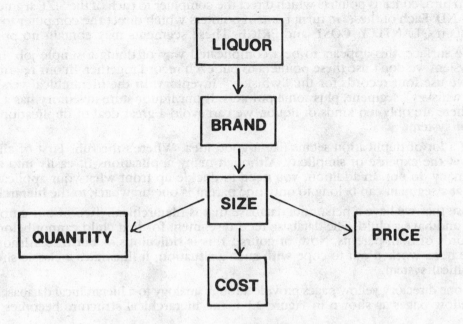

Figure 12-2: A hierarchical database

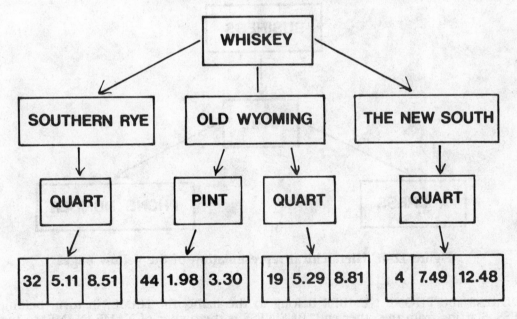

Figure 12-3: A 'whiskey' record in hierarchical representation

sequence number, which is similar in concept to dBASE III's record number.

Each of the four LIQUOR segments contains several pointers. Pointers allow the computer to go directly from segment to segment to assemble the entire record. Each LIQUOR pointer directs the computer to a BRAND segment that belongs to that LIQUOR segment. Each of these BRAND segments, in turn, contains pointers which direct the computer to each of the SIZE segments belonging to that BRAND. Each of these, in turn, contain pointers which direct the computer to the segments which contain QUANTITY, COST, and PRICE. These segments may contain no pointers.

On the surface, this appears to be a complicated way of doing a simple job. In a relational database system we don't use these pointers to put each record together. In our relational example, however, we use four records for the "whiskey" inventory. In the hierarchical version, we need only one "whiskey" segment, plus some pointers. If our liquor store inventory has a thousand entries and there are only ten kinds of liquor, we can avoid a great deal of duplication by using the hierarchical system.

Saving a lot of duplication seems like a good idea. Where's the rub? First of all, duplication is reduced at the expense of simplicity. Although many applications fit easily into a hierarchical structure, many do not. In addition, you need to decide up front what your applications will be. The fact that a segment can belong to only one parent is one drawback to the hierarchical system.

Suppose that we have a personnel database that is hierarchical. Two of our employees marry each other and have a child. The database record segment for that child cannot belong to the personnel records of both parents. Now, of course, this is ridiculous — but true. Although many artifices have been worked out to cope with such a situation, it illustrates a classic shortcoming of the hierarchical system.

Telephone directory yellow pages provide a rough analogy to a hierarchical database. By representing the yellow pages as shown in Figure 12-4, the hierarchical structure becomes apparent.

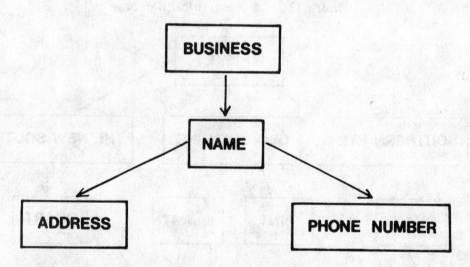

Figure 12-4: Hierarchical representation of the yellow pages

ADDRESS and PHONE NUMBER belong to the name, the NAME, in turn, belongs to the BUSINESS. Starting from the other end, BUSINESS is the owner of NAME. NAME, in turn, is the owner of both ADDRESS and PHONE NUMBER. A segment cannot belong to more than one owner. An owner, however, may own many other segments. For businesses that have more than one address and/or phone number, the structure might be diagrammed as shown in Figure 12-5.

Chapter Twelve

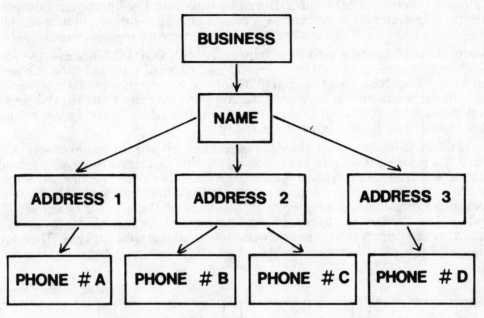

Figure 12-5: An owner of many segments

Unlike relational databases, hierarchical databases can have records of varying sizes. Some records, for example, might have several telephone numbers; others have only one. Though this situation can be handled by a relational database, it requires that you either waste memory or become clever.

Suppose we have a record of new car dealers. The BUSINESS segment contains the title "New Car Dealers," plus pointers to direct the computer to all of the segments that contain names of new car dealers. One such dealer is "Vroom Vroom Motors." The segment for Vroom Vroom Motors contains the company's name, as well as a set of pointers leading the computer to the addresses of the company's facilities. The database system may use the segment ID to keep order within a record (for example, to, keep company names in alphabetical order). Each address segment contains the address and pointers for the phone numbers. A segment will always contain pointers that direct the computer to segments belonging to it. A segment *might* contain a pointer to lead the computer to its owner segment.

There are some possible shortcomings to the hierarchical database system — from the user's viewpoint. First of all, to get an alphabetical listing of all the names in the database would, most likely, require a substantial effort. Second, it is quite possible that a company would belong to more than one business category. Vroom Vroom Motors might very well have a repair shop, a body shop, a parts department, and a used car lot in addition to its new car dealership. In a hierarchical system, a child can have only one parent. To list our sample car dealer under four business categories, the dealership must be entered four times, once in each category.

THE NETWORK DATABASE

Network database management systems are similar to hierarchical systems. One major difference is that, under certain conditions, a child can have more than one parent. Another is that a parent-child relationship such as BUSINESS-NAME can be switched. Finally, the terminology is different from both the relational and hierarchical systems. Again, network refers to a model of the data structure — it does not refer to a database used on a network of computers.

The term *network* is often used interchangeably with CODASYL because the most common network database systems are based upon a proposed national standard for databases, a standard developed by the Data Base Task Group (DBTG) of the COnference on DAta SYstems Languages. CODASYL is the organization that developed the computer language COBOL. The network database is based on the *new math* concept of sets. The network database is even more complex than the hierarchical, but it does provide greater flexibility.

In the network database system, the database is made up of a collection of sets. A set is a group of like items. Each set consists of a collection of records similar to those in a relational system, except that the length need not be fixed. A record can belong to more than one set. Several businesses (NAMES) belong to each business category set (BUSINESS). In the phone book, the new car dealers such as Vroom Vroom Motors belong to, or are members of, the new car dealer set. The "owner" record is thus New Car Dealers. Every set must have an owner record. A set can consist of only one record. A record cannot belong to two occurrences of the same set type. Therefore, the situation in Figure 12-6 is not allowed.

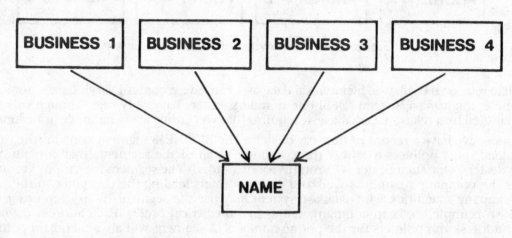

Figure 12-6

Now, this is silly since we all know that a company name can show up under many business categories in the yellow pages. The problem here is that we have a situation where the number of possible relationships is enormous — enormous enough to overwhelm even the largest computer. The network database is comfortable when dealing with one to many relationships. The problem is to restructure the sets so that all relationships are one to many.

In the hierarchical database system, if NAME belonged to BUSINESS, an alphabetical listing of all the names might be difficult to produce. This is because the NAMES are alphabetized for each business category and can be accessed only by business category. In the network system, NAME *can belong* to BUSINESS and at the same time the BUSINESS *can belong* to NAME.

As you might have expected, the network database (Figure 12-7) uses an entirely different terminology from either those of the hierarchical or the relational database systems. The data item is similar to what we have been calling a field. In the hierarchical database example, there might be several phone numbers belonging to an address. This is called a *vector data aggregate*. There

Chapter Twelve

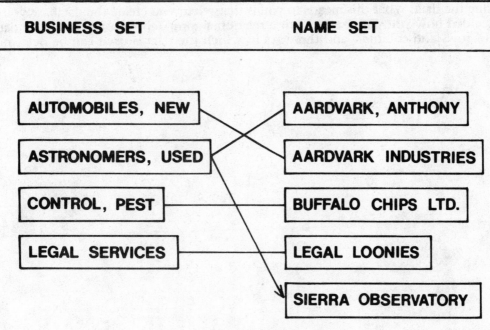

Figure 12-7: Network system

might also be several addresses belonging to a name. Each of the addresses has a phone number. The address-phone number is called a group. If there is more than one group, it is a repeating group.

Both hierarchical and network database systems are substantially different in structure from the relational systems. The way that data records are structured in these systems is much more complex than in the relational system. These systems are well-suited to large, complex database applications. Because of this, they are used extensively on mainframe computers. These systems *can* be very efficient in their use of the computer's resources — CPU time and main memory. The potential for efficiency can become extremely crucial when the database contains tens or hundreds of thousands of records. Because the cost of operating a large mainframe computer system can easily amount to several hundred dollars per hour, the value of efficiency is readily apparent. The cost of professional programmers to work with these database systems is easily justified when their efforts can reduce the cost of using a database management system on this kind of computer installation. This is not usually the case for databases typically used on microcomputers.

As was stated earlier, each of the three database systems can accommodate all of the required database functions. Each has its strengths and weaknesses. The hierarchical and network systems offer the user efficiency and speed. They are conservative in the use of the computer's resources. They are, however, complex and relatively inflexible. They were developed for use on mainframe computer systems where billions of bytes of online disk storage are common. A billion bytes represents from 1,000 to 4,000 eight-inch floppy disks. Just reading that much storage at floppy disk read speed could take a half-million seconds. That is *days*. If your database needs are truly this large, a microcomputer database system may not be for you. You may need either a hierarchical or a network database system and a very large computer.

Each of the three kinds of database systems has things that it does best. Each can perform any database task. The hierarchical and network approaches to database systems require that you represent the data as either a hierarchy or a network by designing your database to satisfy a particular way of using the data. What this means to you is that when you create the database you must have already decided how you will use it. With a relational approach, you represent the data in terms of tables of rows and columns, and the ways in which the data is used can be determined later.

Chapter Twelve

CHAPTER THIRTEEN

MULTI-USER DATABASES

Single-user (personal) computers and multi-user computers are the most frequently used types of computer. With a single-user computer, the user receives all of the computer's resources. With a multi-user computer, the resources are shared among the users. Most large computers (minicomputers and mainframe computers) are multi-user. Most desktop (microcomputers) are single user. Why multi-user? Most large computers are expensive to purchase and to operate. Sharing the computer over a number of users reduces the cost for each user. More importantly, multi-user computers allow users to share programs and information.

Nearly all organizations can profit if the information stored in a database can be shared by a number of users. The airline reservation system, for example, would not be possible without a shared database. On the other hand, multi-user computers are more expensive and usually require more maintenance than single-user systems. They can be delicate and they may require professional staffs for operations and maintenance. And, it's just plain silly to share a $5.00 device like a CPU.

THE NETWORK

Many organizations have begun to connect (single-user) personal computers together to form a *network*. In a network, the advantages of the personal computer are retained, with the addition of many of the advantages of a multi-user computer. A network allows us to share expensive devices such as high-quality printers and plotters. But, more importantly, a network allows us to share information. A typical personal computer network is shown in Figure 13-1.

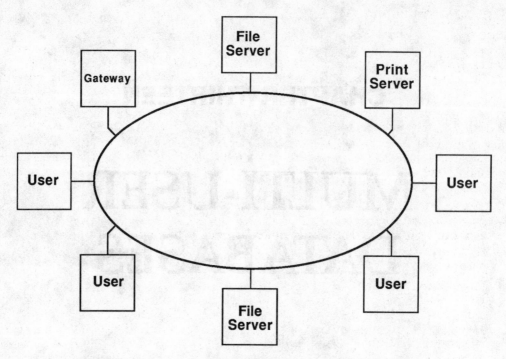

Figure 13-1: A typical personal computer network

The network consists of several personal computers that have been connected together. Each computer can be used with or without the network. Special hardware and software are added to each computer to connect it to the network.

Each of the boxes in Figure 13-1 is a NODE on the network. Each USER node is called a *workstation*. Each workstation is usually a complete, stand-alone personal computer with its own disk drives. A workstation may also have other devices such as a printer or a modem attached directly to it. These are LOCAL devices and belong exclusively to the workstation. The FILE SERVER is essentially a shared disk drive which the workstations can all use just as if it were connected directly to each workstation. The PRINT SERVER is essentially a shared printer. The GATEWAY allows the network to be connected to another network.

The FILE SERVER, the PRINT SERVER, and the GATEWAY may be separate computers that are dedicated to each task. Or, these functions may all be combined within a single computer. On some networks, the SERVERS may even be combined with a workstation. A network can also have several servers. What is important is that the servers represent shared devices.

When a network has a file server, every computer that is connected to the network will appear to have an additional disk drive. Suppose that we have a computer with two floppy disk drives. When the computer is connected to the network it will appear to have an additional disk drive for each server on the network. Server disks, of course, are usually large capacity, high-speed hard disks capable of storing megabytes of data.

SHARED FILES

We can share disk files that are stored on the server (the shared) disk. For example, we can share database files, report form files, label form files, catalogs, and so on. Usually, any number

---

Chapter Thirteen

of users are allowed to view the contents of a database or to use a report form. When it comes to changing database records or modifying a report form, we have another story. When we share files, we do have to make a few minor procedural changes. For example, while several users can view at a database record at the same time, we can allow only one of them to change that record. While multiple users can use a report form, only one user can be allowed to modify that report form. The limitations (or restrictions) involved with shared files all revolve around change.

To share files properly, the database management system must be designed (and installed) as a multi-user DBMS. You may be able to share files that are stored on the network file server if you are using a single-user database manager. But, if you do, you are liable to have trouble because the software wasn't designed to be used with shared files. It doesn't *cooperate* with the other users on the network. For the network system to be effective in sharing data files, all the users must cooperate and operate by the same set of rules.

Let's use the library example again to examine shared database files. Two people cannot take the same book home at the same time. When you check out a book, you don't just walk out with it. You "check out" the book. The librarian keeps track of the book with a book checkout card. When a book that you want is "out", the librarian consults these records to tell you when the book is expected to be returned. The checkout cards, by the way, are *logical* records.

Unlike our library example, our shared database can be "taken home" by two or more users at a time. On the other hand, we cannot allow both of them to change the same record at the same time. Suppose that our shared database contains seating information on airline flights. Two travel agents simultaneously query the database on seat availability on a particular flight. There is only one seat available. We cannot allow both agents to sell the seat. The first agent to "sell" the seat must win. While the transaction is taking place, the second agent must be prevented from using the database record. Once the first agent's sale is complete — the record will be released, but it will no longer be of value to the second agent. This is an example of RECORD LOCKOUT. Multi-user database systems must provide record lockout. Single-user database systems need not.

RECORD LOCKOUT

To prevent two users from changing the same record at the same time, a user must "lock" the record before making a change. The locking action is usually accomplished by pressing a control key — such as Ctrl-O. This action signals the DBMS that the user wants to change the record. The DBMS then re-reads the disk record to make sure that the user's screen display shows the current record content. This protects against the situation where another user has edited a record after the display was created. It also locks the record to prevent others from using that record while it is being changed. When the change is complete, the record is written back to the disk and the "lock" is removed — the record is unlocked.

Figure 13-2 shows the screen display for the dBASE III PLUS EDIT command in the multi-user version. The record lock status is shown on screen. The user is not allowed to change the record without first locking the record.

While the record is locked, other users cannot even read the record. As far as they are concerned, it doesn't exist. To protect against possible error, some database operations, such as SUM, AVERAGE, and COUNT, are prohibited as long as other users have records from the database locked. This prevents a user from obtaining incorrect information from the database.

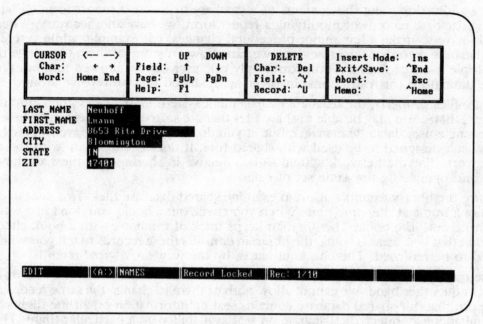

Figure 13-2: Multi-user edit showing lock status

FILE LOCKOUT

There are other cases where we need to lock the entire file. If we are modifying a report form, for example, we don't want another user to be changing that report at the same time. To protect against this case, the entire file is locked. No other user will be allowed to use that report form until you have finished changing it.

There may be other cases where you will want to use a file to prepare a report, or just to make changes without any possibility of another user working on that file. This makes the files that you are using your own "private" property just as if they are stored on your local disk drives. You are said to have *exclusive* use of these files. To make files your exclusive property — for the time being, use the command

. SET EXCLUSIVE ON

The files that you open after you have used SET EXCLUSIVE ON will be yours exclusively. You won't be able to open a file that someone else is using. To release files for use by others, you can either close the files, or you can

. SET EXCLUSIVE OFF

You will also need to use file lockout when changing the database structure — which affects all of the records. Rather than check out each record — we just checkout the entire file. It is reserved for our *exclusive* use.

Chapter Thirteen

PERFORMANCE

A multi-user database will often appear to be slower than a single-user database. There is a lot more going on inside of the blinking box. The more users there are sharing the database files, the slower the system will become. So, there's a trade-off between performance and the convenience of sharing data. When it becomes a problem, a specialist can design a special application program to boost system performance.

USING THE NETWORK PRINTER

In most networks, many of the user workstations may have local printers. Print output is normally directed to the workstation's local printer — even when there is a print server on the network. If there is no local printer the network should be configured so that print output is automatically sent to the shared printer.

dBASE provides the command SET PRINTER to allow you to switch between your local printer and the shared network printer. To make use of this command you must know the *device name* of the network printer. This is a name that is assigned to the remote printer — usually by the person responsible for the network. Suppose that our network printer has the code name FROGGY. We would send printed output to the remote printer with the command

```
. SET PRINTER TO \\FROGGY\PRINTER = PRN
```

Similarly, we could switch back to our local printer with the command

```
. SET PRINTER TO LPT1
```

(See your dBASE manual.) Your network may provide a *hot key* that lets you issue network commands from within a program such as dBASE. A hot key is usually a two-key combination such as Alt-F10. This triggers the network software to provide you with a list of options — usually including switching to the remote printer.

If you are using a network, there will be a person who has been assigned to be the *network administrator*. You should contact that person to obtain the specifics about how to select the network printer from dBASE or any other applications program.

SECTION FOUR
SPECIAL TOPICS

CHAPTER FOURTEEN

A LITTLE LOGIC

Computers and database management systems are built on the use of logic. Most microcomputer database systems are designed so that this use of logic occurs in a very natural way. The use of logic isn't difficult — in fact it's kind of fun. However you feel about it, understanding computer logic allows you to get more from your computer and your database management system.

There are three commonly used logical terms. These are referred to as the *logical operators*:

.AND.
.OR.
.NOT.

These logical operators work in ways similar to their ordinary English counterparts. The periods at each end of the terms are part of the logical operators.

To illustrate the use of these operators, we'll use our liquor store inventory again. The database is shown in Figure 14-1.

Suppose you wished to see all the entries for whiskey and bourbon. The natural tendency is to write the query command as:

. DISPLAY FOR LIQUOR = 'BOURBON' .AND. LIQUOR = 'WHISKEY'

Unfortunately, this command won't get you what you want. It tells dBASE to display all the records where the LIQUOR field contains WHISKEY *and* BOURBON. There are none. The computer applies the request to one record at a time — not to the entire database. The correct command is:

LIQUOR	BRAND	SIZE	QTY	COST	PRICE
SCOTCH	AULD COUNTRY	QUART	23	5.59	9.31
SCOTCH	AULD COUNTRY	2 LITER	7	9.78	16.30
SCOTCH	AULD COUNTRY	PINT	88	2.74	4.56
VODKA	REAL RUSSIAN	QUART	35	3.78	6.30
VODKA	REAL RUSSIAN	2 LITER	9	7.95	13.25
VODKA	REAL RUSSIAN	PINT	75	1.49	2.48
WHISKEY	SOUTHERN RYE	QUART	32	5.11	8.51
WHISKEY	OLD WYOMING	PINT	44	1.98	3.30
WHISKEY	OLD WYOMING	QUART	19	5.29	8.81
WHISKEY	THE NEW SOUTH	QUART	4	7.49	12.48
BOURBON	SOUTHERN ARISTOCRACY	PINT	5	0.99	1.65
BOURBON	SOUTHERN ARISTOCRACY	FIFTH	22	1.78	2.96
BOURBON	SOUTHERN ARISTOCRACY	QUART	21	3.50	5.83
BOURBON	SOUTHERN ARISTOCRACY	1/2 GAL	3	6.89	11.48
BOURBON	SOUTHERN ARISTOCRACY	2 LITER	5	6.47	10.78

Figure 14-1: Liquor store inventory

. DISPLAY FOR LIQUOR = 'BOURBON' .OR. LIQUOR = 'WHISKEY'

The section of the example database to which this applies is shown by the unshaded area in Figure 14-2.

Proper use of the .AND. operator requests the *common area* of two groups. For example, to determine what records contain pints of whiskey, the command is:

. DISPLAY FOR LIQUOR = 'WHISKEY' .AND. SIZE = 'PINT'

The order of the fields doesn't matter. The same result is obtained with the command:

. DISPLAY FOR SIZE = 'PINT' .AND. LIQUOR = 'WHISKEY'

Using .OR. in place of the .AND. in the last example gives an entirely different result.

. DISPLAY FOR SIZE = 'PINT' .OR. LIQUOR = 'WHISKEY'

The unshaded area in Figure 14-3 shows the records that would be displayed from this command.

Chapter Fourteen

LIQUOR	BRAND	SIZE	QTY	COST	PRICE
SCOTCH	AULD COUNTRY	QUART	23	5.59	9.31
SCOTCH	AULD COUNTRY	2 LITER	7	9.78	16.30
SCOTCH	AULD COUNTRY	PINT	88	2.74	4.56
VODKA	REAL RUSSIAN	QUART	35	3.78	6.30
VODKA	REAL RUSSIAN	2 LITER	9	7.95	13.25
VODKA	REAL RUSSIAN	PINT	75	1.49	2.48
WHISKEY	SOUTHERN RYE	QUART	32	5.11	8.51
WHISKEY	OLD WYOMING	PINT	44	1.98	3.30
WHISKEY	OLD WYOMING	QUART	19	5.29	8.81
WHISKEY	THE NEW SOUTH	QUART	4	7.49	12.48
BOURBON	SOUTHERN ARISTOCRACY	PINT	5	0.99	1.65
BOURBON	SOUTHERN ARISTOCRACY	FIFTH	22	1.78	2.96
BOURBON	SOUTHERN ARISTOCRACY	QUART	21	3.50	5.83
BOURBON	SOUTHERN ARISTOCRACY	1/2 GAL	3	6.89	11.48
BOURBON	SOUTHERN ARISTOCRACY	2 LITER	5	6.47	10.78

Figure 14-2

LIQUOR	BRAND	SIZE	QTY	COST	PRICE
SCOTCH	AULD COUNTRY	QUART	23	5.59	9.31
SCOTCH	AULD COUNTRY	2 LITER	7	9.78	16.30
SCOTCH	AULD COUNTRY	PINT	88	2.74	4.56
VODKA	REAL RUSSIAN	QUART	35	3.78	6.30
VODKA	REAL RUSSIAN	2 LITER	9	7.95	13.25
VODKA	REAL RUSSIAN	PINT	75	1.49	2.48
WHISKEY	SOUTHERN RYE	QUART	32	5.11	8.51
WHISKEY	OLD WYOMING	PINT	44	1.98	3.30
WHISKEY	OLD WYOMING	QUART	19	5.29	8.81
WHISKEY	THE NEW SOUTH	QUART	4	7.49	12.48
BOURBON	SOUTHERN ARISTOCRACY	PINT	5	0.99	1.65
BOURBON	SOUTHERN ARISTOCRACY	FIFTH	22	1.78	2.96
BOURBON	SOUTHERN ARISTOCRACY	QUART	21	3.50	5.83
BOURBON	SOUTHERN ARISTOCRACY	1/2 GAL	3	6.89	11.48
BOURBON	SOUTHERN ARISTOCRACY	2 LITER	5	6.47	10.78

Figure 14-3

A Little Logic

Suppose we want to extract those records that are pints of either whiskey or bourbon. The way to set up the command is:

. DISPLAY FOR (LIQUOR = 'WHISKEY' .OR. LIQUOR = 'BOURBON') .AND. SIZE = 'PINT'

The records that qualify under this criteria are shown in the unshaded areas of Figure 14-4.

LIQUOR	BRAND	SIZE	QTY	COST	PRICE
SCOTCH	AULD COUNTRY	QUART	23	5.59	9.31
SCOTCH	AULD COUNTRY	2 LITER	7	9.78	16.30
SCOTCH	AULD COUNTRY	PINT	88	2.74	4.56
VODKA	REAL RUSSIAN	QUART	35	3.78	6.30
VODKA	REAL RUSSIAN	2 LITER	9	7.95	13.25
VODKA	REAL RUSSIAN	PINT	75	1.49	2.48
WHISKEY	SOUTHERN RYE	QUART	32	5.11	8.51
WHISKEY	OLD WYOMING	PINT	44	1.98	3.30
WHISKEY	OLD WYOMING	QUART	19	5.29	8.81
WHISKEY	THE NEW SOUTH	QUART	4	7.49	12.48
BOURBON	SOUTHERN ARISTOCRACY	PINT	5	0.99	1.65
BOURBON	SOUTHERN ARISTOCRACY	FIFTH	22	1.78	2.96
BOURBON	SOUTHERN ARISTOCRACY	QUART	21	3.50	5.83
BOURBON	SOUTHERN ARISTOCRACY	1/2 GAL	3	6.89	11.48
BOURBON	SOUTHERN ARISTOCRACY	2 LITER	5	6.47	10.78

Figure 14-4

Suppose you inadvertently omitted the parentheses in the last example:

. DISPLAY FOR LIQUOR = 'WHISKEY' .OR. LIQUOR = 'BOURBON' .AND. SIZE = 'PINT'

The resulting display — which is entirely different than Figure 14-4 — is shown in Figure 14-5. This result occurs because the .AND. operator takes *precedence* over the .OR. operator.

To return to the earlier example, the logical arrangement resulting in the unshaded areas of Figure 14-4 is due to command structure:

. DISPLAY FOR (LIQUOR = 'WHISKEY' .OR. LIQUOR = 'BOURBON') .AND. SIZE = 'PINT'

Now suppose you really want everything else; it can get messy if you try to write out the logic. However, the .NOT. operator can handle this task with ease:

. DISPLAY FOR .NOT. ((LIQUOR = 'WHISKEY' .OR. LIQUOR = 'BOURBON') .AND. SIZE = 'PINT')

The entire logical expression is placed in parentheses to tell the computer that the .NOT. applies to everything. The result is shown in the unshaded areas of Figure 14-6.

Chapter Fourteen

LIQUOR	BRAND	SIZE	QTY	COST	PRICE
SCOTCH	AULD COUNTRY	QUART	23	5.59	9.31
SCOTCH	AULD COUNTRY	2 LITER	7	9.78	16.30
SCOTCH	AULD COUNTRY	PINT	88	2.74	4.56
VODKA	REAL RUSSIAN	QUART	35	3.78	6.30
VODKA	REAL RUSSIAN	2 LITER	9	7.95	13.25
VODKA	REAL RUSSIAN	PINT	75	1.49	2.48
WHISKEY	SOUTHERN RYE	QUART	32	5.11	8.51
WHISKEY	OLD WYOMING	PINT	44	1.98	3.30
WHISKEY	OLD WYOMING	QUART	19	5.29	8.81
WHISKEY	THE NEW SOUTH	QUART	4	7.49	12.48
BOURBON	SOUTHERN ARISTOCRACY	PINT	5	0.99	1.65
BOURBON	SOUTHERN ARISTOCRACY	FIFTH	22	1.78	2.96
BOURBON	SOUTHERN ARISTOCRACY	QUART	21	3.50	5.83
BOURBON	SOUTHERN ARISTOCRACY	1/2 GAL	3	6.89	11.48
BOURBON	SOUTHERN ARISTOCRACY	2 LITER	5	6.47	10.78

Figure 14-5

LIQUOR	BRAND	SIZE	QTY	COST	PRICE
SCOTCH	AULD COUNTRY	QUART	23	5.59	9.31
SCOTCH	AULD COUNTRY	2 LITER	7	9.78	16.30
SCOTCH	AULD COUNTRY	PINT	88	2.74	4.56
VODKA	REAL RUSSIAN	QUART	35	3.78	6.30
VODKA	REAL RUSSIAN	2 LITER	9	7.95	13.25
VODKA	REAL RUSSIAN	PINT	75	1.49	2.48
WHISKEY	SOUTHERN RYE	QUART	32	5.11	8.51
WHISKEY	OLD WYOMING	PINT	44	1.98	3.30
WHISKEY	OLD WYOMING	QUART	19	5.29	8.81
WHISKEY	THE NEW SOUTH	QUART	4	7.49	12.48
BOURBON	SOUTHERN ARISTOCRACY	PINT	5	0.99	1.65
BOURBON	SOUTHERN ARISTOCRACY	FIFTH	22	1.78	2.96
BOURBON	SOUTHERN ARISTOCRACY	QUART	21	3.50	5.83
BOURBON	SOUTHERN ARISTOCRACY	1/2 GAL	3	6.89	11.48
BOURBON	SOUTHERN ARISTOCRACY	2 LITER	5	6.47	10.78

Figure 14-6

A Little Logic

Now let's suppose we need to see all whiskey and bourbon records for all sizes except quarts. This is accomplished by

. DISPLAY FOR (LIQUOR = 'WHISKEY' .OR. LIQUOR = 'BOURBON') .AND. .NOT. SIZE = 'QUART'

The records affected, all whiskey and bourbon records (except for quarts), are shown in the unshaded areas of Figure 14-7.

LIQUOR	BRAND	SIZE	QTY	COST	PRICE
SCOTCH	AULD COUNTRY	QUART	23	5.59	9.31
SCOTCH	AULD COUNTRY	2 LITER	7	9.78	16.30
SCOTCH	AULD COUNTRY	PINT	88	2.74	4.56
VODKA	REAL RUSSIAN	QUART	35	3.78	6.30
VODKA	REAL RUSSIAN	2 LITER	9	7.95	13.25
VODKA	REAL RUSSIAN	PINT	75	1.49	2.48
WHISKEY	SOUTHERN RYE	QUART	32	5.11	8.51
WHISKEY	OLD WYOMING	PINT	44	1.98	3.30
WHISKEY	OLD WYOMING	QUART	19	5.29	8.81
WHISKEY	THE NEW SOUTH	QUART	4	7.49	12.48
BOURBON	SOUTHERN ARISTOCRACY	PINT	5	0.99	1.65
BOURBON	SOUTHERN ARISTOCRACY	FIFTH	22	1.78	2.96
BOURBON	SOUTHERN ARISTOCRACY	QUART	21	3.50	5.83
BOURBON	SOUTHERN ARISTOCRACY	1/2 GAL	3	6.89	11.48
BOURBON	SOUTHERN ARISTOCRACY	2 LITER	5	6.47	10.78

Figure 14-7

You can often use characteristics of the language to help you avoid some of the more complicated logic. For example,

. DISPLAY FOR LIQUOR $ 'BOURBON   ,WHISKEY   '

will produce the same result as

. DISPLAY FOR LIQUOR = 'BOURBON' .OR. LIQUOR = 'WHISKEY'

The dollar sign is shorthand for "contained in." It is also called a *string operator*. The first statement tells the computer to display each record where the content of the field LIQUOR is contained in the character string, 'BOURBON , WHISKEY '. The blank spaces after WHISKEY and BOURBON are necessary because the computer will compare the entire 10 character field LIQUOR with the character string. The field contains *trailing* blank spaces. If you had omitted the blank spaces, the computer would not find a match with the field content. Blank spaces are as important to the computer as any other character. The comma, in this case, is unnecessary because it is not contained in any LIQUOR field, but it is usually good practice to separate possible matches with some character (such as a comma) that is not a possible match.

If you want to see everything except BOURBON or WHISKEY, the proper command is

. DISPLAY FOR .NOT. LIQUOR$ 'BOURBON   ,WHISKEY   '

The use of the logical operators — .AND., .OR., and .NOT. — allows you to specify exactly what conditions apply to the commands. They improve your efficiency by screening the database to locate specific records. Later in this book, we will discuss procedures that provide even more help from the computer. Logical operators will become even more important when you begin to describe complex tasks that you want the computer to perform for you.

CHAPTER FIFTEEN

OPERATORS AND FUNCTIONS

Operators and functions are tools used when constructing commands. Even if you've never seen a computer before, you are already familiar with most of the dBASE *operators* and what they represent. Functions are provided to perform a variety of standard operations on data. SQRT is an example of a dBASE *function*. This function gives you the square root of a number. In this chapter, we review the operators used in dBASE and discuss some of the functions and then give some examples of how to use them.

OPERATORS

We tend to think of operators such as the plus sign (+) and the equals sign (=) as mathematical symbols. On the other hand, we frequently use these symbols with all kinds of data — not just with numbers. And this is true with dBASE as well as most computer languages. We use the plus sign to join items and we use the equals sign to compare items. All the operators are grouped into four categories: mathematical, relational, logical, and string.

Mathematical Operators

+	Addition
–	Subtraction
*	Multiplication
/	Division
**	Raise To A Power
( )	Grouping

String Operators

+	Join
–	Join (shift blanks)
$	Contained In

Logical Operators

.AND.	Logical AND
.OR.	Logical OR
.NOT.	Logical NOT
( )	Grouping

Relational Operators

=	Equal
#	Not Equal
>	Greater Than
<	Less Than
> =	Greater Than or Equal To
< =	Less Than or Equal To

(The logical operators have already been discussed in "A Little Logic.")

+ and –

The plus (+) and minus (–) signs can be used with character, numeric, and date data types. Their use with date and character data is usually intuitive. The plus sign can be used to join character strings together.

```
. CITY = 'Glendale'
. STATE = 'California'
. MVAR = CITY+', '+STATE
. ? MVAR
Glendale, California

. TWO = '2'
. ? TWO+TWO
22
```

The minus sign allows us to join two character strings where we want to "throw away" the ending blank spaces in the first of the two data items. Let's suppose that we have two database fields, CITY and STATE. The CITY field is 30 spaces wide. Joining CITY and STATE as in the above example would produce the display:

```
. ? CITY + ', ' + STATE
Glendale ,                California
```

Chapter Fifteen

(which looks like it was done by a computer). We really want to "throw away" the blank spaces at the end of CITY. These are called *trailing blanks* because they are at the end of a field. Replace one plus sign with a minus sign:

. ? CITY − (', '+STATE)
Glendale, California

The blank spaces really aren't gone. They have simply been moved to the end of the expression; they come after California where they are not visible. The expression containing the comma and the STATE are enclosed by parentheses so dBASE would treat that part of the expression as a single unit. Otherwise, the blanks would have moved between the comma and the STATE.

Adding and Subtracting From Dates

You can add (or subtract) a number from a date. When you do, the number is taken to be a number of days. The current date is represented by the function DATE( ). To find the date that is 30 days from now, you would use:

. ? DATE( ) + 30

Conversely, to find the date 1,000 days in the past,

. ? DATE( ) − 1000

The result of both of these operations is a new date. We can find the difference (the number of days) between two dates

. ? THISDATE − BIRTHDATE

Grouping

Parentheses are used to group numbers together. dBASE strictly follows the order of precedence rules for arithmetic. Multiplication and division are performed before addition or subtraction. Use the parentheses as grouping symbols if you forget which goes first or you want to modify this rule. For example, suppose we want to add two items together and divide the result.

.? 10 + 6/2
13

Wrong! As you can see from the above example, we didn't get the answer we wanted, we got the *correct* result. dBASE divided first, then added the result of the division to the number 10. To set up this arithmetic problem properly we put parentheses around the numbers being added.

.? (10 + 6)/2
8

The computer will always give you the correct answer. If the answer isn't what we expected, it's because we asked the wrong question. In these two examples, it is easy to see what's wrong. It isn't so easy when we substitute variable names for the numbers.

```
.? COST + MARGIN/2
75
```

If you could easily pick out an error in this case — you don't need a computer. Call us, we need you.

Relational Operators

These symbols are often called the *comparison* operators since they are used to compare two data items. All of these operators can be used with character, date, and numeric data items. The items that are being compared, however, must be of the same data type. You cannot compare apples with oranges (in this case).

When two items are compared, the result of the comparison is either true or false. dBASE will return a logical true (.T.) or a logical false (.F.), depending upon the result of the comparison. When the comparison is performed within a command, the result is used by dBASE in executing the command. For example, in the command

```
. DISPLAY FOR LIQUOR = 'SCOTCH'
```

only the records where the condition LIQUOR = 'SCOTCH' is evaluated as true will be displayed. You can check an evaluation with the ? command:

```
.? LIQUOR = 'SCOTCH'
.T.
```

When you compare dates or numbers, these symbols function just as we learned in grade school. The equals sign means that two data items must be *exactly* equal to each other. The *greater than* sign (>) means that the number to the left is supposed to be greater than the number on the right (the symbol points at the smaller item).

```
. A = 6
. B = 5
.? A > B            Is A greater than B?
.T.                 Yes, it is.
```

When we use these symbols to compare character data, for example two character strings, the comparisons are made character by character — just as you would if you were making the comparison. ABC is "less than" ABX. Characters are compared according to their position in the ASCII chart (see Appendix D). This means that ABC is also "less than" Abc. Spaces count in the comparisons, and a space has the "lowest" value of all of the characters.

When the character strings are not the same length, the comparison is made on the basis of the shorter of the two strings — the extra characters in the longer string are ignored. Therefore, read the equals sign as "begins with" when it applies to character data.

Chapter Fifteen

```
. ? 'ABCDEF' = 'A'      Does ABCDEF begin with A
.T.                     Yes, it does.
```

Because of this, you should take care that the shorter character string is to the right of the equals sign. Although ABCDEF begins with an A, A does not begin with ABCDEF.

```
. ? 'A' = 'ABCDEF'
.F.
```

You need not be concerned about this point when using the other comparison symbols, only with the equal (and not equal) symbols.

$ (Contained In)

This symbol can be used only with character data. We use the symbol to tell dBASE to search a field or a memory variable to see whether a second, smaller string is contained within it. For example, suppose we have a database of NAMES and ADDRESSes. We want to see all of the records where the string 'Robert' is contained *anywhere* in the NAME field. The command looks like

```
. DISPLAY FOR 'Robert' $ NAME        Is Robert contained in NAME?
```

The shorter of the two data items must (in this case) be on the left. The data item being searched must be at least as long as what you are searching for. Because 'Robert' has six characters, the NAME field needs to have six or more characters. Otherwise, Robert cannot be found — it cannot be there.

The $ (contained in) symbol causes the expression to be evaluated as if it were a comparison. You are asking if the expression is true.

```
USE INVENTRY
? 'Scotch' $ LIQUOR
.F.
```

FUNCTIONS

Functions are tools that are provided to perform specific, routine tasks. dBASE is particularly rich in the number and range of the functions that are provided. Each function performs a specific task. There are functions for dates, character strings, and numbers. In addition, there are several functions that perform specialized tests.

Functions have names such as SQRT and ROW. Function names are *always* followed by parentheses. The ROW function is always ROW( ). Many functions have *arguments*. If a function has an argument, the argument is placed within the parentheses. For example,

```
. ? SQRT(4)
2.00
```

In this example, the *argument* is the number 4. An argument can be any legitimate dBASE expression, for example:

```
. ? SQRT(COST)
. ? SQRT(COST * QUANTITY)
. ? SQRT(SQRT(4))
```

Functions can be used within a dBASE expression just as can constants, fieldnames, and memory variables.

Mathematical Functions

The math functions are used to perform special mathematical calculations. Some readers may not be familiar with all of the calculations involved. If you are not familiar with a particular mathematical term, you probably won't need the particular function. The special mathematical functions include:

ABS	Absolute value	MIN	Minimum of two values
EXP	Exponential (ex)	MOD	Modulus
INT	Integer	ROUND	Rounds off
LOG	Logarithm	SQRT	Square root

dBASE displays the results of most mathematical calculations using a fixed number of decimal places. The number of decimals usually displayed is 2. You can change this value by using the command SET DECIMALS TO followed by the number of decimal places you want to have displayed.

Absolute value: The absolute value of a number is its value without regard to its sign. The absolute value of -10 is 10. The ABS( ) function simply returns the absolute value:

```
. AMOUNTDUE = -247.65
    .? ABS(AMOUNTDUE)
   247.65
```

Exponential: The EXP( ) function calculates the value of ex. This function is most commonly used in statistical calculations.

```
. X = 7.3
    . ? EXP(X)
   1480.30
```

Integer: The INT( ) function discards any decimal places in a number.

```
. AMOUNT = 10.47
    .? INT(AMOUNT)
10
```

Chapter Fifteen

Logarithm: The LOG( ) function calculates the natural logarithm of a number.

```
. SET DECIMALS TO 5
    . ? LOG(20)
    2.99573
```

MAX( ): The MAX( ) function returns the larger of two numbers. Suppose a database has two fields. To display the larger of the two, use the command:

```
.? DISPLAY ALL MAX (FIELD1,FIELD2)
```

MIN( ): The MIN( ) function returns the smaller of two numbers. Suppose that a database has two fields. To display the smaller of the two, use the command:

```
.? DISPLAY ALL MIN (FIELD1,FIELD2)
```

MOD( ): The MOD( ) function returns the remainder when we divide two numbers. If the remainder is zero, the numerator is exactly divisible by the divisor. The function is particularly useful in converting between systems of units.

Suppose that we want to display 1,820 seconds in minutes and seconds. Use the INT( ) function to obtain the number of minutes. Then use the MOD( ) function to determine the number of seconds. Straight division would produce the result in decimal minutes (30.33).

```
.? INT(1820/60), MOD(1820,60)
      30              20                    30 minutes, 20 seconds
```

ROUND( ): The ROUND( ) function is used to round a number up or down at a specified digit. The number will be rounded based upon the value of the digit to the right of the specified digit. The number is rounded upward when that digit is 5 or greater, downward otherwise. dBASE III normally rounds upward at the second decimal place. The general syntax for the function is:

ROUND(*number to be rounded,specified digit*)

For example,

```
. ? 3.0000/7
0.42857.
```

```
. ? ROUND(3.0000/7,2)
.43000
```

```
. ? ROUND(1/2,0)
1.00
```

SQRT( ): The SQRT( ) function is used to calculate the square root of a number.

```
. ? SQRT(144)
12.00
```

Character Functions

Character functions allow you to search, manipulate, and transform character data items.

UPPER and LOWER: These two useful functions are used to evaluate a data item as if contained only uppercase or lowercase characters. dBASE treats uppercase and lowercase versions of the same letter as different characters. UPPER AND LOWER can both be used to elude the differences and force dBASE to treat all the characters as if they were uppercase or lowercase. For example, to search the database ADDRESS field for GLENDALE when you're not sure whether you've been consistent when entering the character data:

```
? DISPLAY FOR 'GLENDALE' $ UPPER(ADDRESS)
? DISPLAY FOR 'glendale' $ LOWER(ADDRESS)
```

SUBSTR( ), LEFT( ), and RIGHT( ): A SUBSTRing is just a character string which is a part of another, larger character string. These functions allow you to specify pieces of character strings. LEFT and RIGHT are variations of SUBSTR( ). They specify the first *n* and the last *n* characters in a character string where *n* is a number you also specify. When would we be interested in pieces of fields? Actually, quite often. Let's suppose that you store phone numbers in a field using the form (213) 555-1212. The local exchange is the three characters 555. These are the 7th, 8th, and 9th characters of this field. Let's use the substring function to construct a command to display records with a selected local exchange of 248:

```
DISPLAY FOR SUBSTR(PHONE,7,3) = '248'
```

This command asks dBASE to display the records where the 7th, 8th, and 9th characters of PHONE are 248. The function requires that you provide the FIELDNAME, the starting character position, and the number of characters in the substring.

LEFT allows you to specify the leftmost characters in a sequence. In the phone number example, to display those phone numbers in the 213 area code, use the command:

```
DISPLAY FOR LEFT(PHONE,5) = '(213)'
```

Here we have used the first 5 characters of the phone number as our criteria.

RIGHT can specify the rightmost characters of a field. Use this command to find those records where the phone number ends with 47:

```
DISPLAY FOR RIGHT(PHONE,2) = '47'
```

AT( ): What happens when you don't know the starting character position and you want to use the substring function? Use the AT function. The AT function finds the starting position of one character string inside of another larger character string.

Chapter Fifteen

```
STRING = 'ABCDEFG'
SEARCHFOR = 'CD'
? AT(SEARCHFOR,STRING)          Where is SEARCHFOR within STRING?
3
```

If the search string is not found, the starting position is 0. If the search string occurs more than once, only the first occurrence of the search string will be found. This looks very nice, but is it helpful? Suppose that you have a database that contains the names of people with the last name first (Byers, Robert A.) and you wish to list these names first names first (Robert A. Byers). By combining the SUBSTR and AT functions, we can accomplish this with a single (albeit complicated) command:

```
LIST SUBSTR(NAME,1,AT(',',NAME)+1) – (' '+SUBSTR(NAME,1,AT(',',NAME)–1))
```

This command is long but it does what we want — and it shows you that you can combine functions. The key to our "turn around" is to locate the comma in the name. Then we display the stuff after the comma first. The minus sign joins the expressions containing the first and last names in order to remove any trailing blank spaces.

The VALUE function VAL: There are occasions when we need to make a calculation using a number which has been stored as character data. You can do this with the help of the VAL( ) function. For example, suppose we want to calculate the average value of the zip codes in our database. Normally, of course, these zip codes have no numeric significance to anyone other than the Post Office. However, Snedly Economist has a new, and as yet unproven theory, that the average value of the zip codes in a customer list is directly related to profitability. We can use the AVERAGE command on the zip code field by adding VAL( ) to the command.

```
AVERAGE VAL(ZIPCODE)
```

The VAL function does allow us to use appropriate character data in arithmetic computations.

The STR function: This function allows you to convert numbers to characters when you need to combine numbers with characters in an expression — or when you need to control the width of a numeric display. We've already seen that you are not allowed to combine apples and oranges within a single expression. The STR function is our way around this rule: disguise the apples as oranges. Suppose that we have stored our zip codes as a five-digit numeric field. We can use the STR function to "convert" to a character string and add four blank spaces at the beginning.

```
? STATE+STR(ZIP,9)
```

How about decimal places? We can choose to display decimal places or not — if there are none we can display them anyway — and if there are we can ignore them. Decimal places are displayed by simply adding the number of decimal places to the expression.

```
? STATE+str(ZIP,9,2)
```

Unwanted Blank Spaces: TRIM( ), LTRIM( ), and RTRIM( ) can trim blanks. Suppose that we have a database containing a 30-character CITY field and a two-character STATE field. We want to join these two fields so that the result appears natural. The CITY field can contain trailing blank spaces, so that the display of CITY with STATE looks like

```
? CITY + ',' + STATE
Glendale                           , CA
```

In the discussion on operators, we saw that the minus sign can move these trailing blank spaces to the end of the expression. The TRIM( ) function allows you to make them "disappear."

```
? TRIM(CITY)+', '+STATE
Glendale, CA
```

The TRIM( ) and RTRIM( ) functions are identical. They remove trailing blank spaces. The LTRIM( ) function is used to remove leading blank spaces — blank spaces that occur at the beginning of a data item. The most common use of LTRIM( ) is to remove leading blank spaces from a number that has been "converted" with the STR( ) function. Let's use this function to combine a number with the dollar sign:

```
COST = 1.45
? '$'+LTRIM(STR(COST,9,2))
$1.45
```

How Many Letters in a Name: The LEN( ), length, function is used to tell you the number of characters in a data item. The number of characters includes the trailing blank spaces, if any. Suppose that we want to know the actual length of the name of each city in our database. Of course, we already know the field length. But that's not the same as the length of a *city name*. We can combine the LEN( ) function with the TRIM( ) function to find our solution.

```
DISPLAY ALL CITY, LEN(TRIM(CITY))
```

Substituting Text: Upon occasion, it's convenient — especially in reports, to substitute more descriptive text for the actual content of a database field. For example, we have stored a person's gender as a one-character field GENDER. We can expand this single character into the more descriptive male/female with the IIF function.

```
LIST NAME, IIF( GENDER = 'M', 'Male','Female')
```

There are three parts to the IIF function: The first is a condition; the second and third parts specify the result if it's true or if it's false.

Transforming Text: The TRANSFORM function has many applications in both screen displays and reports; with it, you can use picture functions and picture templates in a display command and in reports. (See Chapter 19 for more on *pictures* and custom screens.) Probably, the most common use of the TRANSFORM function is for formatting numbers for display. Many software programs, including dBASE, do not automatically add commas into the display of numbers. A 4-digit number is displayed as 2434, not 2,434. You can use the TRANSFORM function to insert commas (among other things).

Chapter Fifteen

```
. NUMBER = 9845.66
. ? TRANSFORM(NUMBER,"##,###.##")
  9,845.66
```

The function can be used in an expression list:

DISPLAY ALL BRANDNAME,SIZE,TRANSFORM(COST,"###,###.##")

In this example, the COST will be displayed as a ten-character wide item. A comma will be automatically inserted whenever the COST is 1,000.00 or greater. There will be no comma when the number is less than 1000.00.

Specialized Tests

There are also functions that are available to perform a variety of specialized tests. For example, when you list the contents of the database you end up at the end of the file. There is a function that will tell you whether you are at the end-of-file: EOF( ).

```
? EOF( )
.F.
```

This function ends in parentheses like all functions. In this case however, there is no argument within the parentheses.

Date Functions

The most commonly used date function is DATE( ). This function tells you the current date, according to your computer's clock calendar.

```
? DATE( )
10/31/85
```

All of this is but a sample of the many functions that are available. The functions are helpful, they are fun to use, and they can considerably extend what you can do with dBASE. This chapter has tried to acquaint you with the use of functions and to give you an idea of how they are used and what they can be used for.

THE SET COMMANDS

The SET commands are used to modify the processing parameters used by dBASE. We've used many of these commands throughout this book. Most of the SET commands are included in the single command SET. This command provides you with menu selections containing most of the processing parameters. Entering the command

```
. SET
```

provides the initial menu display shown in Figure 15-1. As in all of the dBASE menu commands, the main menu is shown on the top line of this screen. The Left and Right arrow keys are used to choose the desired menu. The Up and Down arrow keys are used to move a lightbar to highlight a selection within a menu. The highlighted selection is chosen by pressing Return.

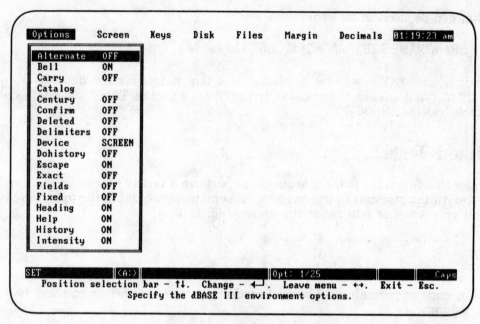

Figure 15-1: Options menu

The Options Menu: This menu allows you to make choices among many routine processing parameters; it provides you with the current status of each of these parameters — and an easy way to make changes.

The Screen Menu: The Screen menu (Figure 15-2) is used to choose from among the characteristics offered by your computer monitor. If you have a color monitor, you can use this menu to set the color combinations in dBASE.

The Keys Menu: The Keys menu (Figure 15-3) shows you the current setting of the F2 through F10 function keys. You can change these settings by moving the lightbar to the key you want to change, pressing Return, and typing in the new key content. Note that the initial values each end in a semicolon. This semicolon acts as the carriage return.

Chapter Fifteen

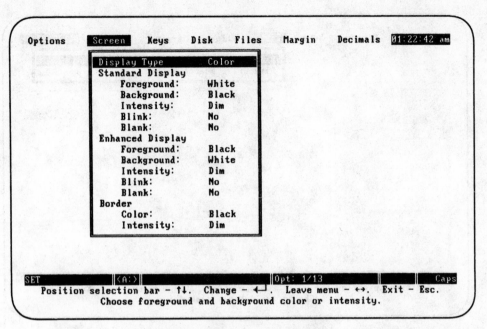

Figure 15-2: Screen menu

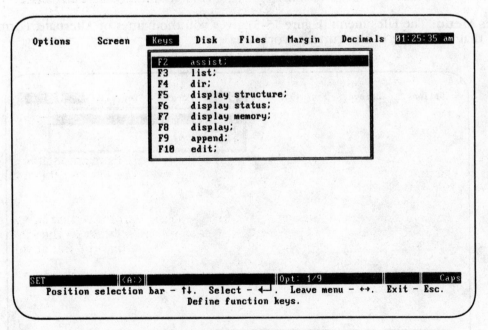

Figure 15-3: Keys menu

The Disk Menu: This menu (Figure 15-4) shows you the *default* disk drive and the disk drive search path. The default drive is initially the disk drive you were logged to when you entered dBASE. This is the disk drive that will be used unless you specify a drive with a filename.

Operators and Functions

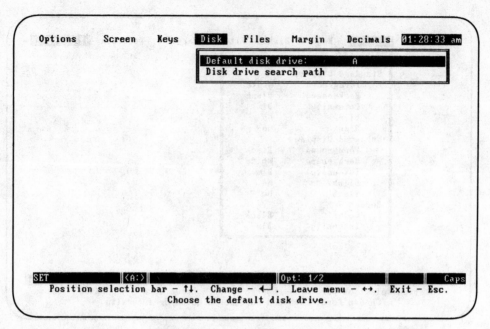

Figure 15-4: Disk menu

The Files Menu: The Files menu (Figure 15-5) gives you the names of Alternate, Format, and Index files that are in use in the current work area.

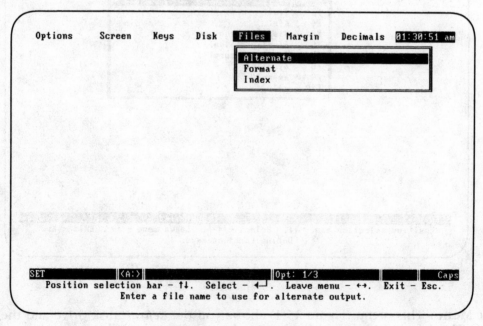

Figure 15-5: Files menu

Chapter Fifteen

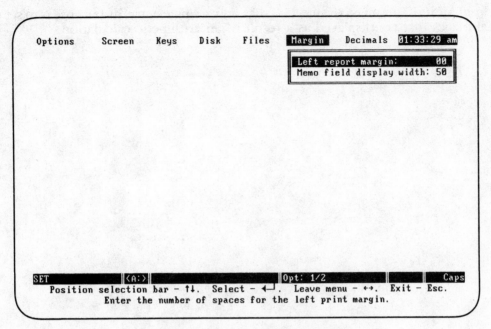

Figure 15-6: Margin menu

The Margin Menu: The Margin Menu (Figure 15-6) is used to set the left margin for all printed output — not just reports. It is also used to establish the width of memo field displays — whether on the printer or on the screen.

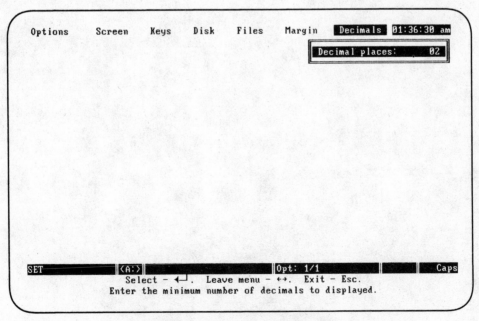

Figure 15-7: Decimals menu

Operators and Functions

The Decimal Menu: This menu (Figure 15-7) has only a single entry. Its purpose is to set the number of decimal places that are displayed as a result of an arithmetic calculation.

Chapter Fifteen

CHAPTER SIXTEEN

DATE, MEMO, AND LOGIC FIELDS

DATE is a special data type, designed to make working with dates as natural with a computer as without one. Although a DATE type may seem to be a necessary part of a database management system, not all systems offer it. dBASE III has a data type for dates, dBASE II does not.

Why the fuss? Most of us are accustomed to working with dates in the more or less standard American format of MM/DD/YY. Europeans prefer a format of DD/MM/YY, whereas Japanese prefer the arrangement of YY/MM/DD. Computers favor the Japanese arrangement which, incidentally, is the standard date format proposed by the American National Standards Institute (ANSI).

Computers read from left to right. What is more important, they also make comparisons from left to right. Unless we conform to the ANSI standard or take some special action, we cannot sort or compare dates and expect to get the correct result. The DATE data type solves this problem. The date is actually stored in a format that the computer prefers, but it is displayed in your preferred format. You don't even need to know that the computer has actually squirreled the information away in Urdu.

A field is identified as a DATE when the database is created or when the structure is modified. To specify a field as a DATE data type, press "D" key when prompted for the field type. The field width of a DATE field is automatically set to 8 bytes (character spaces).

dBASE normally expects dates to be entered using American format of MM/DD/YY. You can, however, work with dates using the date formats of many other countries. The six date formats that can be specified in dBASE are:

American	mm/dd/yy
ANSI	yy.mm.dd
British	dd/mm/yy
French	dd/mm/yy
German	dd.mm.yy
Italian	dd-mm-yy

A special SET command allows you to choose from among these six. To work with dates in the French manner, use the command

. SET DATE FRENCH

dBASE normally expects dates to be entered in the American manner. This is the *default* setting for the date format. If you *always* work with dates in some other specific format, include the SET DATE command in the CONFIG.DB file. (See Appendix C.)

To illustrate the use of dates, let's use the following four-record database:

Record #	NAME	DEPARTED	RETURNED
1	Jim Jones	12/15/83	01/02/84
2	Ed Smith	03/17/84	03/21/84
3	Frank Brown	04/05/84	04/12/84
4	Bill Adams	05/27/84	06/03/84

In the following examples, we'll use the American date format. The operations would be identical with any other date format — only the appearance of the date would change.

DATE DATA ENTRY

A data-entry screen for this database is shown as Figure 16-1. The date separators — the slashes — are already displayed; you do not enter them. You must, however, enter leading zeroes into the three subfields.

Dates are validated upon entry. You are not allowed to enter an invalid (nonexistent) date. An invalid date is not the same as an incorrect date. If you do enter an invalid date such as 15/27/85 (there is no 15th month), an error message is displayed on screen. You cannot move out of the date field until you have entered a valid date. An important exception is the *all blanks* date. You can skip over a date field without entering a value.

WHAT CENTURY IS THIS?

dBASE assumes that you are interested in the twentieth century when you enter data. If you enter the year 01 you may surprised to find that you have entered 1901 and not 2001. This has proved to be an annoyance to historians among others. If you need to work with dates in other than the twentieth century, use the command:

. SET CENTURY ON

Chapter Sixteen

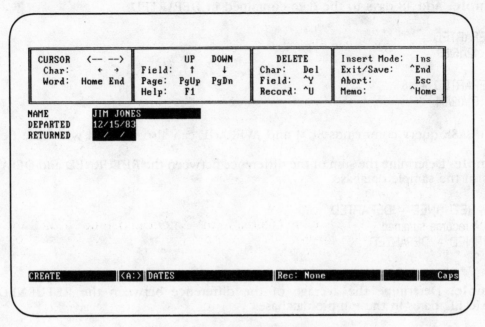

Figure 16-1: Data-entry screen

With the CENTURY ON dates will be displayed with four-digit spaces for the year. Incidentally, dates were always stored in the format YYYYMMDD (the slashes are not stored) we just didn't have access to the first two digits of the year until we SET CENTURY ON.

DATE ARITHMETIC

You can make calculations involving dates directly. A date may be subtracted from another date. The answer is given as the number of days between the two dates.

Example: Subtract the field DEPARTED from RETURNED for the first record in the sample database.

. GO TOP
. ? RETURNED – DEPARTED
       18

A date, however, may not be added to another date. The result is meaningless (just as it is without the computer). If you attempt to add two dates you will receive an error message from dBASE.

A number, however, may be added to or subtracted from a date. The number is treated as a number of days. The result of this calculation is a new date.

Date, Memo, and Logic Fields

Example: Add 18 days to the date contained in DEPARTED.

. ? DEPARTED
    12/15/83

. ? DEPARTED + 18
    01/02/84

The dBASE query commands SUM and AVERAGE can also be used with date fields.

Example: Determine the sum of the difference between the RETURNED and DEPARTED dates in the sample database.

. SUM RETURNED – DEPARTED
    4 records summed
RETURNED – DEPARTED
    36

Example: Determine the average of the difference between the RETURNED and DEPARTED dates in the sample database.

. SUM RETURNED – DEPARTED
    4 records averaged
RETURNED – DEPARTED
9

SORTING

To sort on a date field, just use the name of the date field directly in the SORT command. To illustrate, we want to sort our database chronologically by the contents of the field DEPARTED to the new database file DATESORT. The command is:

. SORT ON DEPARTED TO DATESORT
100% sorted 4 records sorted

INDEXING

To index on date field, we again use the name of the field as the item to be indexed on.

. INDEX ON DEPARTED TO DEPART
100% indexed 4 records indexed

Once the database is indexed on a date field, you can go directly to the first record for a particular date by means of the SEEK command and the CTOD (character to date) function. For example, to position the indexed database to the first record where the content of the DEPARTED field is 04/05/84, use the command:

. SEEK CTOD("04/05/84")

The entire date must be specified when using the SEEK command with the CTOD function. If you will be regularly using a database that is indexed on a date field, you might find it more convenient to use the DATE FUNCTIONS below in the indexing operation:

. INDEX ON STR(YEAR(DEPARTED),4)+STR(MONTH(DEPARTED),2)+
STR(DAY(DEPARTED),2) TO DEPARTED

If you do this, you can find a particular month (say November) by

. FIND 198511

DATE FUNCTIONS

The CTOD (character-to-date) function is only one of several date functions. The date functions are shown in Figure 16-2.

FUNCTION	DESCRIPTION	EXAMPLE
CTOD	Character To Date	
DTOC	Date To Character	
Day	Day of Month	21
Month	Month of Year	10
Year	Year	1984
DOW	Day of Week	3
CDOW	Calendar Day of Week	Tuesday
CMONTH	Calendar Month	January
Date	Current System Date	MM/DD/YY

Figure 16-2: Date functions

These functions make it more convenient for us to work with dates. CTOD, as we have seen, allows us to use a character string as a date. DTOC allows us to use a date in a character string. One use of this function is to embed dates in a text string.

. ? 'He left on '+DTOC(DEPARTED)+' and returned '+dtoc(RETURNED)
He left on 05/27/84 and returned 06/03/84

The DAY, MONTH, and YEAR functions make it convenient for us to specify dates to be used as conditions of dBASE commands. Examples of the use of these functions are shown by the three DISPLAY commands below:

```
. DISPLAY FOR YEAR(DEPARTED) = 1984
. DISPLAY FOR YEAR(DEPARTED) = 1984 .AND. MONTH(DEPARTED) = 9
. DISPLAY FOR YEAR(DEPARTED) = 1984 .AND. MONTH(DEPARTED) = 9 .AND. DAY(DEPARTED) = 21
```

The DOW (day-of-week) function returns a number code for each day of the week beginning with Sunday (1). To display all departing dates that were Tuesdays:

```
. DISPLAY FOR DOW(DEPARTED) = 3
```

CDOW (calendar day of week) and CMONTH (calendar month) allow us to transform dates into forms that are more convenient for us to use in text. As an example, let's use the DEPARTED field from record one.

```
. ? DEPARTED
12/15/83

. ? CDOW(DEPARTED)
Thursday

. ? CMONTH(DEPARTED)
December
```

The system date allows you to read the your computer's clock calendar.

```
. ? DATE( )
07/04/84
```

dBASE cannot change the system date directly. If your computer has more than (the required minimum of) 256K and the file COMMAND.COM is on your dBASE system disk, the date can be changed by:

```
. RUN DATE
```

This command calls the operating system command DATE. When the date has been entered, you will be returned automatically to where you were in dBASE.

It may well be that you would like to print the contents of date fields in the form "calendar month, day, year" (for example, April 9, 1984) from reports and procedures. To do this, use the following instead of the simple field name:

```
CMONTH(FIELDNAME) + STR(DAY(FIELDNAME),3)+","+ ; STR(YEAR(FIELDNAME),5)
```

The above will convert a date such as 04/09/84 to the more convenient form April 9, 1984.

Chapter Sixteen

BLANK DATES

Normally, only DATES that have yet be be entered are blank. These blank fields can present some logic problems. Let's suppose that one of our DEPARTED entries is blank. All comparisons involving this blank field with a real date will be false:

? *Blank date* > DATE( ), *blank date* < DATE( )
.F. .F.

How then, do you specify records that contain a blank date field? The most reliable technique is to use the year function and request those records where the year is 0. For example

. DISPLAY FOR YEAR(DEPARTED) = 0

will display any records where the date field DEPARTED is blank.

MEMO FIELDS

Another special data type allows you to use variable-length fields for storing text. In dBASE, these variable-length fields are called MEMO fields. Examples of the kind of data stored in memo fields would be memoranda, abstracts, general comments, and so forth. Any or all of the 128 fields in a dBASE database file can be memo fields.

A field is identified as being a memo field either when the database is created or when its structure is modified. To specify a field as a memo type, press "M" key when prompted to enter the field type. The fieldwidth of a memo field is automatically set to 10 bytes. This is a little misleading. A memo field can contain up to 4,096 bytes of text. The data is actually stored in a special auxiliary file. The 10 bytes of fieldwidth is used for *pointers* to tell dBASE the location of the field in the auxiliary file. The pointer connects information in the auxiliary file to the data record. The auxiliary file has the same name as the database file, but is given the file extension .DBT to distinguish it from the .DBF database file.

During data entry into the main database file, the data-entry area of a memo field displays MEMO (Figure 16-3). To enter data into a memo field, place the cursor on the M of MEMO. Then, press Ctrl-Home. (Hold down the Ctrl and press the Home key.) The screen clears and displays the current contents of the memo field. The cursor will be positioned to the beginning of any text already in the field.

Data is entered by simply typing in the desired text. When the text has been completely entered, press Ctrl-End to save it or Esc to abandon the entry. No space is taken in the auxiliary text file until data is actually entered into a memo field. Once data is entered, space is allocated, as needed, in 512-byte chunks. The maximum size for memo fields is normally 4,096 bytes.

A word processor is provided to help with data entry and editing of memo fields. When the memo field is entered, the word processor is automatically activated. An external disk file can be read into a memo field by using Ctrl-KR. The contents of a memo field can be copied to an external

---

Date, Memo, and Logic Fields

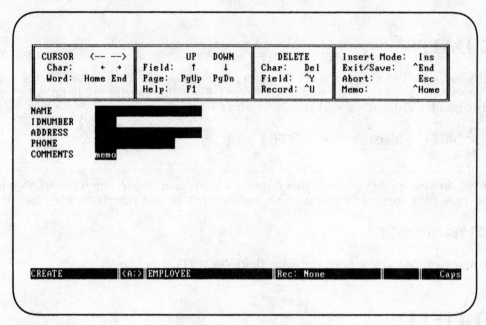

Figure 16-3: MEMO

disk file with **Ctrl-KW**. Other functions that can be performed by use of the **Ctrl** key and/or the special keys are:

KEY	DESCRIPTION
PgUp	Scroll toward the beginning of the text
PgDn	Scroll toward the end of the text
Up Arrow	Move one line toward beginning of text
Down Arrow	Move one line toward end of text
Left Arrow	Move one character space left
Right Arrow	Move one character space right
Ctrl-Left Arrow	Move to beginning of the current line
Ctrl-Right Arrow	Move to end of the current line
Home	Move one word left
End	Move one word right
Ctrl-T	Delete word to right of cursor
Ctrl-Y	Delete current line
Ctrl-N	Insert blank line
Ins	Insert characters
Del	Delete the character cursor is on
Backspace	Delete character to left of cursor
Ctrl-KR	Read in external disk file
Ctrl-KW	Write memo field to external disk file
Esc	Abort changes and return to data entry
Ctrl-End	Save and return to data entry mode

Figure 16-4: dBASE word processor commands

Chapter Sixteen

The memo field can be entered only from one of the dBASE full-screen data-entry commands: APPEND, INSERT, CHANGE, or EDIT. The memo field cannot be entered from the full-screen command BROWSE. When entry or editing of a memo field is completed, you will be returned to the data-entry screen that was used to enter the field.

The content of a memo field can be viewed using the DISPLAY, LIST, ?, and REPORT commands only. When these commands are used, the contents of the specified memo field will be displayed in a 50-character wide format. The memo field must be explicitly named in any of the above commands. The use of DISPLAY or LIST alone will show the word MEMO under the name of the field.

There are severe restrictions on the use of memo fields. They can be changed only manually from the full-screen data entry commands, APPEND, INSERT, and EDIT. They can be viewed only with these commands or DISPLAY, LIST, ?, or REPORT. They cannot be searched automatically for content and they cannot be used as part of a condition for a command.

If your computer has sufficient memory in addition to the 256K required for dBASE, a commercial word processor (such as WordStar) can be used instead of the dBASE word processor for editing of memo fields. To use an external word processor, you must include the statement

WP=filename of the word processor

in the file CONFIG.DB (See Appendix B).

LOGIC FIELDS

Logic fields are special fields that are profitably used when the data can have one of only two possible values. The values are usually expressed as True/False or Yes/No. A good use of a logic field would be to indicate whether or not a check has cleared the bank.

A field is identified as a logic field when the database is CREATEd or when the structure is modified. To specify a field as a logic data type press "L" key when prompted for the field type. The field width of a logic field is automatically set to 1 byte.

The content of these fields is always expressed as .T. or .Y. with the dots emphasizing the fact that they contain logical values. Logic fields are *never* used in comparisons. The comparison is "built-in." Let's suppose that you have a check register database. One of the fields is named CLEARED to indicate whether or not a check has cleared the bank. To view the checks which have cleared, use

. DISPLAY FOR CLEARED

And, to view those that have not, use

. DISPLAY FOR .NOT. CLEARED

Some beginning users have a tendency to write the condition with an explicit comparison — CLEARED = .T. Don't. Logic fields are automatically false until a true value is entered. During data entry, these fields may display a question mark until a value has been entered. The field, however, will be evaluated as false — even though no value has been entered. The banking example above shows this feature clearly — checks are not cleared until we enter either T or Y into the field.

Date, Memo, and Logic Fields

These fields ignore the possibility of "don't know" — a condition that occurs far too often in business. Everyone is either male or female, but we may not know whether Leslie is a boy or a girl. If you need to deal with a situation where the logical value can have one of three states — Yes, No, Unknown — you'll be far better off by choosing to use a character field for the data.

Chapter Sixteen

CHAPTER SEVENTEEN

IMPORTING AND EXPORTING DATA

You may need to move data from one database file to another, or even to move it to an entirely separate software program such as an electronic spreadsheet or a word processor. For example, you might want to include selected parts of a database in a memorandum or report that you are preparing for upper management. In this case you'll want to move data from a database file into a file that can be used directly by the word-processing program.

Similarly, you may need to move data from another program into a dBASE database file. Why would you want to do that? You may have obtained data that was entered into disk files using another software program. Up until now this would have been somewhat of a problem. Different programs often store data in wildly varying formats. One program could not ordinarily make effective use of data stored by another program — there was no software "Rosetta Stone." This is no longer the case. Many programs are now capable of reading data stored by at least the most widely used programs such as dBASE, Lotus 1-2-3, Multiplan, and so on.

COPYING DATA FROM ONE
DATABASE FILE TO ANOTHER

You can copy all or part of a database to a second database file. The dBASE commands to use for copying are: COPY and COPY FILE. What's the difference? The COPY FILE command is used to duplicate an entire database (or any other kind of file). To copy the database FONEBOOK, use the command:

. COPY FILE FONEBOOK.DBF TO NEWFILE.DBF

The name for NEWFILE can be anything that you like — as long as it conforms to the rules for filenames. You might notice that, in this command, we have added the .DBF. file identifier to the filename. The COPY FILE command requires that you use the complete filename. Because you must include the identifier, you can use the command to make copies of any kind of dBASE file: database, index, report, and so on.

When you use this command, neither the file you are copying *from* (the source file) nor the file you are copying *to* (the target file) can be in use. If the target file does not already exist, it will be created. If there is already a file with the same name as the target file, it will be replaced (overwritten) by the target file. But only after dBASE asks you for permission:

NEWFILE.DBF already exists, overwrite it? (Y/N)

The COPY command is used to copy all or selected parts of a database. The source database (the one you want to copy from) must be in USE in the selected work area. The target database cannot be open. To demonstrate this command, we'll use our old standby, the INVENTRY database. To copy the complete database, use the command:

. USE INVENTRY
. COPY TO NEWFILE

Note the differences between this command and the COPY FILE command. The .DBF file identifier is added automatically to NEWFILE. As before, if the target file (NEWFILE) does not already exist, it will be created. If it does exist, dBASE will ask if you want to replace the old version of NEWFILE with this new version.

Unlike COPY FILE, COPY can be used to copy selected parts of the database. To copy only the fields BRAND and QUANTITY, use the command:

. COPY FIELDS BRAND, QUANTITY TO NEWFILE

The new database contains only two fields — the ones we explicitly named in command. Unless you specify which fields are to be copied, *all* fields will be copied. It does contain all the records. You can copy selected records by adding either a FOR *condition* or a WHILE *condition* to the COPY command. To copy only VODKA records, use the command:

. COPY FOR LIQUOR = 'VODKA' TO NEWFILE

In this case, the new database contains only the VODKA records. But all the fields in each record are copied. We can combine the two commands and copy only the fields BRAND and QUANTITY for the VODKA records.

. COPY FIELDS BRAND,QUANTITY FOR LIQUOR='VODKA' TO NEWFILE

Remember, when you use the COPY command, you are still working with the source file. To use the new file you must USE it. The new file consists entirely of what you copied to it. You cannot add to an existing file with the COPY commands. To add records to an existing file, you must use a variation of the APPEND command:

Chapter Seventeen

. APPEND FROM *SOURCE*

The file to which the records are appended is the target file. The file that records come from is the source file. You must be *using* the target file. The source file must *not* be open. Only those fields that have the same name in both the target and source files will be included in the records that are added. In the last copy example above, we created NEWFILE, which contains fields BRAND and QUANTITY and only VODKA records. If we append from NEWFILE we will add a new record to INVENTRY for each record in NEWFILE. All of the fields in the new records will be blank — except for the common fields BRAND and QUANTITY

. APPEND FROM NEWFILE

In Chapter One, we created a file FONEBOOK which contained the names, addresses, and phone numbers of our eight closest friends. There were eight records in that file and three fields. None of the three fields is common with fields in INVENTRY. If we appended from FONEBOOK we would be adding 8 blank records to INVENTRY.

We can specify which records are to be accepted into the target file by using the FOR *condition*. The field that you use in the condition *must* be included in both database files. When this is the case, only those records meeting the condition will be added to the target file. Suppose we have a second inventory file called UPDATE that contains, among other things, WINE and BEER. We want to move only the BEER records into our INVENTRY database. We can do this with

. APPEND FROM UPDATE FOR LIQUOR ='BEER'

The APPEND and COPY commands have been used to move data from one database file to another. These same commands *can* be used to import data used by other programs, such as Lotus 1-2-3, and export data in a form that it can be used by these same programs.

EXPORTING DATA TO OTHER PROGRAMS

Importing data is the process of copying a data file that is used by another program in transforming it into a form that can be used directly by dBASE. Exporting data is exactly the reverse; it is the process of copying data from a dBASE database file and transforming it so that it can be used directly by the other program.

Exporting Data To Lotus 1-2-3

To export data in a form that can be used by Lotus 1-2-3 (and other programs which use the Lotus file structure), we simply add WKS to the COPY command.

. COPY FIELDS BRAND,QUANTITY FOR LIQUOR='VODKA' TO NEWFILE WKS

The COPY command works exactly as explained above in the section on copying except that we have now created a Lotus 1-2-3 WKS file. dBASE automatically adds .WKS to the target filename. Each dBASE record becomes a row and each field becomes a column in the WKS file. The dBASE field names have become the first row in the WKS file. The field name will be truncated if it is longer than the column width.

Exporting Data To Multiplan

To export data in a form that can be used by Multiplan (and other programs which use the Multiplan file structure), add SYLK to the COPY command:

. COPY FIELDS BRAND,QUANTITY FOR LIQUOR='VODKA' TO NEWFILE SYLK

The COPY command works exactly as explained above in the section on copying except that we have now created a Multiplan file. dBASE automatically adds .TBD to the target filename. Each dBASE record becomes a row and each field becomes a column in the SYLK file. The dBASE field names have become the first row in the SYLK file.

Exporting Data To VisiCalc

To export data in a form that can be used by VisiCalc (and other programs which use the VisiCalc file structure), add DIF to the COPY command:

. COPY FIELDS BRAND,QUANTITY FOR LIQUOR='VODKA' TO NEWFILE DIF

The COPY command works exactly as explained above in the section on copying except that we have now created a VisiCalc DIF file. dBASE automatically adds .DIF to the target filename. Each dBASE record becomes a row and each field becomes a column in the DIF file. The dBASE field names have become the first row in the DIF file. The field name will be truncated if it is longer than the column width.

Moving Data To a Word Processor

To move data to a word processor or any program that uses data in *standard data format* (SDF), add SDF to the COPY command. To demonstrate, we will copy the contents of the TEACHERS database that we used in Chapter Nine (Figure 17-1). To copy this database so that it can be used directly by a word processor, use

. COPY TO TEACHERS SDF

Record#	NAME	ROOM	GRADE
1	Chips, Mr.	11	1
2	Brooks, Miss	12	1
3	Crane, Ichabod	22	2
4	Stern, Emma	24	2

Figure 17-1: TEACHERS database file

The results of the COPY command are shown in Figure 17-2.

Chapter Seventeen

Chips, Mr.	111
Brooks, Miss	121
Crane, Ichabod	222
Stern, Emma	242

Figure 17-2: Text of the TEACHERS database file

The COPY command works exactly as explained above in the section on copying except that we have now created a file that can be used by just about any word processor. dBASE automatically adds .TXT to the target filename. Each dBASE record becomes a line in the target file. Note, however, there is no longer any *field structure*. There is no way to differentiate between columns except where there happen to be blank spaces at the end of a field.

Moving Data To Other Programs

Many programs, such as WordStar's MailMerge and most programs written in BASIC use a variation of the SDF format that preserves the field structure. To export data to one of these programs, add DELIMITED to the COPY command.

. COPY FOR LIQUOR='VODKA' TO NEWFILE DELIMITED

The COPY command works exactly as explained above in the section on copying except that we have now created a *delimited* text file. dBASE automatically adds .TXT to the target filename. Each dBASE record becomes a row and the fields are seperated by commas. Character fields are enclosed by double quotation marks (" ")and trailing blank spaces are discarded. The result of this COPY operation is shown in Figure 17-3.

"VODKA" , "REAL RUSSIAN" , "PINT" , 75, 1.49, 2.48
"VODKA" , "REAL RUSSIAN" , "2 LITER" , 9, 7.95, 13.25
"VODKA" , "REAL RUSSIAN" , "QUART" , 35, 3.78, 6.30

Figure 17-3: Output file using the *delimited* option

To change the character-string delimiters (the double quotation marks) to some other delimiter, such as colons (: :), add the statement WITH followed by the character to be used to the command. It is important to know that this does *not* affect the character used for a field separator — that is always a comma.

. COPY FOR LIQUOR='VODKA' TO NEWFILE DELIMITED WITH :

Exporting Data To PFS: FILE

To export data in a form that can be used by PFS: FILE, use the new dBASE command EXPORT. This command is similar to COPY but is used *only* to move data from dBASE to PFS: FILE.

Importing & Exporting Data

To EXPORT the VODKA records to PFS: FILE, use the command as shown below.

. EXPORT FOR LIQUOR='VODKA' TO NEWFILE PFS

The EXPORT command above creates a file named NEWFILE that can be use directly by the PFS FILE. The difference between EXPORT and COPY is that EXPORT does not allow you to specify which fields are to be copied. To copy field selectively with the EXPORT command, the database being copied must be used in conjunction with a **format file**. A **format file** is used to create a custom screen in dBASE. Format files and their use are discussed in the "Custom Screens" chapter.

IMPORTING DATA FROM OTHER PROGRAMS

If you already have data that was entered into your computer, you can probably move that data into dBASE III files. The same is true if you obtain data from some outside source. dBASE provides specific means for moving data from Lotus 1-2-3, MultiPlan, VisiCalc, PFS FILE, most word processors, and many standard business applications programs.

Importing Data From Lotus 1-2-3

To import data from Lotus 1-2-3 (and other programs which use the Lotus file structure), add WKS to the APPEND FROM command. To illustrate, let's move data from the Lotus 1-2-3 file named 123FILE.WKS.

. APPEND FROM 123FILE.WKS WKS

Data records from the Lotus 1-2-3 WKS file will be added to the database file you are using. The fields in your receiving database must be in the same order as the columns in the Lotus file. Column 1 in the Lotus file will be added to Field 1 in the dBASE file, Column 2 to Field 2, and so on. Each row in the Lotus file will become a record in the database file. The field width of each dBASE field must be at least as large as the corresponding Lotus column. If not, the data content will be truncated during the transfer operation.

Importing Data From Multiplan

To import data from Multiplan (and other programs which use its structure), add SYLK to the APPEND FROM command:

. APPEND FROM MPFILE SYLK

Data records from the Multiplan file will be added to the database file you are using. The fields in your receiving database must be in the same order as the columns in the Multiplan file. Column 1 in the Multiplan file will be added to Field 1 in the dBASE file, Column 2 to Field 2, and so on. Each row in the Multiplan file will become a record in the database file. The field width of each dBASE field must be at least as large as the corresponding Multiplan column. If not, the data content will be truncated during the transfer operation.

Importing Data From VisiCalc

To import data from VisiCalc (and other programs which use the VisiCalc file structure), add DIF to the APPEND FROM command.

. APPEND FROM VFILE DIF

Data records from the VisiCalc file will be added to the database file you are using. The fields in your receiving database must be in the same order as the columns in the VisiCalc file. Column 1 in the VisiCalc file will be added to Field 1 in the dBASE file, Column 2 to Field 2, and so on. Each row in the VisiCalc file will become a record in the database file. The field width of each dBASE field must be at least as large as the corresponding VisiCalc column. If not, the data content will be truncated during the transfer operation.

Moving Data From a Word Processor

To move data from a word processor or any program that uses data in *standard data format* (SDF), add SDF to the APPEND FROM command. To demonstrate, we will move the data shown in Figure 17-4 to a database. The database structure that we need to accept this data is shown in Figure 17-5.

. APPEND FROM TEACHERS.TXT SDF

Chips, Mr.	11	1
Brooks, Miss	12	1
Crane, Ichabod	22	2
Stern, Emma	24	2

Figure 17-4: Source text file

Field	Field Name	Type	Width	Dec
1	NAME	Character	20	
2	ROOM	Character	2	
3	GRADE	Character	5	
** Total **			28	

Figure 17-5: Database structure to receive data from Figure 17-4

When we move data from a standard text file such as the one above, each row becomes a record in the receiving database. It's sometimes important to know that a "row" is the text between carriage returns. A "row" may wrap around on your screen and appear on two or more screen lines. Because there is no field structure, dBASE assigns characters to each field, in order, until the fields are full. Character 1 goes to character 1 of field 1, character 2 to character 2 of field 1, and so on, until field 1 is full. Then we start assigning characters to field 2. This process continues until we run out of either characters or fields. Putting your data into what appear to you as columns doesn't count. The blank spaces are just as relevant to dBASE as any other character. It's your responsibility to assign column widths to match the data — or edit the data to match the column width.

Moving Data From Other Programs

Many applications programs, such as accounting packages, are written in a conventional language such as BASIC. To import data files that are used by these programs, add the word DELIMITED to the APPEND FROM command:

. APPEND FROM BASFILE DELIMITED

Each row in the source file becomes a record in the database file. Each item separated by commas is considered to be a field. Fields from the source file are moved, in order, into the file you are using. Field 1 goes to field 1, field 2 to field 2, and so on. Again, your database file must match the data you are importing. dBASE assumes that character fields are additionally enclosed by double quotation marks — as shown in Figure 17-6. These quotes will be automatically discarded as the data is accepted into dBASE. If character fields are delimited by other than quotes, such as colons, you need to identify the character used by adding the character-field delimiter to the command:

. APPEND FROM BASFILE DELIMITED WITH :

It is important to know that the colon (:) is *not* the field delimiter (field separator). It is only used to identify the delimiter used in place of the double quotation marks in Figure 17-6.

```
"VODKA" , "REAL RUSSIAN" , "PINT" , 75, 1.49, 2.48
"VODKA" , "REAL RUSSIAN" , "2 LITER" , 9, 7.95, 13.25
"VODKA" , "REAL RUSSIAN" , "QUART" , 35, 3.78, 6.30
```

Figure 17-6: BASFILE.TXT source file

Importing Data From PFS: FILE

To import data from PFS: FILE, use the new dBASE command IMPORT. The IMPORT command creates a new database file. The new database file will have the same eight character name as the PFS FILE file. You should not have a file in use when you invoke the IMPORT command. Close any open database file with CLOSE DATABASE or USE. To IMPORT the PFS FILE PAYMENTS, use

. CLOSE DATABASE
. IMPORT FROM PAYMENTS PFS

This IMPORT command creates a new database file of the same name: PAYMENTS. The new file is automatically placed in USE. The original PFS FILE version is unaffected by the command. In addition, a dBASE *format file* (a custom screen) is automatically created, as is a VIEW. VIEWs are discussed in Chapter Twenty-Two and FORMAT files are discussed in the Chapter Twenty.

Chapter Seventeen

SECTION FIVE
SPECIAL FEATURES

CHAPTER EIGHTEEN

REPORTS

To get the most out of your database manager, you'll need to master its *report generator*. The report generator is used to prepare formal reports, using the content of your database files. In Chapter Two, we used the dBASE Report Generator to prepare the report shown as Figure 18-1. In this chapter, we'll use this same report to discuss the features of the dBASE Report Generator in greater depth. In addition, we'll discuss some of the advanced features of the REPORT commands and show you how to prepare a report similar to the one in Figure 18-2.

The dBASE III Report Generator makes use of three commands:

CREATE REPORT
MODIFY REPORT
REPORT

These are among the most powerful and easy to use of all the dBASE commands. There is no end to the possibilities provided by the REPORT commands. You can use them to prepare status reports on inventories, customer lists, class rosters, and so on.

As we saw in Chapter Two, reports are prepared with the help of a *report form*. The report form is a disk file that contains the information to prepare the report. Since it's a disk file, you can use it over and over again and make as many copies of the report as you like — whenever you want to. Since the database is the source of data, any changes in data content are automatically reflected in the final report. Report forms are prepared using CREATE REPORT and changed with MODIFY REPORT. The two commands are essentially identical. Once a report form has been created, the report itself is prepared by REPORT.

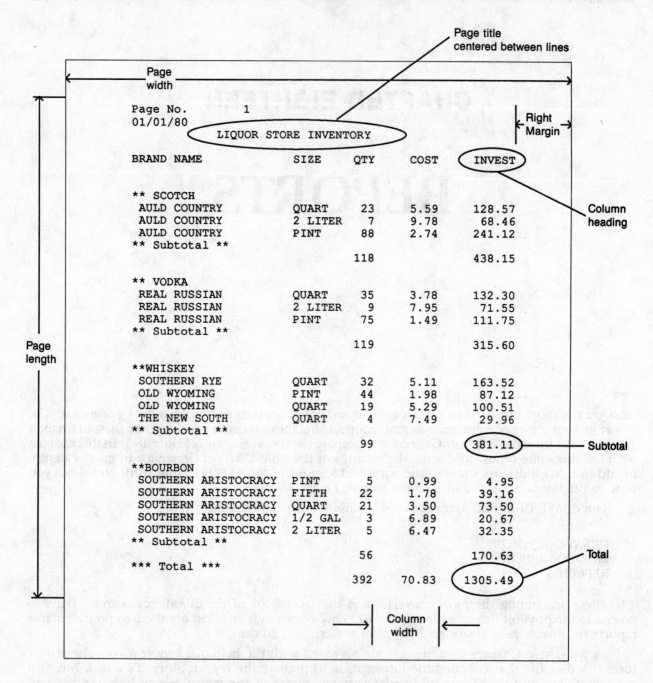

Page title
centered between lines

Page width

Right Margin

Column heading

Column width

Subtotal

Total

Page length

```
Page No.        1
01/01/80
            LIQUOR STORE INVENTORY

BRAND NAME              SIZE     QTY     COST     INVEST


** SCOTCH
  AULD COUNTRY          QUART     23     5.59     128.57
  AULD COUNTRY          2 LITER    7     9.78      68.46
  AULD COUNTRY          PINT      88     2.74     241.12
** Subtotal **
                                 118              438.15


** VODKA
  REAL RUSSIAN          QUART     35     3.78     132.30
  REAL RUSSIAN          2 LITER    9     7.95      71.55
  REAL RUSSIAN          PINT      75     1.49     111.75
** Subtotal **
                                 119              315.60


**WHISKEY
  SOUTHERN RYE          QUART     32     5.11     163.52
  OLD WYOMING           PINT      44     1.98      87.12
  OLD WYOMING           QUART     19     5.29     100.51
  THE NEW SOUTH         QUART      4     7.49      29.96
** Subtotal **
                                  99              381.11


**BOURBON
  SOUTHERN ARISTOCRACY  PINT       5     0.99       4.95
  SOUTHERN ARISTOCRACY  FIFTH     22     1.78      39.16
  SOUTHERN ARISTOCRACY  QUART     21     3.50      73.50
  SOUTHERN ARISTOCRACY  1/2 GAL    3     6.89      20.67
  SOUTHERN ARISTOCRACY  2 LITER    5     6.47      32.35
** Subtotal **
                                  56              170.63
*** Total ***
                                 392    70.83    1305.49
```

Figure 18-1: Sample report

Chapter Eighteen

```
Page No.      1
08/30/85
                      CUSTOMER LIST
                     BOB'S BETTER BOOKS
                  10150 W. JEFFERSON BOULEVARD
                  CULVER CITY, CALIFORNIA  90230


NAME AND ADDRESS                      PHONE NUMBER
================================      =============


52ND STREET BOOK SHOP                 (212)266-4410
SHIPPING
126 E. 18TH ST.
NEW YORK, NY  10003


A-1 BOOKS                             (303)925-1234
77 E. COPPERFIELD
ASPEN, CO  81611


AARDVARK ASSOCIATES                   (201)267-1000
KAREN
121 STONE CT.
NORTHVALE, NJ  07647


ABC BOOK SELLERS                      (214)344-3740

9715 MINERS AVENUE
DALLAS, TX  75231


ABC BOOK SELLERS                      (313)425-7711
CAROLINE SIMMONS
12510 FRONTIER
LIVONIA, MI  48154


ACME BOOKS                            (312)741-3380
ALBERT LONGMAN
115 S. WEST ST.
ELGIN, IL  60120


ACRIMONY                              (503)284-9876
MORT EASTON
2512 NE COLUMBIA
PORTLAND, OR  97232
```

Figure 18-2: Columns with multiple items

PREPARING THE REPORT FORM

To create a report form, you must give dBASE information about the *page layout* as well as about what is to go into the report. Let's look at how we use CREATE REPORT to enter this information. When you create a report, you must be using (USE) the database that you will be reporting on.

```
. USE INVENTRY
. CREATE REPORT
Enter report file name: INVENTRY
```

Report forms are disk files; so, each report form needs its own disk filename. A report filename must conform to the same rules as any other disk files. dBASE automatically assigns a *.FRM* file identifier to the filename. Once we have assigned a name to the report form, we'll be presented with the screen form shown in Figure 18-3. On the top line of this screen are the names of five *pull-down* menus: Options, Groups, Columns, Locate, and Exit. All the information used to prepare the report is entered via these five menus.

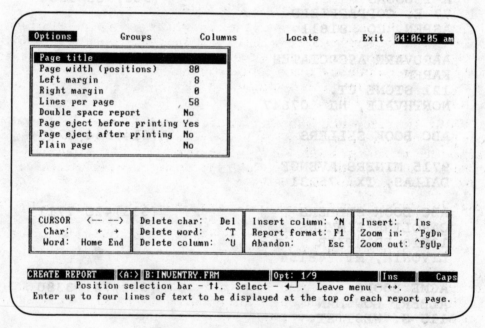

Figure 18-3: Options menu

The current selections are highlighted: on the menu name and on a selection within the selected menu. The selection is changed by using the arrow keys to move the highlights. The Left and Right arrow keys control the menu selection. The Up and Down arrow keys control the selection of items within the menu. As we change menus, the previously selected menu will be replaced by the newly selected menu.

To enter data into a menu item, use the Left or Right arrow key to select the menu. Then use the Up and Down arrow keys to select an item within the menu. Press the Return key to enter the selection. Type in the new information. Then, press the Return key to exit from the selection.

Chapter Eighteen

The Options Menu

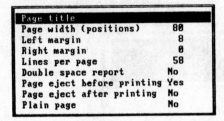

Page Title: The page title consists of up to four lines. Each line can be up to 60 characters long. Each title line will be automatically centered *between the margins*. If the body of the report does not take up the full space — margin to margin, then the title will *not* be centered over the body of the report. If this is the case, adjust either the content of the report or the right margin to get the title to appear centered.

To enter the title, use the arrow keys to highlight *Page Title*. Press Return. You'll be presented with the screen shown as Figure 18-4. The cursor is placed at the beginning of the box provided for entering the title automatically. This box is only 36 characters wide. As you enter a title line that is longer than 36 characters, the line will scroll to the left as you enter the title. This is to allow you full use of the title width. When finished with the title, press PgDn.

Page Width: The page width is the number of *character positions* for the total width of your page, including margins (shown in Figure 18-1). dBASE assigns an initial value of 80 characters to the page width. You'll want to change this value if you are using either wide paper or small print. dBASE will not allow you to use more characters in your report than the value entered into page width.

Left Margin: The left margin is given in character positions. dBASE assigns an initial left margin of 8 character spaces. The left margin is indicated on screen by the > > > > symbols on the first line in the box for REPORT FORMAT (see Figure 18-5). Each > indicates one character position in the left margin.

Right Margin: The right margin is also given in character positions. dBASE assigns the initial value of zero to the right margin (no right margin). When you assign a right margin dBASE displays < < < < symbols on the first line in the box for REPORT FORMAT. Each > symbol indicates one character position in the right margin.

Lines per page: Practically speaking, this value sets the bottom page margin. The *lines per page* value is the total number of lines, including the page header, that dBASE will print for each line of the report. The page header includes the page number, date, page title, and column headings (as shown in Figure 18-1). The report begins one line down from the top of the page. Most printers use 11-inch paper and are set to 6 lines per inch (66 lines per page). The standard setting of 58 lines provides a 7-line bottom margin.

You *cannot* use this setting to change the paper length. That is done by your printer. To use paper that is not 11 inches, you must change *both* this setting and the form length adjustment on your printer.

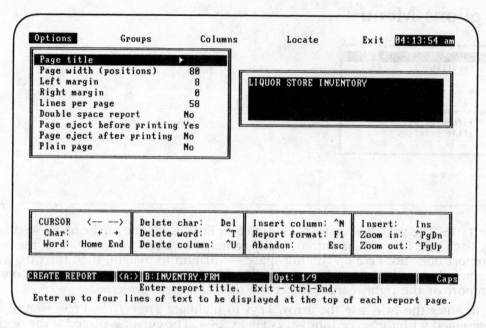

Figure 18-4: Entering the report title

Top Margin: No adjustment is provided for the top margin. To move the report "down" on the paper, you must adjust the paper in the printer.

Double-spacing: Normally, one record (or a part of one record) is printed on each line of the report. As we'll see later, you can use more than one line for each record (see Figure 18-2). A *yes* entry for this item will insert a blank line between records.

Page eject before printing: dBASE normally ejects one page from the printer before beginning the report. This make sures that your report will always begin at the top of a page (just in case you have a partially printed page in the printer).

Page eject after printing: The last page in the report is not normally ejected. This feature allow comments to be printed at the end of the report.

Plain page: Each page of the report is normally printed with a full page heading; page number, date, and page title. If you select *plain page*, the page number, and date will not be printed at all, while the page title will be printed on the first page only.

The Groups Menu

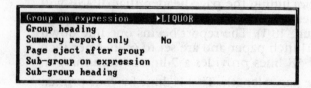

This menu allows us to *group* like items together in a report. If you look at Figure 18-1, you will see that the records for each kind of liquor are *grouped* together. To take advantage of this feature, the database must be arranged so that the records in a *group* are adjacent to one another. To group records together, we can enter them in order, sort the database, or index the database.

Group on expression: This selection is used to identify the field (or fields) that the report is to be grouped by. The database is usually sorted or indexed on this field. In Figure 18-1, the records were grouped by the contents of the field LIQUOR.

When records are grouped, any numeric columns that are to be totalled will be automatically subtotalled by the group (as in Figure 18-1).

Group heading: The content of the *grouping* field is automatically printed at the beginning of the group as in Figure 18-1. The group heading allows you to add additional text just before this automatic group heading. For example, if we had entered "KIND OF LIQUOR:" for the group heading, it would be printed just before and on the same line as the kind of liquor.

Summary report only: A summary report consists of only the *group* field and the subtotals, if any. It's a good way to get a quick overview of a large report. A summary report using the same data as Figure 18-1 is shown as Figure 18-4.

Page Eject after group: This feature is used when you want each group to begin on a fresh page.

Sub-group: Sub-groups are simply groups which occur within larger groups. In our liquor store example, it's conceivable that (if we had a larger store) that we would want to group items by BRAND within each liquor category. To be able to do this, we would need to have the database indexed (or sorted) by both LIQUOR and BRAND.

. INDEX ON LIQUOR + BRAND TO BRAND

If brand is to be the sub-group, then it must occur in second place in the index or sort order.

When sub-groups are identified, numeric columns that are to be totalled will be automatically sub-subtotalled by sub-group. Had we identified BRAND as a sub-group, QUANTITY and INVESTMENT would be sub-subtotalled.

Sub-group heading: This is text that is to be displayed just before the sub-group field data.

The Columns Menu

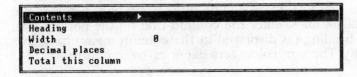

```
Page No.       1
08/31/85

                    LIQUOR STORE INVENTRY

     BRAND NAME            SIZE   QTY    COST     INVEST

  **   BOURBON
  ** Subtotal **
                                    56            170.63

  **   SCOTCH
  ** Subtotal **
                                   118            438.15

  **   VODKA
  ** Subtotal **
                                   119            315.60

  **   WHISKEY
  ** Subtotal **
                                    95            351.15

  *** Total ***
                                   388           1275.53
```

Figure 18-4

This menu is used to define each of the columns in the *body* of the report. You must fill out this menu "form" for each of the columns in the report. Columns are defined one at a time. When a column is defined, you must use the PgDn key to advance to the next column. Use the PgUp key to backup to a previous column definition.

Contents: This item determines *what* is to go into the column. This will usually be a field from the current database or an expression involving one or more fields from that database. You must be using the database that you want to report on when you create (or change) the report form.

If you forget the name of a field, press F10. This adds help information to the column definition screen — as shown in Figure 18-5. As you can see, the help is provided by two onscreen boxes. The first lists the field names in the database. If there are more fields than can be displayed at a time, you can *scroll* through additional fieldnames by pressing the PgDn key. One of these fields will be highlighted. Information about the highlighted field is displayed in the second box. Use the Up and Down arrow keys to move the light bar to another field name.

Column Heading: A column heading is optional. If you elect to enter a column title you are provided with a box in which to enter the heading. This box (as shown in Figure 18-6) has space for four lines. If you enter the heading into the first line, there will be three blank lines between the heading and the data. To eliminate these blank lines, enter the column title on the bottom line. When you do, you will find that column heading (as displayed in the column menu) has three semicolons in front of it (;;;BRAND NAME). The semicolon acts like a carriage return.

Width: This value is the number of character spaces to be allocated to the column. The standard value is exactly the width of the column contents or the column heading (whichever is wider). You can elect to use either more or fewer character spaces. If you use additional spaces, they will be added to the right for character fields and to the left for numeric fields. This provides you with one way to adjust the spacing between columns. If the column width is less than the width of

Chapter Eighteen

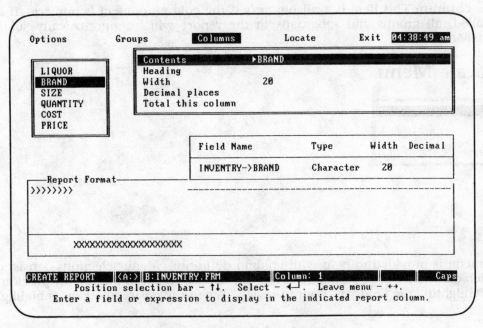

Figure 18-5: Field help information

the content, the content will "wrap" within the column boundaries and be printed on multiple lines.

Decimal places: This value is the number of decimal places to be displayed in the column. It is normally the number of decimal places in the field (fields) involved in the column. However, you can choose to use either more or fewer decimals than the database contains.

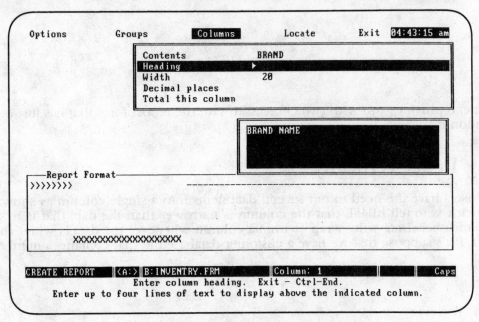

Figure 18-6: Enter column heading

Reports

Total this column: This item is available *only* if the column content is numeric. If a column is to be totalled, all groups and subgroups in the report will be automatically subtotalled and sub-subtotalled.

The Locate Menu

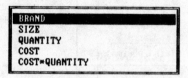

This menu is provided to help with column definition. Menu selections consist of the contents of each defined field. You can go directly to the column definition for any previously defined field by highlighting the field you want to review. When the desired content is highlighted, press Return.

The Exit Menu

This menu provides you with two choices: to save the report form that has just been defined or to abandon it.

Printing Items Vertically

Many users have the need to put several data items into a single column as shown in Figure 18-2. The trick is to tell dBASE that the column is narrower than the data that is to go into the column. Remember: Data will "wrap" within a column whenever the data is wider than the column width. Let's suppose that we have a customer database file that contains a number of fields, including:

Field Name	Type	Width
NAME	Character	30
ATTN	Character	30
ADDRESS	Character	25
CITY	Character	20
STATE	Character	2
ZIP	Character	5
PHONE	Character	14

We want to prepare the report shown in Figure 18-2 from this database. Without this technique, you would need to use either wide paper or tiny print to get all of this information on a single page. The reporting tools that we will use are:

- Date wraps when the data is wider than the column width.
- Text can be entered if enclosed by quotes
- Character fields can be concatenated (added together)
- Semicolons will force the data to wrap

The first column of Figure 18-2 contains NAME, ATTN, ADDRESS, CITY, STATE, and ZIP. We'll put all this into one column by entering

```
NAME + ATTN + ADDRESS + ';' + TRIM(CITY)+ ',' + STATE + ' ' + ZIP
```

as the contents of column 1. dBASE will protest a little since the width of this item is larger than the page width. Ignore the protest and set the column width to 30. Why 30? This value happens to be the width of the widest field that we want displayed. Data will wrap at the column width. In this case we want each field to be displayed without wrapping. The NAME field takes the first line of the column and ATTN the second. The ADDRESS field begins the third line, but has only 25 characters — not enough to fill the line. The semicolon (enclosed in quotes) is used to "force" a wrap after ADDRESS. This places CITY at the beginning of line 4.

TRIM( ) is a dBASE function. It is used to discard "trailing" blank spaces from data items. The contents of CITY are not the same length. "El Paso" is shorter than "San Francisco." By using the TRIM( ) function with CITY we are able to place a comma correctly after the name of the city (see Figure 18-2). The comma and a single blank space separate CITY from STATE. These are inserted into the expression by enclosing them in quotes. The semicolon is also enclosed by quotes, but it doesn't appear in the report.

To separate the records in the printout, the report is double-spaced. This does not affect the line spacing within the record.

Substituting Text

There is another trick that you might want to use here. The ATTN column is often blank. This prints out as a blank line within the record. You can prevent dBASE from printing the blank by replacing ATTN in the column expression with iif(ATTN = space(30), chr(0), ATTN)

This instruction becomes embedded and it says: *If ATTN is empty don't print it, otherwise do.* Chr(0) is a null; it is exactly nothing and takes no space.

In this example we have substituted nothing for all blank spaces. A more common use of text substitution is to translate data. For example, suppose you use a one-character field to represent a person's gender: M for male, F for female. To print the words Male and Female in the report, we would enter

iif(GENDER= 'F', 'Female','Male')

to describe the column content.

You can use this technique to do "exception" reporting. For example, suppose that you have a database which is a check register. One of the items is a logic field (CANCEL) that indicates whether a check has "cleared" or not. When we report on this field, we want no comment for checks that have cleared, and the word "open" when the check has not cleared. It's easier to spot the open items in a printout when you use this technique. Use

iif(.NOT.CANCEL,"open",""   ")

to describe the column content.

Column Headings

The column heading appears to be limited to 4 lines. You can use the semicolon to obtain column headings that are more than 4 lines long. Simply insert a semicolon whenever you want a new heading line.

THIS;IS;A;SIX;LINE;TITLE

produces a column heading that looks like

THIS
IS
A
SIX
LINE
TITLE

Grouping Data Items

Sometimes you'll need to group data items from more than one field. Let's suppose that we have a database of elementary school children. Among the fields in the database are NAME, ROOM and GRADE. We want a report form to prepare class rosters. A class roster is an alphabetical list of the children in each room and grade. Some of the rooms have children from two grade levels. To arrange the records into alphabetical groups of ROOM and GRADE (ROOM and GRADE are character fields), use

Chapter Eighteen

. INDEX ON ROOM + GRADE + NAME TO CLASS

With the database records properly arranged we can have the report *group* the students by class. The entry into *group by expression* would be

ROOM + GRADE

A "better" entry for this data item would be:

"Room: "+ ROOM + " Grade: "+ GRADE

The text inside of the quotes doesn't affect the grouping. Only the contents of the listed fields are used. The advantage in using the latter approach is that the text will be printed together with the field content.

Room 21B Grade: 6

Reporting From Multiple Databases

Your report can contain information from more than one database file. The database files should be linked together by the SET RELATION command. When specifying a data item from another database file, use the *alias* for the work area of the other file, the – > and the fieldname.

alias– >fieldname

Under certain circumstances, you can group records by a field in a linked database. To do so, the current database must be sorted by the field used to link to another database. Any field in the linked database can be specified as the grouping field.

To illustrate this point, let's examine an elementary school database system. The STUDENT file contains NAME, ROOM, and GRADE. The TEACHERS file contains NAME, ROOM, and GRADE also. Both files, of course, contain other fields. Both files are indexed on GRADE and ROOM. To link these files together, we use

. SELECT STUDENTS
. SET RELATION TO GRADE+ROOM INTO TEACHERS

Now we can prepare the class rosters by entering the field name NAME from the TEACHER'S database into *group on expression*. This gives us exactly the same result as if we had grouped directly on GRADE+ROOM — except that the teacher's name will appear at the beginning of each class roster.

The REPORT Command

The report command itself provides you with a set of options. The command options allow you to:

- specify *which records* are to be included
- print a special *page heading*
- specify that the report is to be *printed*
- specify that the report is to go to a *disk file*

Selecting Records

You can specify which records are to be included in the report by adding a *for* or *while* clause to the report command. To include only the SCOTCH records in the report of Figure 18-1, use

. REPORT FOR LIQUOR = 'SCOTCH'

Page Heading

You can define a page heading in addition to the title. This additional heading is printed at the top of each page — beginning on the line that displays the page number. Use this feature to *label* a report. For example, we could add the heading "Preliminary Report" to our liquor store inventory with the command

. REPORT HEADING "Preliminary Report"

Reporting To A Printer

A report is always displayed on screen. To route the report to a printer add the words TO PRINT to the report command.

. REPORT TO PRINT

Saving Report Output On Disk

You can send the report output to a disk file instead of the screen or a printer. If you do so, you can *edit* the report using a word processor. To "save" a report as a disk file, use

. REPORT TO *filename*

The filename can be any legitimate disk filename you desire. dBASE will add the file identifier .TXT to the filename.

As you have seen, you can use the REPORT commands to create *report forms* that can be used over and over again to produce reports that contain information about the contents of your database files. Try experimenting with the REPORT commands; you'll find them a great resource.

CHAPTER NINETEEN

LABELS

In this chapter we will discuss the specialized commands that dBASE III provides to help you prepare and print standard labels. These commands are:

. CREATE LABEL
. MODIFY LABEL
. LABEL FORM

Printed labels have long been a favorite of time-conscious business people. Although there are many uses for printed labels, the most common is the old-fashioned mailing label. Let's suppose that we have a database of customer names, addresses and other information. The filename for our customer database is CUSTOMER. To prepare mailing labels, we use the following fields:

FIELDNAME	TYPE	WIDTH
NAME	Character	30
ADDRESS	Character	25
CITY	Character	20
STATE	Character	2
ZIP	Character	5
ATTENTION	Character	30

Representative contents for this database are shown in Figure 19-1. (This figure was prepared with the REPORT command. See Chapter Eighteen.) Labels prepared from this database are shown in Figure 19-2.

Page No.   1
08/30/85

CUSTOMER LIST
BOB'S BETTER BOOKS
10150 W. JEFFERSON BOULEVARD
CULVER CITY, CALIFORNIA 90230

NAME AND ADDRESS   PHONE NUMBER
=   = = = = = = = = = =

52ND STREET BOOK SHOP   (212)266-4410
SHIPPING
126 E. 18TH ST.
NEW YORK, NY 10003

A-1 BOOKS   (303)925-1234
77 E. COPPERFIELD
ASPEN, CO 81611

AARDVARK ASSOCIATES   (201)267-1000
KAREN 121 STONE CT.
NORTHVALE, NJ 07647

ABC BOOK SELLERS   (214)344-3740
9715 MINERS AVENUE
DALLAS, TX 75231

ABC BOOK SELLERS   (313)425-7711
CAROLINE SIMMONS
12510 FRONTIER
LIVONIA, MI 48154

ACME BOOKS   (312)741-3380
ALBERT LONGMAN
115 S. WEST ST.
ELGIN, IL 60120

ACRIMONY   (503)284-9876
MORT EASTON
2512 NE COLUMBIA
PORTLAND, OR 97232

Figure 19-1: Customer database contents

Computer labels come in standard sheets of rows and columns. The total number of labels on each sheet varies according to label size and the layout of the labels on the sheet. The number of columns across a sheet of labels is called the *number of labels*. What kind of labels should you choose? First of all, they need to be big enough. After that, it will depend on how you are going to use them. If you will be printing hundreds of labels at a time, you will be happier with three or four across. Most printers can print multi-column labels faster than single-column labels because it takes time to advance the printer for each new line. On the other hand, if you are going to print only a handful of labels, you might be happier with single-column labels.

```
52ND STREET BOOK SHOP          A-1 BOOKS
SHIPPING                       77 E. COPPERFIELD
126 E. 18TH ST.                ASPEN CO 81611
NEW YORK NY 10003


AARDVARK ASSOCIATES            ABC BOOK SELLERS
KAREN                          9715 MINERS AVENUE
121 STONE CT.                  DALLAS TX 75231
NORTHVALE NJ 07647
```

Figure 19-2: Mailing labels

To print labels, you choose and fill in a LABEL FORM to tell dBASE what kind of labels you are using and what to print on each label. To fill out a label form, use the command:

```
. CREATE LABEL
Enter label file name: CUSTOMER
```

dBASE requests a name for the new label form. Your label form will be saved on the disk as a disk file. The rules for label form names are the same as for all other disk files — they can be up to eight characters long, they can contain letters and numbers but no embedded blank spaces. dBASE automatically adds .LBL to the filename as the file identifier. For our example, we have chosen to name this label form CUSTOMER.

Once you have created a LABEL FORM you can make changes to it at any time with MODIFY LABEL. This command works exactly like CREATE LABEL. Remember, the LABEL FORM is stored on the disk and you can retrieve it to either print labels or make changes to it whenever you want.

THE LABEL FORM

We fill out the label form with the help of three *pull-down* menus: Options, Contents, and Exit. These three menus are shown in Figures 19-3, 19-4, and 19-5. The menu titles are shown at the top of each screen. You select from among these three menus with the Left and Right arrow keys. You select from among the options for each menu with the Up and Down arrow keys. The active menu and the active menu choice will be highlighted.

At the bottom of each menu screen is a *help* menu. This menu tells you which keys you can use for some onscreen functions. You must be using the database that the labels will be prepared from. You can view the field structure for that database file by pressing function key F1. This will replace the key help menu with a field help menu. Press F1 again to restore the key help. Various messages will be displayed at the screen bottom to help guide you through the process of filling out the LABEL FORM.

The Options Menu

With the Options menu, you enter the size and configuration of the labels. There are seven items on the Options menu, as shown in Figure 19-3.

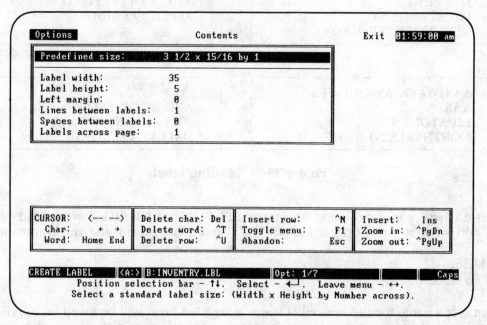

Figure 19-3: Label options

Predefined size: There are five predefined sizes supported by dBASE. These are (width by height by number of labels):

3½ x 15/16 by 1
3½ x 15/16 by 2
3½ x 15/16 by 3
4 x 1 7/16 by 2
3 2/10 x 11/12 by 3 (Cheshire)

The default size is the first one in the list above. To select another from this list, use the Up or Down arrow key to highlight the choice *Predefined size*. Then, press the Return key. Each time you press Return the predefined size selection will advance by one through the list. When you get to the bottom of the list, the program automatically cycles back to the beginning of the list.

As you cycle through the predefined size list, the other menu options, such as *Label width*, are automatically assigned values to match the particular selection. All the options assume that your printer is set to print 10 characters per inch and 6 lines per inch.

Computer printers can print at just about any print density. The three most common are 10, 12, and 17 characters per inch (pica, elite, and compressed). If your printer is set to other than 10 characters per inch (cpi) and 6 lines per inch, you will need to make appropriate adjustments in the options settings. The option settings below will need to be changed *only if* your printer is set to a nonstandard configuration or if you are not using one of the dBASE standard label sizes.

To change any of the label options, use the Up or Down arrow key to move the highlight to the desired option. Press the Return key to *enter* the option. Type in the new value. Then press Return to leave the option.

Figure 19-3 shows a typical label layout. This diagram helps to explain some of the option terms.

Label width: This is the label width in characters — it is *not* the length of the content of the label.

Label height: This is the number of lines that *can* be printed on the label — not the number that *will* be. Standard settings assume 6 lines per inch.

Left margin: This is the number of character spaces to be placed between the leftmost position of the printhead and the first printed character on each line. dBASE has a SET command that is often used to provide a standard left margin for all printed output SET MARGIN TO *N*. If you have used SET MARGIN, any value that you assigned will be added to the left margin setting in the Options Menu when the labels are printed.

Lines between labels: Most label layouts leave a little space between each row of labels. For example, 15/16-inch — high labels usually leave a 1/16 space between rows. This means that the labels are on 1-inch centers. With normal line spacing (6 lines per inch) you would choose a 5-line *label height* and 1 *line between labels*.

Spaces between labels: Label layouts usually leave a little space between each column of labels. You account for this blank space by entering a number of character spaces. For example, if your printer is set to 10 cpi and the space between labels is 2/10ths of an inch you would enter a 2 in this space.

Labels across page: This is just the number of columns of labels on the printed output.

Contents

Once you have given dBASE the necessary information about the size and configuration of your labels, you can tell dBASE what to put on the labels. Use the Left or Right arrow key to highlight the word *Contents* at the top center of the screen.

This menu option presents you with the screen shown as Figure 19-4. This screen allows you to define what goes on each line of a label. To space down from the top of a label, leave lines blank. In the sample (Figure 19-4) we left label line 1 blank.

On line two of this label we want to print the contents of the NAME field. All we need to do is enter what we want to print — in this case — just the single field name NAME. On line 3 we want to print the content of the ATTENTION field. So we have entered the fieldname ATTEN-

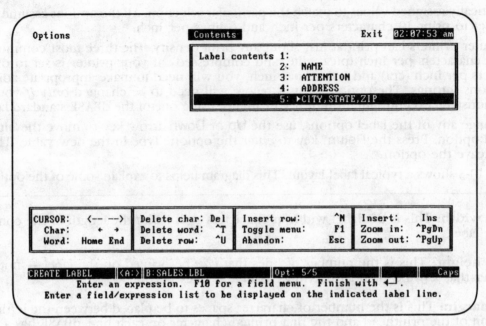

Figure 19-4: Label contents

TION for label contents 3. ATTENTION is a field that is sometimes left blank. If you look at figure 2 you will see that some labels have 4 printed lines, and some have 3. If the ATTENTION field is blank, the label will "close down" — which means that the item above the blank field (NAME) will be printed on this line.

For label line 4, we want to print the contents of the ADDRESS field. For label line 5, we have CITY, STATE, and ZIP. Note that these three fieldnames are separated by commas (a *comma-delimited* list). When there are multiple items on a line, any trailing blank spaces in a field are discarded. If you examine Figure 19-4, you will see that the trailing blank spaces in CITY have been discarded so that the label is printed just as you would desire.

Exit

This menu provides you only two choices — Save and Abandon. Move the highlight to your selection with the Up or Down arrow key. Then press Return (Figure 19-5).

USING THE LABEL FORM

To print the labels according to the label form that you have prepared, use the LABEL FORM command:

. LABEL FORM CUSTOMER TO PRINT SAMPLE

There are actually several parts to this command.

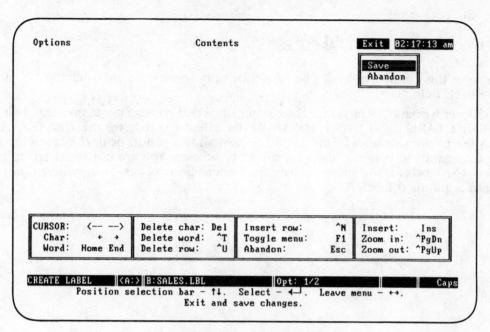

Figure 19-5: Exit menu

LABEL FORM is the part of the command that informs dBASE that we want to use one of the label forms that we have already prepared. This is followed by the filename of the label form that we want to use. In this example, we want to use the label form CUSTOMER.

TO PRINT tells dBASE to direct the labels to the printer — as well as to the video screen. If you omit this phrase, labels will be displayed *only* on the screen.

SAMPLE prints a row of sample labels. No data is actually printed — X's are used to show the data area. You use this option to align the labels in your printer. After the sample has printed, you will be asked if you want another sample. You can print samples until you have properly aligned the labels in the printer.

There is another option available with this command: You can create a disk file of the label "images." You can use this disk file with your favorite word processor. To send the labels to a file, add TO DISKFILE to the command. The name of this file can be anything you like — as long as it conforms to the rules for filenames. dBASE will add the .TXT file identifier to the filename.

Printing Selected Labels

LABEL FORM can also be used to print selected labels using either FOR *condition* or WHILE *condition* or both. The FOR and WHILE condition statements are used just as explained in Chapter Eight, "Using a Database." For example, suppose that you want to print labels for customers in New

York. Here's the command:

. LABEL FORM CUSTOMER TO PRINT SAMPLE FOR STATE = 'NY'

The output from this command would be labels for only those customers having NY as the content of the STATE field.

In this chapter we have examined the three commands that you can use to prepare labels: CREATE LABEL, MODIFY LABEL, and LABEL FORM. We have learned that we use CREATE LABEL and MODIFY LABEL to prepare label forms. LABEL FORM allows you to print the labels. You can use these three commands to prepare labels for a variety of uses. You are not restricted to preparing mailing labels. Use labels for inventory shelves, file folders, book plates — anywhere that you might otherwise use a gummed label.

Chapter Nineteen

CHAPTER TWENTY

CUSTOM SCREENS

Creating special customized screens such as that shown in Figure 20-1 was once a source of woe for computer users. Beginners couldn't do it and programmers hated doing it. The result was nearly always dull screens with terse messages. Today, an increasing number of software packages are making it easy for anyone to create special screens.

Custom screens offer more than just a pleasing appearance. These screens allow you to make better use of the limited screen space. They can also provide some checking of the data. A typical standard screen used by dBASE III PLUS is shown as Figure 20-2. This screen is very good for a built-in screen. Since you know what you want the screen to look like, you can, however, always improve on a built-in form.

dBASE III PLUS provides an easy-to-use tool for producing special screens. To invoke this *screen editor*, type CREATE SCREEN after a dot prompt or select CREATE and Format if you are using the dBASE Assistant. Let's use this command to prepare the screen shown in Figure 20-1.

```
. CREATE SCREEN
Enter screen file name: INVENTRY
```

CREATE SCREEN gathers the information that dBASE needs to produce this custom screen and stores the information in a disk file. The filename for this screen form must conform to the standard rules for disk filenames. dBASE will automatically add the .SCR file identifier to this filename. When the screen has been completely defined, dBASE uses the screen file to produce a second file. This second file is called a FORMAT FILE. dBASE will automatically assign the format file the same name as the screen file, but uses a .FMT file identifier.

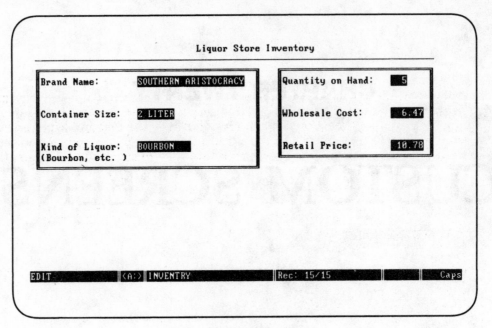

Figure 20-1

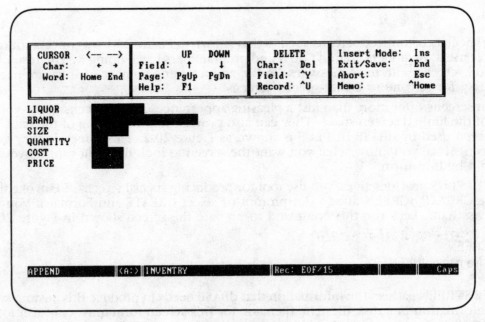

Figure 20-2

Chapter Twenty

CREATING A CUSTOM SCREEN

CREATE SCREEN provides four menus to help you define your custom screen. The names of these menus are shown on the top line of Figure 20-3. The bottom three lines of the screen provide information to help you through the screen-definition process. The screen-creating menu system works in the same way as the other dBASE menu programs. Use the **Left** and **Right** arrow keys to select a menu from the top of the screen. Use the **Up** and **Down** arrow keys to position the lightbar so that the desired option is highlighted. Press the **Return** key to select the highlighted option.

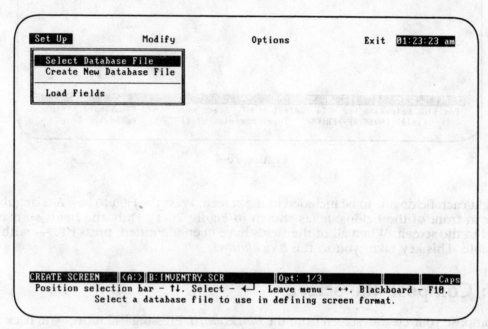

Figure 20-3

Now let's go through the process of creating the custom screen shown in Figure 20-1.

STEP 1: Select a database

To create a custom screen, you *must* be using the database that the custom screen is to be used with. If you were not using that database when you entered CREATE SCREEN, you can select that file from the *Set Up* menu.

STEP 2: Choose the database fields

You must identify which database fields are to be included in the custom screen. Do this with the help of the *Load Fields* option. This option produces a menu consisting of all the fieldnames as shown in Figure 20-4.

Custom Screens

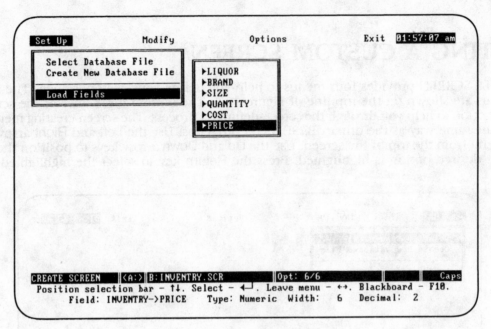

Figure 20-4

Highlight each fieldname to be included in the screen. Press the Return key. A triangular marker will appear in front of the fieldname (as shown in Figure 20-4). Only the fields so marked will be included in the screen. When all of the fields have been identified, press F10 — with the field list still visible. This key takes you to the *blackboard*.

STEP 3: Compose the screen

You compose your custom screen from the *blackboard*. Pressing F10 moves you back and forth between the blackboard and the menu screen. The blackboard should initially resemble Figure 20-5. This is the starting point for creating the custom screen. Note that the field areas are shown in reverse video. Character fields are filled with Xs and numeric fields are filled with 9s.

Moving the cursor

You can move the cursor to any position on screen with the help of the cursor control keys. The Left and Right arrow keys move the cursor one space in the direction of the arrow. The Up and Down arrow keys move the cursor one line up or down. To move the cursor to the beginning (or the end) of the line, press the Ctrl key and the Left or Right arrow at the same time. The status bar keeps track of the cursor position. For our demonstration, we will move the standard display down on the screen and put the new display at the top of the screen.

Adding blank lines

Move the cursor to the top left corner of the screen. Press Ctrl-N. (Hold the Ctrl key down

---

Chapter Twenty

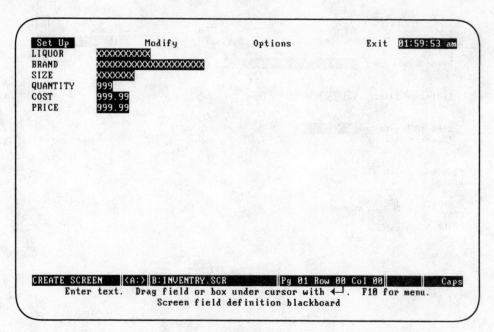

Figure 20-5

and press "N" at the same time.) Each time you do this, the standard display will move down one line. What you are doing is adding new blank lines to the beginning of the screen. Add several blank lines to the beginning of the screen to accommodate the screen title and the new screen design.

Entering Text

To enter text on the screen, move the cursor to where you want the text to be and type it in. In the example we can add the text *Brand Name:* by moving the cursor to the beginning of line 2 and then simply typing it in.

Inserting Text

You can add characters between other characters if *Insert* is *On*. To turn it on, press the Ins key. The status bar will display the letters "Ins" in the second element from the right. To turn it off, press the Ins key again. When *Insert* is on, characters can be added at the current position of the cursor. Any characters to the right will automatically move to the right.

Moving Fields

You can put the fields anywhere on the screen — and in any order. Figure 20-6 shows the screen partly completed and with the first three fields moved to their new locations.

Note that field 1 (LIQUOR) has been moved to the third position. To move a field, place the cursor on the field area. Then, press the Return key. Move the cursor to where you want the field

---

Custom Screens

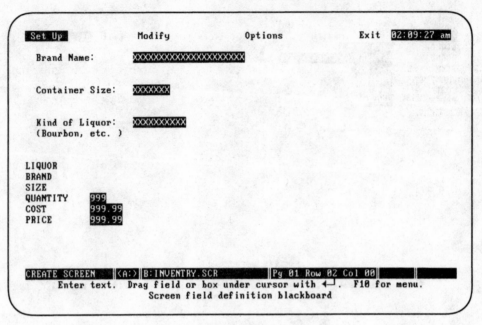

Figure 20-6

to be. Press the Return key. The field will move to the new position. Figure 20-7 shows our screen partly finished with all of the fields in the new locations.

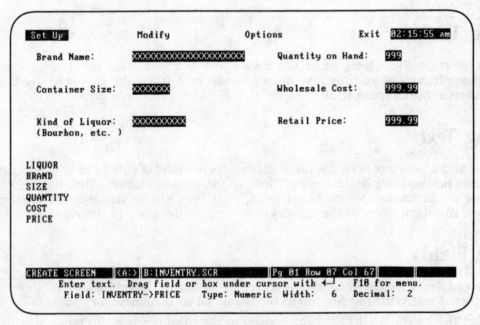

Figure 20-7

Chapter Twenty

Drawing Boxes

To draw the boxes, press function key **F10**, then select the options menu (Figure 20-8). Highlight *Double bar*. With this selection, you can draw one double-line box each time you use it. The *Single bar* selection will draw one single-line box. When you make your selection you are automatically back in the blackboard.

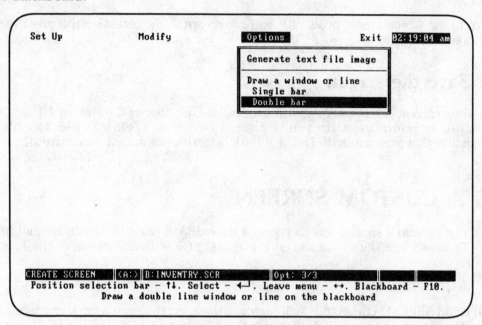

Figure 20-8

Move the cursor to where you want the upper left corner of the box. Press **Return**. Now move the cursor to where you want the lower right corner of the box. Press **Return**. Repeat this process for each box. To erase a box, place the cursor at any point on the box perimeter and press **Ctrl-U**.

Drawing Lines

Lines are nothing more than very thin boxes. To draw a horizontal line, follow the procedure used to draw a box. Move the cursor to the left end of the line. Press **Return**. Move the cursor to the right end of the line. Press **Return** again. To draw a vertical line, move the cursor to the top of the line and press **Return**. Then move the cursor to the bottom of the line and press **Return**.

Erasing Lines

Once the basic screen has been assembled, you will be left with the fieldnames at the bottom of the screen as in Figure 20-6. Move the cursor to the line that you want to erase. Press **Ctrl-Y**. (Hold the **Ctrl** key down and press "Y" at the same time). Each time you press **Ctrl-Y**, the line that the cursor was positioned to will be deleted.

Custom Screens

Erasing Words

To erase a single word, place the cursor on the word and press Ctrl-T.

STEP 4: Return to the menu

To return to the screen menu, press F10. You can return to the blackboard at any time by pressing this same key.

STEP 5: Save the screen

To save your screen, select the *Save* option on the *Exit* menu (Top line of Figure 20-3). This tells dBASE to use the information that you've entered and create a FORMAT file. This file will have the same filename that was entered. The .FMT file identifier is added automatically.

USING A CUSTOM SCREEN

Once you've created a special screen you can have dBASE use this screen instead of the standard screen. To do so, use the command SET FORMAT TO with the name of the format file.

. SET FORMAT TO INVENTRY

The EDIT and APPEND commands will now use the special screen format in place of the standard display. To turn off the special format, use the command CLOSE FORMAT. If you close the database you are using, the FORMAT file will automatically close. When you reopen the database, you must again use the SET FORMAT TO command with the format filename to reestablish the custom screen.

If you are using several databases files at the same time, you can have a custom screen for each. That means that you can have a separate format file in each dBASE work area. Remember that each custom screen counts as an additional file in use and you can have only 15 files open at any one time.

Controlling Data Entry

dBASE naturally provides a limited measure of control to facilitate data entry. Only numbers can be entered into numeric fields and only valid dates can be entered into date fields. We can, however, provide a great deal more control for data entry through the custom screen. For example, we can restrict the data entry for character fields to the letters a-z, and we can force the entry to uppercase (A-Z). We can also restrict the entry of date or numeric data to a *range* of values. This can be done with the help of the Picture Function, Picture Template, and Range selections on the *Modify* menu of SCREEN.

Let's modify our existing screen INVENTRY to incorporate these features into a screen. Use the MODIFY SCREEN command to change an existing screen design.

. MODIFY SCREEN
Enter screen file name: INVENTRY

dBASE uses the screen form with the .SCR identifier to make the modifications. You can erase this file *only* if you are certain that you won't want to make changes. It does take space in your disk directory. Once you have your screen exactly as you want it, you can eliminate the .SCR file.

When you modify an existing screen, the fields are already loaded. The blackboard looks just as it did when you saved the screen. You must, however, be using the database file that the screen is to be used with.

Selecting A Picture

First, select the blackboard. Next, move the cursor so that it is positioned to the field you want to work with (the reverse video area). In our example, we would move the cursor to the LIQUOR field. With the cursor positioned to the LIQUOR field, press **F10**. This will take you to the *Modify* option of the menus (Figure 20-9).

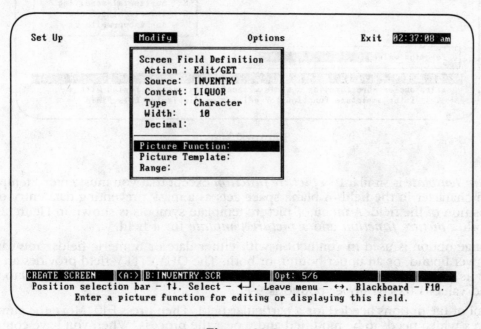

Figure 20-9

A word of caution: You can use this menu to modify the structure of your database. You can add fields, and change the characteristics (fieldwidth, and fieldtype) of existing fields. Experiment with this menu using a small, expendable database.

Once in the *Modify* menu you are faced with a variety of choices. The first option toggles the field between EDIT/GET and DISPLAY/SAY. EDIT/GET allows you to edit the field. DISPLAY/SAY is used when the field is to be displayed without the ability for editing.

Custom Screens

Highlight *Picture Function:* and press Return. This will provide you with a menu of *picture functions*. A picture function applies to every character in the field. Enter the desired picture functions in the space labeled *Function value*. Figure 20-10 shows the entries to select the first two picture functions (! and A). The ! symbol forces all alphabetical characters to uppercase. The A symbol prevents the user from entering anything other than an alphabetical character into the field.

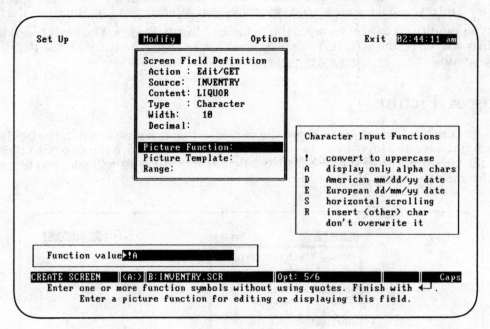

Figure 20-10

A *Picture Template* is similar to a *picture function* except that you must enter a template symbol for each character in the field. A blank space acts as a mask preventing data entry or display into that position of the field. A menu of picture template symbols is shown in Figure 20-11. You can have both a *picture function* and a *picture template* for a field.

The Range option is used in conjuction with either date or numeric fields. You can choose to enter a lower bound, or an upper bound, or both. The QUANTITY field provides an excellent example for its use. We want to restrict entries in the QUANTITY field to the range 0 to 999. The lower bound value is 0. The upper bound is 999.

Select all of the options needed for a particular field. Then press F10. Move the cursor to the next field area which needs to be modified and repeat the process. When you have completed all field modifications, use the *Exit* menu to save the changes to the custom screen.

Now, let's take a look at the format file INVENTRY.FMT. This file, shown as Figure 20-12, can be created and modified by most word processors. dBASE has a built in word processor. To use this built-in word processor, type the command MODIFY COMMAND followed by the *complete* filename (including the file identifier) of the file that you want to edit. You can only edit text files with this word processor. You cannot edit screen (.SCR), report (.FRM), label (.LBL), view (.VUE), query (.QRY), or database (.DBF) files.

Chapter Twenty

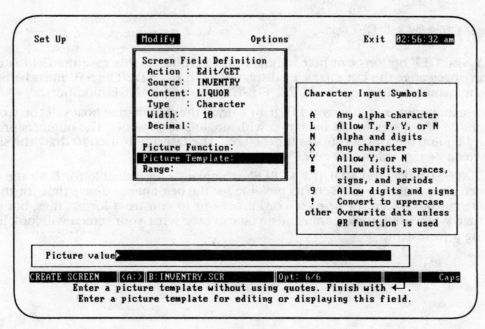

Figure 20-11

```
@2,28,   SAY "Liquor Store Inventory"
@5,2     SAY "Brand Name:"
@5,18    GET INVENTRY->BRAND
@5,46    SAY "Quantity On Hand:"
@5,64    GET INVENTRY->QUANTITY RANGE 0, 999
@7,2     SAY "Container Size:"
@7,18    GET INVENTRY->SIZE
@7,46    SAY "Wholesale Cost:"
@7,64    GET INVENTRY->COST
@9,2     SAY "Kind of Liquor:"
@9,18    GET INVENTRY->LIQUOR FUNCTION "!A"
@9,46    SAY "Retail Price:"
@9,64    GET INVENTRY->PRICE
@10,2    SAY "(Scotch, etc.)"
@4,1     TO 11, 39 DOUBLE
@4,44    TO 10, 73 DOUBLE
@3,1     TO 3, 73
```

Figure 20-12: INVENTRY.FMT

Each entry in this file is a dBASE command. This format file is really a little program that dBASE has written in dBASE. The basic command is the @ command. It is most often used in this form:

Custom Screens

```
@ row,column SAY "display text" GET field
```

The SAY and GET options can be combined on one line. In this case the field is displayed one character space after the last character displayed with the SAY. The SAY must be before the GET. Each command can include PICTURE, FUNCTION, and RANGE modifiers.

The commands containing the word DOUBLE draw the double-line boxes. If the word DOUBLE were omitted, the boxes would be drawn with single-line symbols. The numbers provide the beginning and ending screen coordinates for the box. The last line is used to draw the single line across the screen — just below the title.

The CREATE SCREEN and MODIFY SCREEN commands are valuable for both the beginner and the expert. They make custom screens possible for the beginner and save time for the expert. You can create custom screens by using a word processor to construct format files, but it's much more work than when using these commands: you can't see what your screen will look like while you're writing a format file.

Chapter Twenty

CHAPTER TWENTY-ONE

DIRECTORIES, CATALOGS, AND DICTIONARIES

As you use your computer and its database management system you will accumulate a large number of files of all kinds: database files, index files, report form files, label form files, and so on. How do you keep track of all of these files? What did you call the file? Which index goes with which database? You *must* know the names of the files that you want to use.

Your computers's operating system, called DOS (Disk Operating System), keeps a list of all the files on each disk that you are using. These lists are called the *disk directories*. Each time you create a new file, its filename is added automatically to the disk directory. Both dBASE and DOS provide you with access to this list of filenames through their DIR (directory) commands.

dBASE also provides you with the means to *catalog* your dBASE files. A dBASE catalog helps you to remember which indexes, report forms, and other dBASE files belong to each database file. The dBASE catalog is semiautomatic. If you want dBASE to keep track of these files for you, you must *turn* the catalog feature on. Once *on*, each new file is automatically added to the catalog — until you turn it off.

Some systems, usually those intended for use on large computers, also employ a *data dictionary*. A data dictionary contains all the information about all the files on your database — including the structure for each separate *relation*. The dictionary is most useful when you have a very complex database with from tens to hundreds of separate relations, reports, and so on. In this chapter we'll focus on using directories and catalogs. We will also discuss ways that you can *organize* your disks to make working with your computer a little easier.

The DOS Directory

DOS maintains a collection of information about each of your disk files. This information includes: the filename, the time and date that the file was last changed, the size of the file, and where the file is located on your disk. You can view the first four of these items with the DOS command DIR. A sample directory is shown in Figure 21-1.

```
Volume in drive C has no label
Directory of  C:\

COMMAND  COM    23210    3-07-85    1:43p
CONFIG   SYS       40    6-03-85    6:54p
AUTOEXEC BAT       78    8-20-85    2:20p
ANTON         <DIR>      8-19-85    7:37p
LAUREN        <DIR>      8-19-85    7:38p
MYFILES       <DIR>     11-01-85    3:10p
DBASE    EXE   138240   12-26-85    9:42a
DBASE    MSG    12276   12-17-85    9:07a
DBASEINL OVL    27648   12-26-85    9:42a
DBASE    OVL   272384   12-26-85    9:41a
HELP     DBS    66560   12-17-85   12:36p
ASSIST   HLP    17648   11-01-85   10:57a
INVENTRY DBF     3409    1-05-86    9:15a
INVENTRY FRM     1990    1-05-86    9:30a
FONEBOOK DBF     2438    1-05-86    7:17a
       15 File(s)  18230400 bytes free
```

Figure 21-1: Sample DOS directory

DIR normally provides you with a single long list of filenames. If you have more than 22 files on your directory, the first files will scroll upward off the top of the screen — leaving only the last 22 filenames visible on the screen. To view more than 22 filenames at a time, add a /W to the DIR command as shown in Figure 21-2. This will display the filenames in 5 columns. With the /W option, you can view 110 filenames on screen before any filenames scroll up off screen and out of view.

You can cause the directory display to pause after every screenful by adding /P to the command.

A> DIR/P

Among the more annoying features of the directory system is that the filenames are usually presented in the order that the files are actually stored on the disk. For our purposes, they appear in essentially random order. You can get the filenames to appear in alphabetical order — however, you will need a special program to do this. SORT.COM comes with your operating system. If SORT.COM is on the disk you are using, you can sort your directory display.

A> DIR ¦ SORT

Chapter Twenty-One

```
Volume in drive C is PC-AT
Directory of  C:\BIN

                          ANSI     SYS    LIBPATH  SYS    UDISK    SYS
WS       COM    WSOVLY1  OVR    WSMSGS   OVR    DBASE    OVL    DBASE    EXE
DOSEDIT  COM    EXE2BIN  EXE    LINK     EXE    DEBUG    COM    ATTRIB   EXE
FIND     EXE    JOIN     EXE    SHARE    EXE    SORT     EXE    SUBST    EXE
ASSIGN   COM    BACKUP   COM    BASIC    COM    BASICA   COM    CHKDSK   COM
COMMAND  COM    COUNT    COM    DISKCOMP COM    DISKCOPY COM    EDLIN    COM
FDISK    COM    FLOPPY   COM    GRAFTABL COM    GRAPHICS COM    KEYBFR   COM
KEYBGR   COM    KEYBIT   COM    KEYBSP   COM    KEYBUK   COM    LABEL    COM
MODE     COM    MORE     COM    PRINT    COM    RECOVER  COM    RESTORE  COM
SELECT   COM    SYS      COM    TREE     COM    NETSU    COM    10NET    COM
LOGIN    EXE    LOGOFF   EXE    MOUNT    EXE    UNMOUNT  EXE    NETSTAT  EXE
NETLOG   EXE    10SPOOL  EXE    XTREE    EXE    DCALC    EXE    DCALC    HLP
HPR      EXE    FORMAT   BAT    MASM     EXE    D        COM    123      EXE
123      HLP    123      CNF    CLEAN    BAT    DBC      COM    DBL      COM
LOTUS    COM    GREP     BAT    VTREE    COM    LIST     COM    WHEREIS  COM
DBRUN    EXE    DBRUN    OVL    DIFF     EXE    TD       DRV    GD       DRV
KB       DRV    PR       DRV    WSCOLOR  BAS    XDIR     EXE    BOX      BIN
          85 File(s)  26800128 bytes free
```

Figure 21-2: DIR/W

This command doesn't actually sort the directory. It just sorts the directory display. (The *Norton Utilities*, published by Peter Norton, include a program called Filesort that you can use to actually sort your directory.)

Subdirectories

In Figure 21-1, there are three files displayed with < DIR > following the filename. These three are called subdirectories.

ANTON   <DIR>
LAUREN <DIR>
MYFILES <DIR>

Each subdirectory is a special "compartment" of a disk directory that you *can* use to hold some of your disk files. Use subdirectories to group files together and avoid cluttering up the "main" directory. In this example, the subdirectory ANTON contains all the files belonging to my son Anton. The subdirectory LAUREN contains all of the files belonging to my daughter Lauren.

Creating a new subdirectory: You can create a subdirectory of the subdirectory we are currently using with the DOS command MKDIR (for *make directory*). To create a subdirectory named CLIENTS, we would use:

MKDIR CLIENTS

Using a subdirectory: To use a subdirectory, use the DOS command CD (Change Directory) from your operating system. To use the subdirectory *myfiles* we would use:

Directories, Catalogs, and Dictionaries

CD MYFILES

The contents of *MYFILES* are shown in Figure 21-3. As you can see, this subdirectory contains more subdirectories. DOS allows you to organize your disk into a number of smaller subdirectories to make the task of managing your disk files a little easier. It's a little like having a filing cabinet with as many drawers and compartments as you desire.

```
Volume in drive C has no label
Directory of  C:\MYFILES

.
..
SOFTWORD    <DIR>      8-20-85    2:20p
LIBRARY     <DIR>      8-19-85    7:37p
BANK        <DIR>      8-19-85    7:38p
PRIMER      <DIR>     11-01-85    3:10p
BUSBOOK     <DIR>     12-26-85    9:42a
COOKBOOK    <DIR>     12-17-85    9:07a
UNIXBOOK    <DIR>     12-26-85    9:42a
CLIENTS     <DIR>     12-26-85    9:41a
OFFICE      <DIR>     12-17-85   12:36p
ASSYCODE    <DIR>     11-01-85   10:57a
      13 File(s)  18230400 bytes free
```

Figure 21-3: MYFILES subdirectory

All of the subdirectories on your disk are automatically arranged into *hierarchy* as shown in Figure 21-4. The top box in this diagram is called the *root* directory, possibly because the diagram resembles an upside-down tree. The subdirectory has a filename — just like any other disk file. When you first use a disk, you are automatically in its root directory. To use one of the subdirectories, you must use the DOS command CD. To move back up the tree when you have finished with the directory, use CD followed by two dots:

CD ..

This command will move us "up" one level in the directory. When we are "in" a subdirectory, the DIR command will show us only the names of the files in that subdirectory. However, DOS provides us with a way to use any file in any subdirectory.

Paths and Pathnames

In Figure 21-4. there is a heavy black line connecting some of the boxes on the diagram. This line traces a *path* from the root directory to the file BILLINGS.DBF. The "complete" name of

Chapter Twenty-One

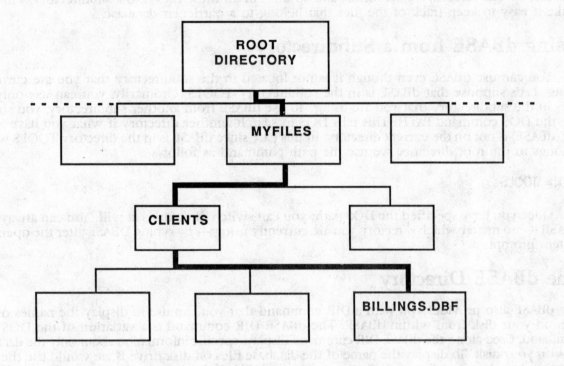

Figure 21-4: Diagram of directory system

BILLINGS consists of its filename *and* the names of all the directories (seperated by backslashes) from the root directory to the file.

\MYFILES\CLIENTS\BILLINGS.DBF

This is the *absolute pathname* of the file BILLINGS.DBF. We can gain access to any file in any subdirectory by using its absolute pathname. For example, we can display all the filenames in the directory CLIENTS by means of its absolute pathname.

DIR \MYFILES\CLIENTS

If we trace a path downward from the directory we are using, we obtain the *relative pathname* of a file. For example, if we are using the directory MYFILES, the relative pathname of BILLINGS.DBF is:

CLIENTS\BILLINGS.DBF

The absolute pathname of a file always begins with a backslash (for the root directory). The relative pathname must begin with the name of a subdirectory of the directory that we are currently using.

Subdirectories provide us with a convenient means for organizing the files on a disk. Put the files that belong together into a separate directory. Let's suppose that you have a database for your department's budget. Along with this budgetary database, you have a large number of ancillary files —

Directories, Catalogs, and Dictionaries

indexes, special screens, report forms, and so on. Put all these files into a subdirectory. This will make it easy to keep track of the files that belong to a particular database.

Using dBASE from a Subdirectory

You can use dBASE even though it is not located in the subdirectory that you are currently using. Let's suppose that dBASE is in the subdirectory TOOLS. Ordinarily, you can use only the files in the subdirectory that you are using. To use dBASE from another subdirectory, you should use the DOS command PATH. This tells DOS to search another directory if what you have asked for (dBASE) is not on the current directory. In this case since dBASE is in the directory TOOLS which belongs to the root directory we use the path command as follows:

PATH= \TOOLS

Once you have specified the DOS path, you can switch directories at will. You can always use dBASE — no matter which directory you are currently using — by typing DBASE after the operating system prompt.

The dBASE Directory

dBASE also provides you with a DIR command that you can use to display the names of the files on your disk from within dBASE. The dBASE DIR command is a variation of the DOS DIR command. Used alone, the dBASE DIR command displays specific information about only the database files on your disk. To display the name of the database files on disk drive B we would use the DIR command as shown in Figure 21-5. As you can see, dBASE displays the filenames, the number of database records, the date that each database was last changed, and the size of each file in bytes.

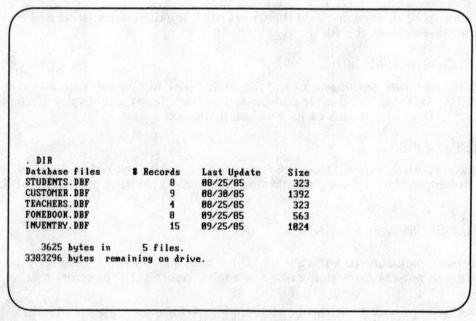

```
. DIR
Database files       # Records    Last Update    Size
STUDENTS.DBF             8         08/25/85        323
CUSTOMER.DBF             9         08/30/85       1392
TEACHERS.DBF             4         08/25/85        323
FONEBOOK.DBF             8         09/25/85        563
INVENTRY.DBF            15         09/25/85       1024

   3625 bytes in       5 files.
3383296 bytes   remaining on drive.
```

Figure 21-5: Displaying database file data

Chapter Twenty-One

Using Wildcards

The basic dBASE directory shows only the names of the database files because all your work with dBASE revolves around these files. You can view the names of other files on your disk by adding to the basic command. For example, to view the names of all the files on your disk, use the DIR command as shown in Figure 21-6. The asterisk (*) is a *wildcard* character that we use to substitute for *all* sequences of characters. The directory display will automatically pause each screenful.

```
. DIR *.*
ANSI.SYS         LIBPATH.SYS      VDISK.SYS        WS.COM
WSOVLY1.OVR      WSMSGS.OVR       DBASE.OVL        DBASE.EXE
DOSEDIT.COM      EXE2BIN.EXE      LINK.EXE         DEBUG.COM
ATTRIB.EXE       FIND.EXE         JOIN.EXE         SHARE.EXE
SORT.EXE         SUBST.EXE        ASSIGN.COM       BACKUP.COM
BASIC.COM        BASICA.COM       CHKDSK.COM       COMMAND.COM
COUNT.EXE        DISKCOMP.COM     DISKCOPY.COM     EDLIN.COM
FDISK.COM        FLOPPY.COM       GRAFTABL.COM     GRAPHICS.COM
KEYBFR.COM       KEYBGR.COM       KEYBIT.COM       KEYBSP.COM
KEYBUK.COM       LABEL.COM        MODE.COM         MORE.COM
PRINT.COM        RECOVER.COM      RESTORE.COM      SELECT.COM
SYS.COM          TREE.COM         NETSU.COM        10NET.COM
LOGIN.EXE        LOGOFF.EXE       MOUNT.EXE        UNMOUNT.EXE
NETSTAT.EXE      NETLOG.EXE       10SPOOL.EXE      XTREE.EXE
DCALC.EXE        DCALC.HLP        HPR.EXE          FORMAT.BAT
MASM.EXE         D.COM            123.EXE          123.HLP
123.CNF          CLEAN.BAT        DBC.COM          DBL.COM
LOTUS.COM        GREP.BAT         VTREE.COM        LIST.COM

1736736 bytes in     72 files.
26791936 bytes remaining on drive.
```

Figure 21-6: Displaying all disk files

We can use the asterisk (*) and another *wildcard* character, the question mark (?) to limit this directory display to just certain kinds of files, such as report form files, or files that begin with the letter D, and so on.

Here are some examples of restricting the directory display with the use of the asterisk.

. DIR D*.*   Filenames beginning with D
. DIR DB*.*   Filenames beginning with DB
. DIR *.   Filenames without a file extension
. DIR *.FRM   All Report Form Files
. DIR *.LBL   All Label Form Files
. DIR *.NDX   All Index Files

The question mark substitutes for a particular character position. Suppose that we want to display all filenames where the third character is a "D." Or, perhaps, we want to see only those filenames that begin with "D" but have five or fewer characters. These are cases where we would use the question mark to substitute for individual characters.

. DIR ??D* . *	Files with D as the third character
. DIR ?????. *	Files with 5 or fewer characters
. DIR * . ?	Files with a one-character extension
. DIR MENU?. *	Five-character files beginning with MENU

These *wildcard* characters are used to help narrow down the display — to help us to locate the files that we want from among the large number that may be on your disk. The *wildcard* characters are used in the same manner with either the dBASE or DOS versions of DIR. As long as you have only a few files, none of this has much value. But if you make use of your computer, you will have a very large number of files. You can count on it.

The wildcard characters * and ? can help you to identify which files are indexes, which are report forms, and so on. If you've got 50 report forms, you will, however, almost certainly end up forgetting which report form belongs to which database file. The same is true with index files and the other services that we use in dBASE.

As we mentioned before, you can organize your disk into subdirectories. dBASE allows you to use files in subdirectories other that the ones that you are currently using. For example, suppose that you are in the subdirectory MYFILES and you want to use a particular database file, say CHARGES, that is in the subdirectory LAUREN. To use this file, simply refer to it by its absolute pathname.

. USE \LAUREN\CHARGES

Similarly, you can use files in subdirectories that lie on a path below the directory you are in by means of the relative pathname. For example, if we are in MYFILES, we can use the database BILLINGS with the command:

. USE CLIENTS\BILLINGS

because CLIENTS is a subdirectory of MYFILES.

To view the names of files in another subdirectory, you should follow the directory name with a backslash. To view database files in the subdirectory CLIENTS you would use the command:

. DIR CLIENTS\

To view other files in the subdirectory, use the wildcard characters as described above. For example, to view index files in the subdirectory CLIENTS you would use the command:

. DIR CLIENTS* .NDX

One small drawback to the dBASE version of DIR is that it does not allow you to see the names of subdirectories. If you do need to look at subdirectory names, you must either leave dBASE — or (if you have enough memory) you can use the run command. The RUN command allows you to execute DOS commands and use other programs from within dBASE. To use the DOS command DIR you would use the command:

. RUN DIR

To use this command, your computer must have at least 320 kilobytes of main memory — and the logged disk drive must have the DOS program COMMAND.COM. If you have this command you can change directories while using dBASE with :

. RUN CD CLIENTS

dBASE Paths

There is another way to make use of files from other subdirectories without either changing subdirectories or using pathnames. You can simply specify one or more *paths* that dBASE should search for the files that you want. Let's suppose that we frequently use files from the MYFILES subdirectory CLIENTS as well as from LAUREN's directory. We can specify that dBASE is to always look in the subdirectories *as well as the current subdirectory* with the command:

. SET PATH TO CLIENTS, \LAUREN

Once we have done this, we can use Lauren's file CHARGES with this command:

. USE CHARGES

dBASE first searches the current directory MYFILES. If CHARGES is not there, CLIENTS is search-ed. If the file CHARGES is still not found, the subdirectory LAUREN is searched. Note that CLIENTS is a relative pathname while LAUREN is an absolute pathname.

Another advantage of using subdirectories is that you can have two or more files with the same name — if you try to put both of them in the same subdirectory. You can even use files with the same name at the same time by using an ALIAS. An ALIAS is an alternative name assigned to a work area at the time a database is opened. Let's imagine that we have two files named PAYMENTS. One is in the subdirectory \LAUREN and the other in \MYFILES\CLIENTS. To open both payments files at the same time, we would use:

. USE \LAUREN\PAYMENTS ALIAS PAY1
. SELECT 2
. USE \MYFILES\CLIENTS\PAYMENTS

In order to do this we *must* assign an alias to the first of the two files. If we do not assign an alias to the first file, dBASE will not allow us to open the second file of the same name — even if we attempt to assign an alias to the second file.

THE dBASE III PLUS CATALOG

Beginning with dBASE III Plus, dBASE offers another tool that you can use to help you keep track of your database files and all their ancillary files. We can use the dBASE *catalog* to help us remember what each database file is for, and to keep track of all the files that belong to each database file. Each database can have several supporting files; indexes, report forms, label forms, views, queries, and custom screens. A CATALOG is used to keep an inventory of each database and its supporting files. To help you keep track of what each file is for, the catalog also lets you enter a 76-character description of each file.

To use this feature, you must first turn it on. Once on, it's all automatic. The CATALOG is turned on with the command:

```
. SET CATALOG TO CATALOG
     Enter File Title:
```

which is used to tell dBASE that you want to use the *master* catalog. This master catalog is a disk file named CATALOG.CAT. If it doesn't already exist, it will be created and you will be asked (one time only) for a file title — this is a description of the file. In *this* case you might enter something like "master catalog." If you are using floppy disks, it might be advisable to enter a description of what the particular floppy disk is for.

Once the catalog has been activated, each time you create a new dBASE database file, or a supporting file such as a report form, the name of the file will be added to the catalog and you will be asked for a description of the file. Similarly, whenever you use a database file that is not yet in the catalog (such as the files we created earlier in this book) the filename will be added to the catalog, and you will be asked for a description of the file.

Once your files have been catalogued, you can go through the catalog to make use of them. For example, when you want to use a database, you can employ the familiar USE command — followed by a question mark rather than a filename:

```
. USE ?
```

This command produces the screen display shown in Figure 21-7. This display shows you the names of all the database files in the catalog together with the file description of the filename that is highlighted. Use the Up and Down arrow keys to move the highlight. Each time a different filename is highlighted, the description for that file will appear in the box in the lower right-hand section of the screen. To select a file, you simply highlight the filename and press Return. To escape from the display, press Esc. You can still use any files in the old-fashioned way.

The real value of the catalog lies in its ability to keep track of all the supporting files that you have for each of your database files. Each database file can have index files, report form files, format (custom screen) files, view files, query files, and label form files. If you have several of these supporting files for each of your database files, the disk directory will become cluttered, and you might have difficulty remembering what each file is for and which database it belongs to. The catalog does this remembering for you. When the catalog is activated, you can substitute a question mark wherever you might otherwise use a filename. For example, when you want to run a report, use the command:

```
. REPORT ?
```

and you will automantically obtain a list of all of the reports that belong to the database file in use — together with a description of each. The commands for producing catalog displays are:

```
. USE ?
. SET INDEX TO ?
. REPORT FORM ?
. LABEL FORM ?
. SET FORMAT TO ?
. SET VIEW TO ?
. SET FILTER TO FILE ?
. SET CATALOG TO ?
```

Chapter Twenty-One

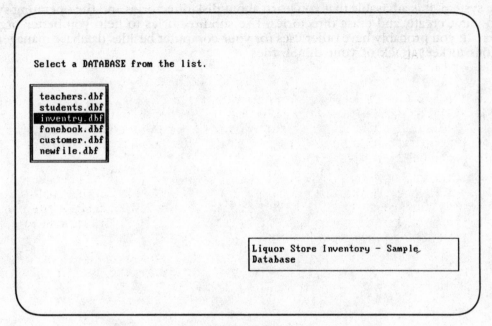

Figure 21-7

When you are using dBASE with an active catalog, the catalog uses work area 10. The catalog is actually a database file that dBASE uses in a special way. Normally, dBASE maintains the catalog, adding, deleting, and editing as necessary. Whenever you delete a file, the filename will be removed from the catalog. However, if you should happen to get rid of a file from outside of dBASE the catalog won't know that. In this case you will need to do your own maintenance of the catalog. Use the delete and pack commands to remove unwanted files from the catalog. You can use all the commands that have been described in this book to edit the catalog.

You can turn the catalog *on* and *off*. For example, suppose that you want to create a temporary file. Rather than add it to the catalog we can temporarily turn the catalog off with the command:

. SET CATALOG OFF

While the catalog is turned off, changes that we make to our database environment will not be incorporated into the catalog. To turn the catalog back on, use the command:

. SET CATALOG ON

You can have more than one catalog. It may be more convenient for you to create *special-purpose* catalogs to monitor groups of files that are normally used together. One example of such a group might be an inventory management system where we have separate database files for the inventory itself, suppliers, and items on order. These files and their supporting files might be contained in a special inventory catalog to keep track of the fact they are to be used together. If you do have more than one catalog, you must still have the master catalog — named CATALOG.CAT.

In this chapter we have discussed some of the techniques that you can use to keep track of your database files and all their supporting files. Some of the tools that you can use are provided by your operating system. Although dBASE does not require that you know anything about the

Directories, Catalogs, and Dictionaries

operating system, it is advisable that you learn about disk directories and the operating system commands to view, create, and erase directories. Use subdirectories to help you better organize your data. After all, you probably have other uses for your computer besides database management. And, use catalogs to keep track of your dBASE files.

CHAPTER TWENTY-TWO

FILTERS, QUERIES, AND VIEWS

The databases files used in this book are small; they have only a few fields and not many records. In the real world, the databases that you'll be working with will have many records. Some may have a very large number of fields. You will find that working with these large database files can be, at times, cumbersome. Fortunately, the designers of database management systems are aware of this and provide you with tools that you can use to make your database (temporarily) smaller and more manageable. The tools that dBASE provides are filters, queries, and views.

FILTERS

As we have seen, you can *select* the records that are to be used with each command. For example, to display only the SCOTCH records from our INVENTRY database we use

. DISPLAY FOR LIQUOR = 'SCOTCH'

Each time we select these particular records we need to add the clause FOR LIQUOR = 'SCOTCH' to the command. We can, however, cause dBASE to pretend that the database contains *only* these records. We do this by setting a *filter*. When a filter is in effect the database will seem to contain only the records that have been specified. To set a filter so that the database seems to contain only SCOTCH records, use

. SET FILTER TO LIQUOR = 'SCOTCH'

```
. SET FILTER TO LIQUOR = 'SCOTCH'
. DISPLAY ALL
Record#  LIQUOR     BRAND                 SIZE      QUANTITY   COST   PRICE
      1  SCOTCH     AULD COUNTRY          QUART           23   5.59    9.31
      2  SCOTCH     AULD COUNTRY          2 LITER          7   9.78   16.30
      3  SCOTCH     AULD COUNTRY          PINT            88   2.74    4.56
. SUM
      3 records summed
   QUANTITY       COST        PRICE
        118      18.11        30.17
.
Command Line    │<A:>│INVENTRY                    │Rec: EOF/15              │          │ Caps
```

Enter a dBASE III PLUS command.

Figure 22-1

Figure 22-1 shows the effect of the DISPLAY and SUM commands with a filter. In both cases, we could use the command without specifying a condition because the condition is already specified in the SET FILTER command.

To limit the database to only QUARTS of SCOTCH, *change* the filter setting to

. SET FILTER TO LIQUOR = 'SCOTCH' .AND. SIZE = 'QUART'

To turn off the filter to view the entire database again, use the SET FILTER command *without* any condition:

. SET FILTER TO

When you leave dBASE, or USE another database file, any filter in use is automatically forgotten by dBASE.

FIELD "FILTERS"

In a similar manner, you can view *selected* fields from your database by adding a *field list* to your command. For example, to display *only* the three fields BRAND, SIZE, and QUANTITY, use

. DISPLAY BRAND,SIZE,QUANTITY

If you want to use these fields in successive commands, you must add the field list to each command. Another way is the field "filter" SET FIELDS. This command is similar to the SET FILTER command except that you specify the fields that you want to use. After you enter this command,

. SET FIELDS TO BRAND,SIZE,QUANTITY

dBASE will pretend that only these fields are in the database. In fact, if you specifically request another field, you will be told that it doesn't exist. Figure 22-2 shows the response to the DISPLAY command (with record filter on) with SET FIELDS in effect.

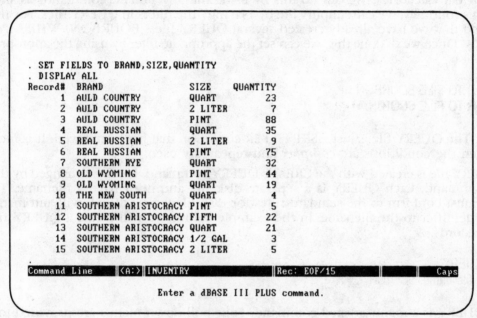

```
. SET FIELDS TO BRAND,SIZE,QUANTITY
. DISPLAY ALL
Record#  BRAND                SIZE      QUANTITY
       1  AULD COUNTRY         QUART           23
       2  AULD COUNTRY         2 LITER          7
       3  AULD COUNTRY         PINT            88
       4  REAL RUSSIAN         QUART           35
       5  REAL RUSSIAN         2 LITER          9
       6  REAL RUSSIAN         PINT            75
       7  SOUTHERN RYE         QUART           32
       8  OLD WYOMING          PINT            44
       9  OLD WYOMING          QUART           19
      10  THE NEW SOUTH        QUART            4
      11  SOUTHERN ARISTOCRACY PINT             5
      12  SOUTHERN ARISTOCRACY FIFTH           22
      13  SOUTHERN ARISTOCRACY QUART           21
      14  SOUTHERN ARISTOCRACY 1/2 GAL          3
      15  SOUTHERN ARISTOCRACY 2 LITER          5
```
```
Command Line    <A:> INVENTRY              Rec: EOF/15              Caps
```
Enter a dBASE III PLUS command.

Figure 22-2

SET FIELDS offers an important advantage when you are working with multiple database files. Let's suppose that you are working with a STUDENTS file and a TEACHERS file. The STUDENTS file is *related* to the TEACHERS file by the content of a field ROOM. (This is the example used in the chapter on Multiple Databases). If you need to specify fields from both files, it is often more convenient to use SET FIELDS. The field list can contain field names from *more* than one file.

. SET FIELDS TO STUDENTS->NAME,TEACHERS->NAME

To change the field list, just use the SET FIELDS command with the new field list. To "turn off" the SET FIELDS command, you must use

. SET FIELDS OFF

which, you should notice, is different from the way you turn off a record filter. On the other hand, the command

. SET FIELDS ON

Filters, Queries, and Views

will restore your field filter.

QUERIES

In many cases, we will want to work with just selected parts of a database at a time. In our liquor store inventory example, it might be reasonable to work, in turn, with records from each of the LIQUOR categories. We can do this by using the SET FILTER commands as shown above. If we do this routinely, we can simplify life by "saving" the filters in QUERY files. For the moment, let's pretend that we have already created several QUERY files: BOURBON, WHISKEY, SCOTCH, and VODKA. Once we've done this, we can set the appropriate filter by using the appropriate QUERY file:

. SET FILTER TO FILE BOURBON
. SET FILTER TO FILE SCOTCH

and so on. The QUERY file is just a SET FILTER condition that has been saved. It is most practical to use when the conditions are *complex* and repeatedly used.

A QUERY file is created with the CREATE QUERY command. It can be changed by the MODIFY QUERY command. Each QUERY is a separate disk file and must have a filename. The QUERY filenames must conform to the standard rules for disk filenames. dBASE will automatically add a .QRY file identifier to the filename. In the example below, we will create a QUERY file to select SCOTCH records.

. CREATE QUERY
Enter Query file name: SCOTCH

CREATE QUERY is a menu-assisted command. Four pull-down menus are provided to guide you through the process of creating a QUERY file. The initial menu is shown as Figure 22-3. Use the Left and Right arrow keys to select from among the four menus shown on the top line of Figure 22-3. Use the Up and Down arrow keys to move the light bar to highlight a particular menu selection. Choose the highlighted selection by pressing Return.

We need to go through the steps to specify the condition LIQUOR = 'SCOTCH' as the content of our QUERY file SCOTCH.

Step 1 identifies the field to be used in the query. Highlight the SET FILTER selection *Field Name*, then press Return. A submenu of fieldnames appears. Move the highlight to the desired fieldname — in this case LIQUOR. Press Return again and the field is selected.

Step 2 identifies the operator to be used. In this case the operator is the = sign. Highlight *Operator* as shown in Figure 22-4. Press Return. A submenu containing the list of possible operators appears. In this case we can choose either of the = equal sign selections: *Matches* or *Begins with*. That will not always be the case. *Matches* means that the field contains only blank spaces following the specified item, in this case the letters SCOTCH. *Begins with* allows nonblank spaces to follow what we specify.

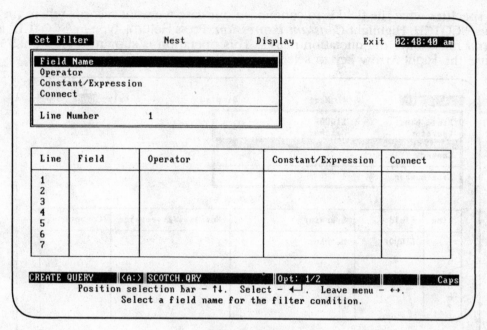

Figure 22-3

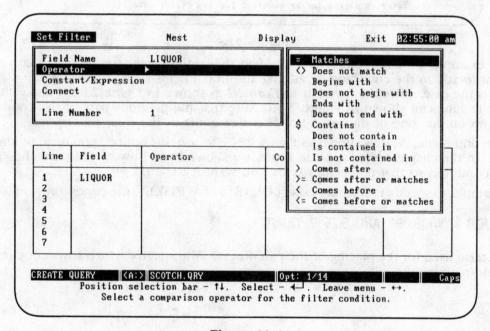

Figure 22-4

Filters, Queries, and Views

Step 3 specifies what the field is to contain. In our case we want records where the LIQUOR field matches SCOTCH. Highlight *Constant/Expression*. Press Return. Type in 'SCOTCH' as shown. Note that *you* must enter the quotation marks. This operation is shown in Figure 22-5. To save our filter, use the Right Arrow key to select the Exit menu.

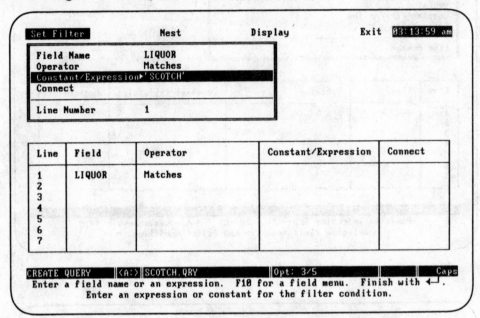

Figure 22-5

In our example, we have completely specified the condition for the filter. In many cases we would want to add to the condition by adding additional items such as .AND. SIZE = 'QUART'. When this is the case, move the light bar to *Connect* as shown in Figure 22-6. Press Return. This gives you the submenu shown in Figure 22-6. Note that the previous part of the condition has been built up on line one of the seven-line box that contains the filter description.

The second menu, *Nest*, is shown as Figure 22-7. To use this option, you need to know what a "nest" is. In the chapter called A Little Logic, we showed you how to put parentheses around parts of a condition so that it specifies what you want it to.

For example, to specify everything except QUARTS of WHISKEY, the condition would look like

. .NOT. (LIQUOR = 'WHISKEY' .AND. SIZE = 'QUART')

Nest is the term used for the placing of the parentheses. You specify which rows contain the starting and ending parentheses.

Chapter Twenty-Two

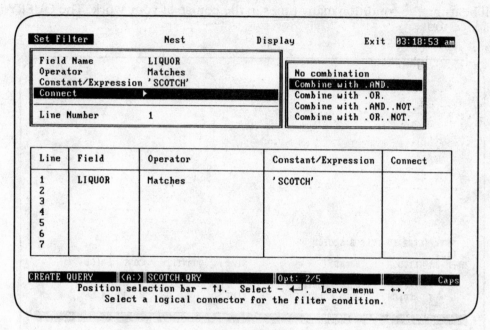

Figure 22-6

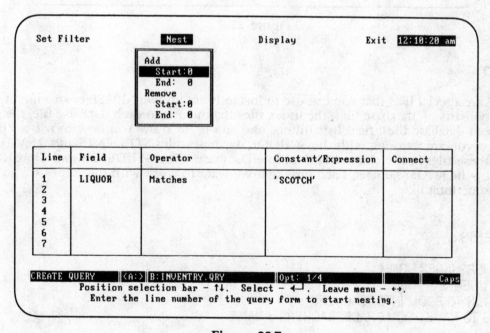

Figure 22-7

As shown in Figure 22-8, we can use this QUERY whenever we want to limit the database to SCOTCH records. Sometimes it takes more time to construct this filter than to simply specify the filter from the keyboard. The value of the QUERY file comes when the condition is *complex*

Filters, Queries, and Views

and you will be using the condition many times in the course of your work. The QUERY in dBASE is a convenience tool.

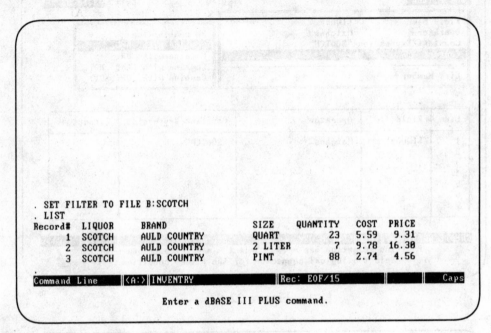

```
. SET FILTER TO FILE B:SCOTCH
. LIST
Record#   LIQUOR    BRAND           SIZE      QUANTITY   COST   PRICE
      1   SCOTCH    AULD COUNTRY    QUART           23   5.59    9.31
      2   SCOTCH    AULD COUNTRY    2 LITER          7   9.78   16.38
      3   SCOTCH    AULD COUNTRY    PINT            88   2.74    4.56
.
```

| Command Line | ⟨A:⟩ INVENTRY | Rec: EOF/15 | | Caps |

Enter a dBASE III PLUS command.

Figure 22-8

VIEWS

VIEWS are special files that you can use to instantly set up your dBASE environment. The environment consists of: database files, the index files that belong to each database file, the relationships between database files, field lists, filters, and so on. To show you how to use a VIEW, let's suppose that you are working with the SCHOOL databases files STUDENTS and TEACHERS. We developed these files in the chapter on Multiple Databases. The STUDENTS and TEACHERS files are related by the ROOM number. Each time that we want to work with these files we go through a process something like

```
. SELECT 1
. USE STUDENTS
. SELECT 2
. USE TEACHERS INDEX ROOM
. SELECT STUDENTS
. SET RELATION TO ROOM INTO TEACHERS
. SET FIELDS TO NAME,ROOM,GRADE,TEACHERS->NAME
```

This process becomes even more complex if we have more database files and relationships between files — and still more complex if we add in filters and format files (Custom Screens). We still haven't done any work — we've just set up our initial operating environment. If we do this all the time, it can become a bother. dBASE provides a way that you can accomplish all this with a single command:

Chapter Twenty-Two

. SET VIEW TO SCHOOL

In this command, SCHOOL is a VIEW file which was created by the CREATE VIEW command.

. CREATE VIEW
Enter view file name: SCHOOL

Each VIEW is contained in a separate disk file. The names of VIEW files must conform to the standard rules for disk filenames. dBASE will automatically add the file identifier .VUE to the filename. An existing VIEW file can be changed with the MODIFY VIEW command.

CREATE VIEW leads you through the process of creating a VIEW with a series of five menus. The names of each of the five menus are shown on the top line of Figure 22-9, the initial menu selection. Menus are selected by using the Left and Right arrow keys. Options within menus are chosen by first moving the light bar to highlight an option, then pressing the Return key.

The Set Up Menu

The Set Up Menu is a list of database files. The first step in creating a VIEW is to choose the database files that are to be included. Highlight a filename that you want included in the VIEW. Press the Return key. A small triangular marker will appear to the left of the filename. A submenu of possible index filenames will be displayed to the right of the Set Up menu (shown in Figure 22-9). Highlight the name of each index file to be included. Press Return. (You can only select index files that belong to the currently selected database). To return to the database menu, press the Left Arrow key.

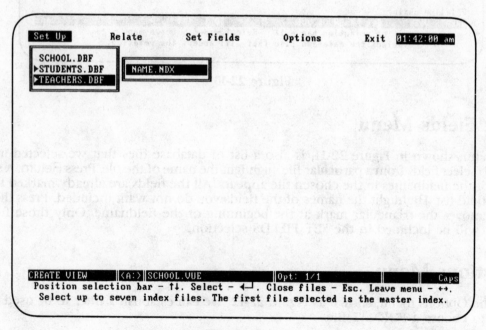

Figure 22-9

Filters, Queries, and Views

The Relate Menu

The Relate Menu is a list of database files selected with the help of the Set Up Menu. Select the STUDENTS file. Press Return. The remaining selected files will be displayed in a submenu as shown in Figure 22-10. Move the light bar to highlight the name of the file that is to be related to STUDENTS — TEACHERS. Press Return. The next step is to identify how STUDENTS and TEACHERS are related. Enter the name of the field in STUDENTS that is to link the two files together — ROOM.

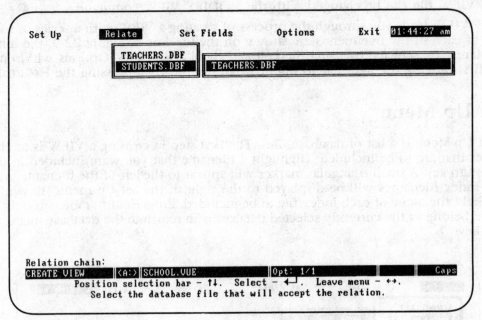

Figure 22-10

The Set Fields Menu

The menu, shown in Figure 22-11, is also a list of database files that we selected in the Set Up menu. To select fields from a particular file, highlight the name of the file. Press Return. A submenu consisting of the fieldnames in the chosen file appears. All the fields are already marked for inclusion in the field list. Highlight the names of the fields you do not want included. Press the Return key. This removes the triangular mark at the beginning of the fieldname. Only those fields that are marked will be included in the SET FIELDS selection.

The Options Menu

With the Options menu, shown as Figure 22-12, we can establish a filter to be used with the VIEW and to choose a FORMAT file.

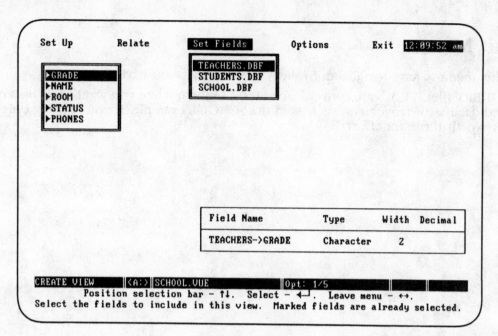

Figure 22-11

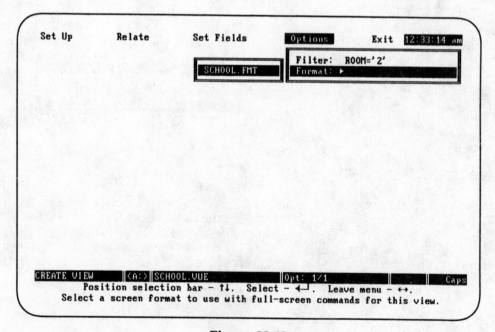

Figure 22-12

Filters, Queries, and Views

The Exit Menu

Use this menu to save (or abandon) the VIEW file that you have just created.

Like QUERY files, VIEWS are convenience files. Use them when you want to set up a relatively complicated database arrangement, such as in the SCHOOL example. If you're using only a single file, it isn't worth the extra effort.

CHAPTER TWENTY-THREE

dBASE ASSISTANT

The dBASE Assistant provides you with access to all of the basic database management operations through a series of menus. Many software designers feel that it is easier to learn to use the database by selecting from a list of options than to enter commands directly. For many users, this is true. However, the command mode (entering commands from the dBASE dot prompt) is preferable for frequent users. The menu mode (the Assistant) becomes invaluable for the new and the occasional user. The Assistant provides the ability to:

- Create and use database files
- Create and use catalogs, views, filters, and custom screens
- Prepare reports and labels
- SORT, INDEX, and COPY
- Add to, delete from, and edit database files
- Obtain information
- Copy, delete, and rename disk files

Beginning with dBASE III PLUS, dBASE automatically *comes up* in the Assistant mode (Figure 23-1). To leave the Assistant, press the Esc key. You will then be in the command mode. To return to the Assistant, press F2 or enter the command

. ASSIST

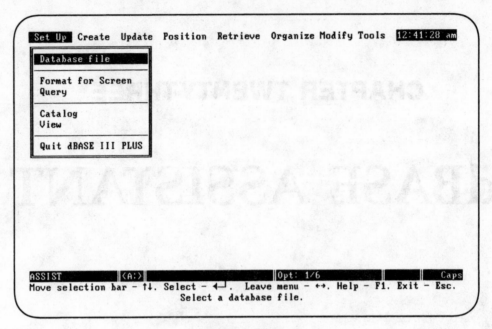

Figure 23-1

For those readers who would prefer to have dBASE come up in the command mode (the dot prompt), change the name of the file CONFIG.DB, which is located on the disk with the dBASE program to CONFIG.SAV.

The Assistant provides you with a selection of eight menus. The names of these menus are shown on the top line of Figure 23-1. The top line of the assistant is the *main menu* — a menu of menus. Upon entering the Assistant, the *Set Up* menu is already selected for you. The menu name *Set Up* is highlighted, and the content of the *Set Up* menu is displayed.

To select a different menu, use the Left or Right arrow keys. Each time you press one of these keys, the light bar that highlights the name of the current selection will move one selection in the direction of the arrow key. The contents of the new menu selection will be displayed on screen. You can also select a menu by pressing the key corresponding to the first letter of the menu name. For example, to move to the *Position* menu, press "P".

To select an option from within a menu, use the Up and Down arrow keys. Each time you press one of these keys, the highlight within the menu will move one selection in the direction of the arrow key. When the desired selection is highlighted, press the Return key. This activates the highlighted selection.

If you would like information about a menu selection, press F1 *before* you make the selection. This action will provide you information about the dBASE command associated with the menu item. Figure 23-2 shows the help information belonging the menu selection shown in Figure 23-1.

Each menu selection is associated with a dBASE command. As you make each selection, the dBASE command will be displayed on the line just above the status bar. By observing this line you will gradually become familiar with the dBASE command language. This line displays the same command that you would use from the dot prompt.

Information about which keys can be used, and what they do, is always displayed just below the status bar — at the bottom of the screen.

Chapter Twenty-Three

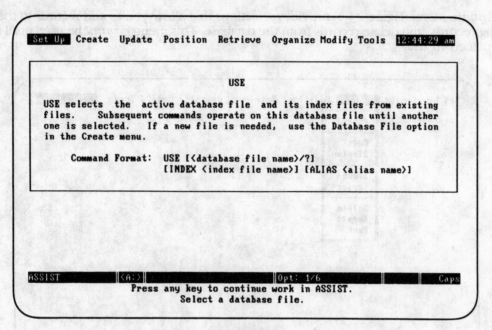

Figure 23-2

The **Create** Menu (Figure 23-3) allows you to create six different kinds of dBASE files: databases, format or custom screen files, views, queries, report forms, and label forms. Creating a file from the Assistant is just the same as creating the file from the dot prompt.

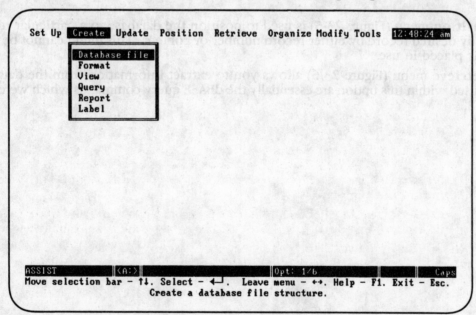

Figure 23-3

The **Update** menu (Figure 23-4) provides selections that allow you to add records to the database, edit existing records, and delete records from the database. This menu *cannot* be used until a database has been placed in use.

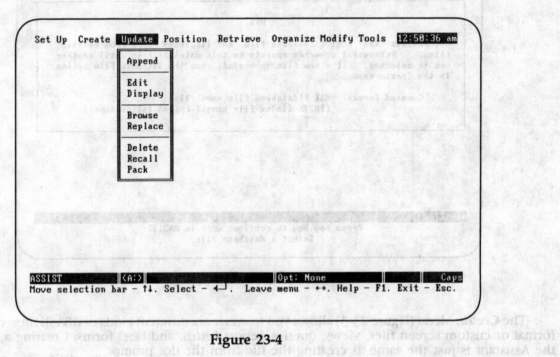

Figure 23-4

The **Position** menu (Figure 23-5) is used to position the database to a particular record. You can locate any desired record by either record number or content. This menu cannot be used until a database is placed in use.

The **Retrieve** menu (Figure 23-6) allows you to extract information from the database. The commands used within this option are essentially the dBASE query commands which were discussed in Chapter 8.

Chapter Twenty-Three

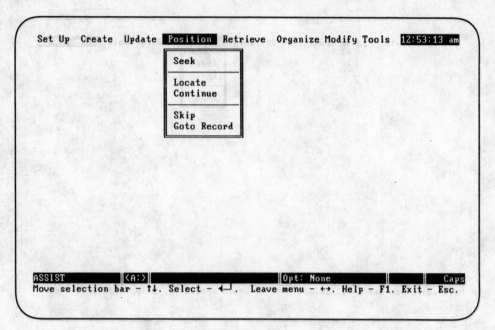

Figure 23-5

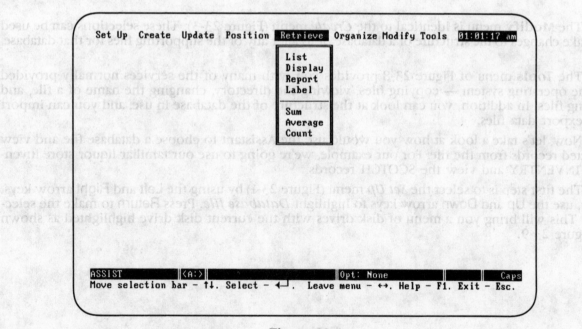

Figure 23-6

The **Organize** menu shown in Figure 23-7 is used to index or sort the database that you are currently using. You can also use this particular selection to make a copy of all or any part of the current database.

dBASE Assistant

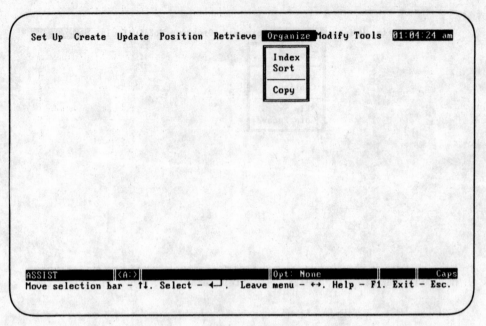

Figure 23-7

The **Modify** menu is identical to the *Create* menu (Figure 23-3). These selections can be used to make changes to the structure of a database or to alter any of the supporting files for that database.

The **Tools** menu of Figure 23-8 provides you with many of the services normally provided by the operating system — copying files, viewing the directory, changing the name of a file, and erasing files. In addition, you can look at the structure of the database in use, and you can import and export data files.

Now, let's take a look at how you would use the Assistant to choose a database file and view selected records from the file. For our example, we're going to use our familiar liquor store inventory INVENTRY and view the SCOTCH records.

The first step is to select the *Set Up* menu (Figure 23-1) by using the Left and Right arrow keys. Next, use the Up and Down arrow keys to highlight *Database file*. Press Return to make the selection. This will bring you a menu of disk drives with the current disk drive highlighted as shown in Figure 23-9.

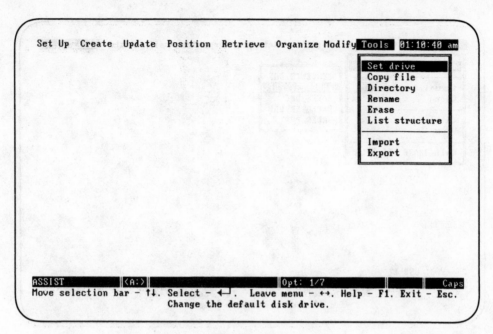

Figure 23-8

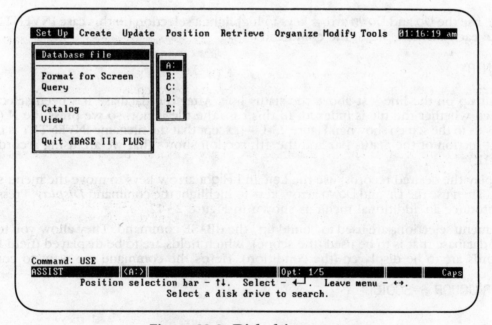

Figure 23-9: Disk drive menu

Use the Up and Down arrow keys to highlight the disk drive that the database is on. Press Return. The disk drive menu will be replaced by a menu of database files (Figure 23-10).

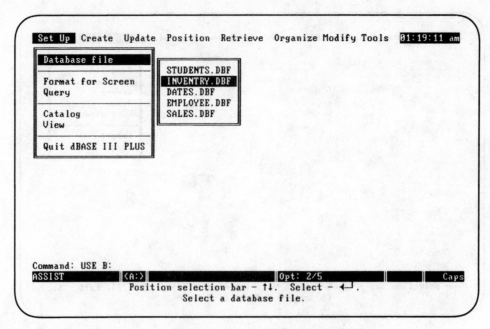

Figure 23-10: Menu of database files

Once again, use the Up and Down arrow keys to highlight a selection (in this case INVENTRY.DBF). As you take each of these steps, the command

USE B:INVENTRY

will be built up on the line just above the status line. After the database has been selected, you will be asked whether the file is indexed. In this case the file is not, so we press the N (No) key. This returns us to the screen shown in Figure 23-1 — except that the filename INVENTRY is displayed in the third section of the Status Bar and the 4th section shows that we are using record 1 of 15 (Figure 23-11.)

To display the desired records, use the Left and Right arrow keys to move the menu selection to *Retrieve*. Then use the Up and Down arrow keys to highlight the command *Display*. Press Return. This will produce an additional menu as shown in Figure 23-12.

These menu selections are used to "build up" the dBASE command. They allow you to specify the part of database that is to be used (the scope), which fields are to be displayed (field list), and which records are to be displayed (the condition). Here's the command we want to construct:

DISPLAY FOR LIQUOR = 'SCOTCH'

Chapter Twenty-Three

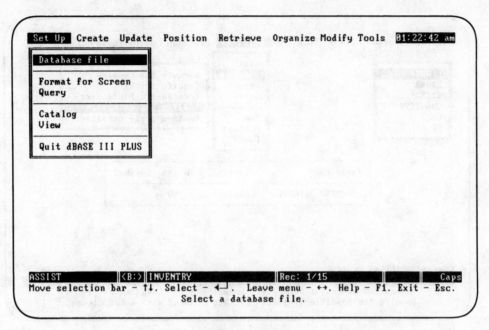

Figure 23-11

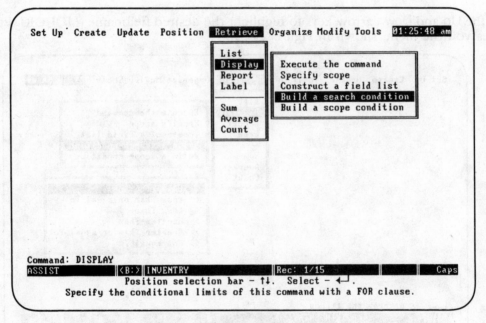

Figure 23-12

Use the Up and Down arrow keys to highlight *Build a search condition*. Press Return. This provides you with a menu of fields from your database (Figure 23-13).

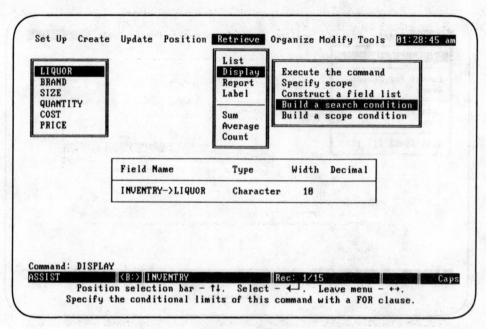

Figure 23-13

Use the Up and Down arrow keys to highlight the desired fieldname (LIQUOR). Press Return. This gives you the menu shown in Figure 23-14.

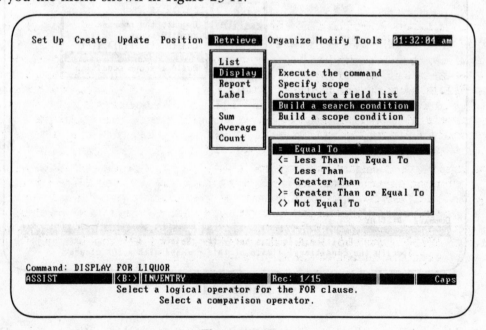

Figure 23-14

This is a menu of operators. Use the Up and Down arrow key to highlight = Equal To. Press Return. You will be asked to enter a character string (Figure 23-15).

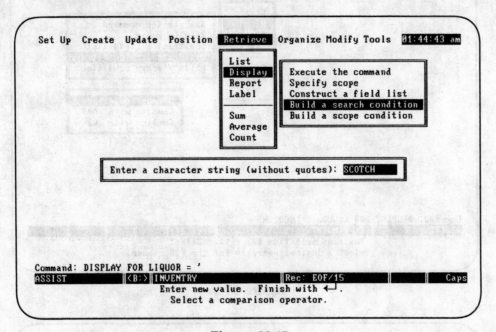

```
Set Up  Create  Update  Position  Retrieve  Organize Modify Tools   01:44:43 am
                      List
                      Display
                      Report        Execute the command
                      Label         Specify scope
                                    Construct a field list
                      Sum           Build a search condition
                      Average       Build a scope condition
                      Count

         Enter a character string (without quotes): SCOTCH




Command: DISPLAY FOR LIQUOR = '
ASSIST        <B:> INVENTRY            Rec: EOF/15              Caps
                    Enter new value.  Finish with ⏎ .
                    Select a comparison operator.
```

Figure 23-15

Enter the characters SCOTCH. This will give you a menu that allows you to tack on additional conditions to your command (Figure 23-16).

Note that our desired command has already been built up on the line above the status bar. In this case we don't want to add any more conditions. Highlight the top selection *No more conditions*. Press Return. We're back to Figure 23-12. Highlight *Execute The Command* and press Return. This displays the desired records as shown in Figure 23-17. Remember, this command sequence is only an example. You can build any condition, using the menus, that you require to extract any information available in the current database. All that is required of you is that you know what you want or need and Assist does almost all the rest.

As you can see, the Assistant has "walked" you through the process of constructing the command. As in all menu systems, there are limits to what you can do. Suppose you wanted to display COST * QUANTITY. You can't. As menu systems go, the Assistant is very good. Menu systems are not usually well-suited for general-purpose use. They are excellent when dealing with closed systems — such as defining a report. However, the Assistant is an excellent way to learn the basic construction of dBASE commands. And, it also provides an invaluable tool for the infrequent dBASE user who may forget the details of the command language between uses.

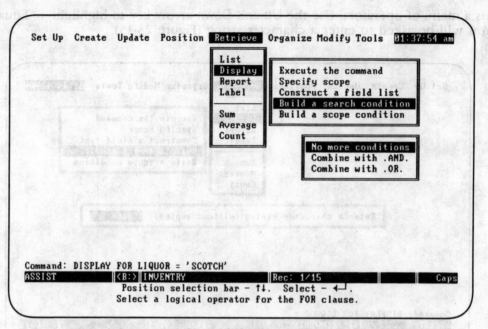

Figure 23-16

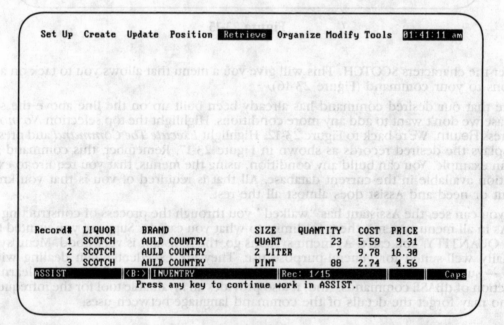

Figure 23-17

SECTION SIX
INTRODUCTION
TO PROGRAMMING

Section Six is about power, speed, and ease. The computer's capabilities can be dramatically enhanced by teaching it some tricks. It is not hard to teach the computer tricks — and you can customize these tricks to support your specific information storing and reporting needs.

We'll use familiar database examples to define menu options, to make use of DO WHILE clauses, and to automate routine activities that customize our system, giving us a greater "reach" and saving us time and energy. The customization gives us the very useful ability to produce specific reports.

CHAPTER TWENTY-FOUR

THE FINE ART OF PROCEDURES

Most database management systems have a query language processor and a report writer. These two DBMS features can probably satisfy most, if not all, of your needs. Any further need is easily accommodated using simple procedures. In previous chapters, we discussed several examples of procedure-generated special processes. You can use procedures to construct exactly what you want the computer to do for you in a specific circumstance. This process not only provides custom, deluxe, "designed-for-you" computer output, but also provides a practical way to save you work.

To illustrate how a procedure can save you effort, we will work through a simple example of a check-register database. This sample database, B:CHECKREG, has a plan which is shown as Figure 24-1. In this particular example we have chosen to have a logic field indicate whether the amount is for a check or a deposit. A "Y" indicates that the amount is a deposit. To calculate the account balance, proceed with the query language dialogue in Figure 24-2.

FIELD	FIELD DESCRIPTION	FIELDNAME	TYPE	WIDTH	DECIMALS
1	Check Number	CHECKNO	N	4	
2	Paid To	PAIDTO	C	20	
3	Amount of Check or Dep	AMOUNT	N	7	2
4	Deposit or Check	DEPOSIT	L	1	
5	Deductible (Y/N)	DEDUCT	L	1	
6	Cancelled (Y/N)	CANCEL	L	1	
7	Date (mm/dd/yy)	DATE	D	8	

Figure 24-1: Check-register database plan

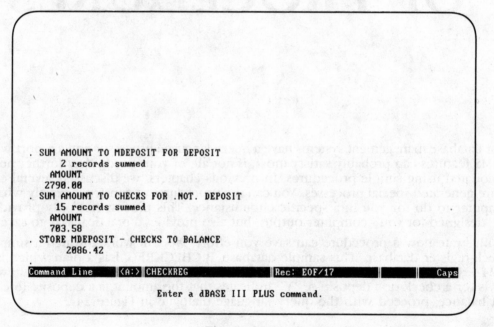

Figure 24-2

The memory variable that stores the sum of the deposits is called MDEPOSIT. The temptation to name the variable DEPOSIT is unfortunate: a data field and a memory variable should not have the same name. It will confuse the computer.

Note: In this example, we add all the checks and all the deposits each time we calculate the balance. In a conventional checkbook, we usually keep a running balance. With the computer it is often easier to calculate the balance each time than to keep a running balance.

As you can see, there are three instructions required to determine the bank balance. We will likely want to know the bank balance often. To save ourselves the work and nuisance of typing three instructions each time we want to know the balance, we will create a means for the com-

Chapter Twenty-Four

puter to remember the instructions: a procedure.

We help the computer to remember a procedure by placing the instructions on a special disk file. This file, containing the instructions, is available whenever we want to use it. In dBASE, this special file is called a *command file*. A command file provides the capability to *save* a group of commands so that we can use them, as a group, without retyping them each time. To get the computer to remember a procedure, you must first tell it that you are going to write one. In dBASE, this is done with the command MODIFY COMMAND:

. MODIFY COMMAND

The computer responds with a request for a filename. The same filename rules apply as have applied for database files and report files. A filename must have 8 or fewer characters and must begin with a letter. You should also identify which disk drive the procedure is to be stored on by using a disk drive identifier. In this example we will call the command file BALANCE, and place it on the B drive.

Enter filename: B:BALANCE

The video screen then clears and displays

dBASE Word Processor

in the upper left-hand corner of the screen. There will be no dot prompt. There is nothing wrong — this is a special screen provided for this command. Type in the instructions one after another just as though you were typing on a blank sheet of paper (Figure 24-3).

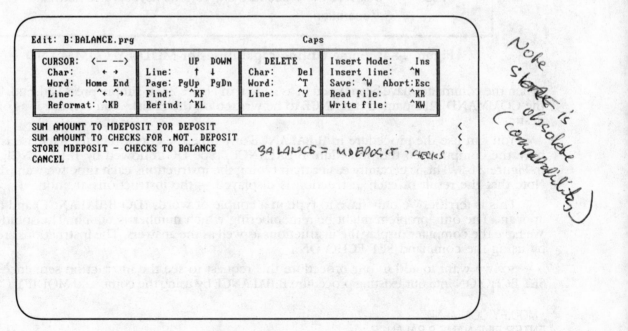

Figure 24-3

The Fine Art of Procedures

Note that an extra line has been added to the end of the procedure. This line contains the single word CANCEL. This is to return control of the computer to the keyboard after the computer has completed the procedure.

The computer will not execute the instructions while you are writing a procedure. Because most of us are not perfect typists, the system provides a limited editing capability through use of the control and arrow keys. Editing capabilities and the associated control keys are shown in Figure 24-4.

KEY	EDITING ACTION
←	Moves cursor 1 character left
→	Moves cursor 1 character right
↑	Moves cursor 1 line up
↓	Moves cursor 1 line down
^N	Makes a blank line
^Y	Deletes a line
^T	Deletes a word
Del	Deletes a character
Ins	Inserts characters
^End	Saves the procedure on disk and returns the keyboard to normal operation
Esc	Discards the procedure and returns keyboard to normal operation

Figure 24-4: Some editing capabilities of MODIFY COMMAND

When the commands have been typed in as shown in Figure 24-3, simply press Ctrl-End. This causes the COMMAND FILE named BALANCE to be written on the B disk: you can use it as often as you desire.

You can use the procedure in B:BALANCE any time the check register database is in use. To have the computer do the procedure B:BALANCE, type DO followed by B:BALANCE, as shown in Figure 24-5. This is certainly easier than typing the instructions each time we want the balance. Note that the result of each instruction is displayed — the instructions are not.

This is terrific. We only have to type in a couple of words (DO B:BALANCE) and the answer appears. The only problem might be remembering which number is which. The solution is easy: We have the computer display the instructions as well as the answers. The instructions are displayed by using the command SET ECHO ON.

So, we want to add to our procedure this request to see the instruction sequence. We insert SET ECHO ON into our existing procedure B:BALANCE by using the command MODIFY COMMAND.

```
. MODIFY COMMAND
ENTER FILE NAME:B:BALANCE
```

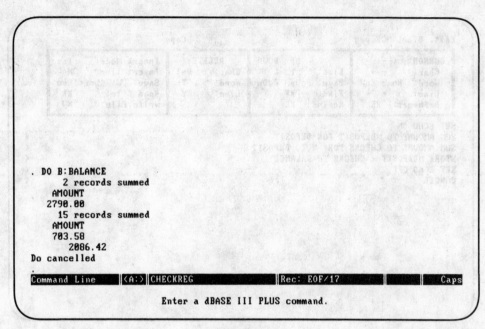

Figure 24-5

The screen will be erased and the existing file, B:BALANCE, will be displayed. The cursor will be positioned at the upper left-hand corner of the screen directly on the "S" of the first SUM. The command SET ECHO ON is placed on the first line by pressing Ctrl-N, which provides a blank line — and then typing SET ECHO ON. Move the cursor to the first C of the word CANCEL. Press Ctrl-N which provides you with a blank line, then type in SET ECHO OFF (the normal condition). The screen should appear as shown in Figure 24-6.

The Fine Art of Procedures

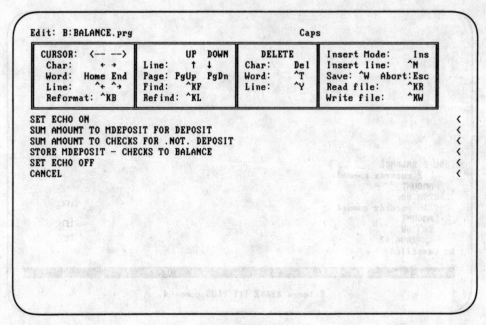

Figure 24-6

Press **Ctrl-End** to save the new command file BALANCE on disk drive B. Now, whenever you have the computer execute the procedure B:BALANCE, the results will appear as shown in Figure 24-7.

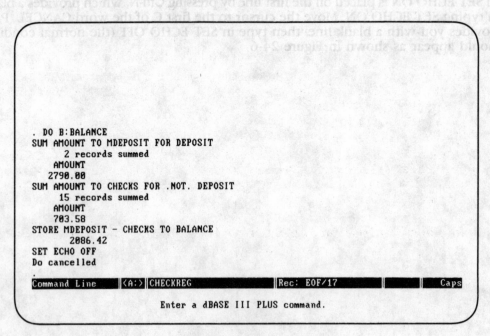

Figure 24-7

Chapter Twenty-Four

Writing a procedure uses the same mechanics as writing a letter. The difference, of course, is that a procedure is written on the computer using a language the computer understands. Most microcomputer database management systems allow you to write procedures in two ways: with an internal feature of the DMBS or with a separate word processor.

A word processor is special software designed specifically for working with text. When you use an external word processor to write a dBASE procedure, you must add a file identifier .PRG to the filename. When you use the internal word processor to write a procedure, dBASE will automatically add the identifier .PRG to the filename. The dBASE file identifier used with procedures is .PRG. So the complete name of our sample procedure is B:BALANCE.PRG.

Even if the procedure can be written from within the database system, it is often advantageous to write it with a word-processing system. Word processors generally offer significantly greater editing capabilities than are available with a DBMS. After all, editing is what word processors are for, and editing features are of great value when writing lengthy procedures.

Word processors usually provide a special mode for use when preparing material to be read by the computer. All procedures, command files, and computer programs prepared on a word processor must be written using this mode. The normal word-processing mode for preparing letters and documents adds formatting symbols that don't show on the screen. These are for the word processor's internal use in editing, and subsequently printing, the letters and documents. These extra symbols will cause problems if they are inadvertently included in a procedure. If you are not sure which mode to use, consult your user's manual.

SAVE YOURSELF SOME TIME . . .

. . . *AND MINOR IRRITATION.* When the computer executes an instruction such as SUM, it must read the entire database from the disk. The time it takes to read the database depends primarily on the size of the database and the kind of disk drive. A typical floppy disk drive might read the database at 2,300 characters per second. A very small database of 23,000 characters will take ten seconds each time that it is read. A database of 230,000 characters will take 100 seconds.

If you are entering commands manually, you will find that the short delay for the computer to read the database becomes very annoying if the delay is more than about five seconds. Because of this *read* time, it is beneficial to group commands. Whenever entering a number of manual commands, it is often convenient to place the commands into a procedure. This frees you from the annoying short waits of a few to several seconds for each instruction.

The idea behind establishing a procedure is to have the computer do all (or at least most) of the work. You give it a list of single instructions, and it does them for you all at once. If you often sit before a computer terminal and interrogate the computer about the contents of your database, you can save yourself a lot of time if you write a procedure to do the same tasks automatically.

For instance, suppose you want to acquire a lot of information about scotch and gin from our liquor store inventory database. You can sit at the keyboard and enter a series of commands *or* you can write a procedure that is a list of those commands and have the computer run through the commands for you.

```
COUNT FOR LIQUOR='SCOTCH'
COUNT FOR LIQUOR='GIN'
COUNT FOR LIQUOR='SCOTCH'.AND.SIZE='FIFTH'
```

If you enter these commands from the keyboard, it takes the computer a few seconds to respond to each of them. If the database is large, it may take many seconds for each response. If you enter the commands as a procedure, you can relax and have a cup of coffee while the computer gets you the answers you want. The time it takes the computer might not be any less, but *you* aren't sitting around twiddling your thumbs between commands while the computer searches for the answers.

A computer follows the set of instructions you give it literally. If the computer is to follow the procedure, you must write the instructions in a way the computer can understand. Remember, the computer may be very, very fast, but it isn't very bright. A computer procedure must be written clearly. Do not assume that the computer "knows" anything.

To really get a feeling for this, consider the following example. If we ask a very small child to count to three, he or she can probably manage to do it. To get the computer to count to three is something else. The computer can only count to three if we give it a procedure to count to three. Even after it's done it once, it won't be able to do it again unless the procedure is used. An ordinary English version of a computer procedure to count to three is shown below. This procedure is very similar to the procedure a person might follow if using a hand calculator with a memory.

Step 1: Store a zero in memory.
Step 2: Add 1 to the contents of the memory and store the result in memory.
Step 3: Display the contents of the memory.
Step 4: Add 1 to the contents of the memory and store the result in memory.
Step 5: Display the contents of the memory.
Step 6: Add 1 to the contents of the memory and store the result in memory.
Step 7: Display the contents of the memory.

When we want the computer to perform this procedure, it must be written differently. The translation of our English to a computer language will be different for each computer language, just as it would differ if we were translating into some other language such as French or German. Here is the dBASE version:

Step 1:	STORE 0 TO X
Steps 2 and 3:	STORE X + 1 TO X
Steps 4 and 5:	STORE X + 1 TO X
Steps 6 and 7:	STORE X + 1 TO X

(The procedure itself contains only the terms starting with the word STORE. The step numbers are shown so that you can easily see the correspondence between the two versions of the procedure.)

You should notice two things about this sample procedure.

• We are doing the same thing over and over.
• This approach wouldn't be very practical for doing the same thing a large number of times — like counting to a thousand.

The English version can be rewritten in the form:

Chapter Twenty-Four

Step 1:	Store a zero in memory.
Step 2:	Add 1 to the contents of the memory and store the result in memory.
Step 3:	Display the contents of the memory.
Step 4:	Repeat step 2.
Step 5:	Repeat step 3.
Step 6:	Repeat step 2.
Step 7:	Repeat step 3.

In *Winnie The Pooh*, Winnie and Piglet discover footprints in the snow in front of Piglet's house. Dreaming of great adventure, the two set out to follow the tracks and see where they might lead and what sort of creature might have made them. They follow these footprints on and on until, at last, they find themseves back at Piglet's house. There they find three sets of footprints leading away from Piglet's house. One set is much smaller than the other two. After some debate, they speculate that they are tracking a woozle and a wizzle. Off they go again following the footprints. After a time they find two more sets of footprints have joined the first three. Piglet becomes quite concerned over his safety and discovers he has work to do at home. He leaves. Winnie the Pooh finally determines the footprints are their own. They have been travelling in circles.

In the case of Winnie the Pooh and Piglet, going in circles might have been high adventure, but it really got them nowhere. In our case, however, it turns out that going in circles will get us farther faster. Circles facilitate writing simple procedures.

DO WHILE...ENDDO

Simplification #1

Step 1:	Store a zero in memory.
Step 2:	Add 1 to the content of the memory and store the result in memory.
Step 3:	Display the content of the memory.
Step 4:	If memory is less than 3, go to step 2.

Simplification #2

Step 1:	Store a zero in memory.
Step 2:	Do steps 3 and 4 as long as the content of the memory is less than 3.
Step 3:	Add 1 to the content of the memory and store the result in memory .
Step 4:	Display the content of the memory.

The first example is typical of the way you might write a procedure in one of the traditional computer languages such as FORTRAN, COBOL, or BASIC. The latter is representative of the modern languages such as Pascal, PL/1, and dBASE. Writing our simple counting example (Simplification #2) in dBASE, we get:

```
STORE 0 TO X
DO WHILE X<3
STORE X+1 TO X
ENDDO
```

The Fine Art of Procedures

The symbol < is arithmetic shorthand for *less than*. The statement beginning with DO is read as "do while X is less than 3." The symbol > means *greater than*. DO WHILE 3>X would mean "do while 3 is greater than X." The two statements DO WHILE X<3 and DO WHILE 3>X mean exactly the same thing.

This new example has just as many instructions as the original did. There is one important difference, however — we can cause the computer to count to a hundred or a thousand or a million just by changing the "3" to the any counting goal. The command DO WHILE X<3 tells the computer that you want it to keep repeating the following instructions as long as the value of X is less than three. ENDDO signifies the end of the group of instructions begun by DO WHILE. Each DO WHILE must have an ENDDO. DO WHILE/ENDDO is one way of telling the computer to perform the same set of instructions over and over as long as some condition (such as X<3) is valid. The group of statements beginning with DO WHILE and ending with ENDDO is called a **loop**.

INITIALIZING THE LOOP

Immediately in front of the loop we used an instruction that stored the value zero in the memory variable X. You know if you count to three, you begin at one. The computer doesn't know where to begin. It must be told where to begin — as well as how to count. This single instruction — STORE 0 TO X — does two things:

• It stores the value of 0 to X
• It also creates the memory variable X

You are not allowed to use a memory variable in a procedure until the variable has been created. Also, you are not allowed to create the memory variable without giving it an initial value. In this case the variable was created and assigned an initial value with the instruction STORE 0 TO X. The statement *initialized* the loop by providing the starting place and creating the variable X.

ACCUMULATOR: A BASIC CONCEPT

A simple little counting procedure is an accumulator. The accumulator forms the basis of the ordinary adding machine and the hand-held electronic calculator. The basic concept is often used in procedures in database systems business applications.

To accomplish more complex tasks, you use a group of simple procedures. As an example, suppose you want to count by ones to ten and then by tens to one hundred. One way to do this is to use two simple counting loops in succession.

```
STORE 0 TO X
DO WHILE X<10
STORE X+1 TO X
ENDDO

DO WHILE X<100
STORE X+10 TO X
ENDDO
```

AN ALTERNATIVE PROCEDURE: IF

Another way to achieve exactly the same result is to have the computer take different actions for different values of X. This is, of course, what occurs above, however this procedure takes advantage of the fact that we know everything about X, and about what we want to happen. The computer is capable of making decisions — albeit limited ones. We can take advantage of this capability and write an equivalent procedure.

```
STORE 0 TO X

DO WHILE X<100

IF X<10
   STORE X+1 TO X
ENDIF

IF X>=10
   STORE X+10 TO X
ENDIF

ENDDO
```

IF is the word we use when we want the computer to make a decision about whether or not to do something. It's used in exactly the same way we ordinarily use *if*. *If* it's raining, take an umbrella. *If* the gas tank is getting low, stop and get gasoline. We use IF when the action to be taken (or conclusion to be drawn) depends on some condition.

In the example, the action is to add one number to another. The condition is the value stored in X. When the computer makes each decision, it doesn't know about the other IF. Each IF must have an ENDIF just as each DO WHILE must have an ENDDO. The information after IF (X is less than ten, X is greater than or equal to ten) is the condition the computer must make a decision about. The decision that it makes after the first IF is whether or not X is less than ten. If it is, the IF applies, and the computer will execute the instruction STORE X + 1 TO X. If it isn't, the computer won't store X + 1 to X.

DO WHILE and IF are the basic tools that can be used for a procedure. These examples employ the specific terminology of dBASE. The concepts, however, are universal and are used in all computer languages. This terminology is similar to that used by modern languages such as PL/1 and Pascal.

To give you a better idea of how you can use DO WHILE and IF, we will write a procedure using these two features that accomplishes the same things as B:BALANCE. We will also take this opportunity to demonstrate how you can exert more control over the displays produced by the computer. The new B:BALANCE is shown as Figure 24-8. In the example, we use instructions which may be unfamiliar to you:

```
SET TALK OFF/ON
SKIP
DO WHILE.NOT.EOF
?
```

```
Edit: B:BALANCE.prg                          Caps
USE CHECKREG                                                    <
SET TALK OFF                                                    <
STORE 0 TO MDEPOSIT,CHECKS                                      <
DO WHILE .NOT. EOF()                                            <
 IF DEPOSIT                                                     <
   STORE AMOUNT+MDEPOSIT TO MDEPOSIT                            <
 ENDIF                                                          <
 IF .NOT. DEPOSIT                                               <
   STORE AMOUNT+CHECKS TO CHECKS                                <
 ENDIF                                                          <
SKIP                                                            <
ENDDO                                                           <
? 'TOTAL DEPOSITS ',MDEPOSIT                                    <
? 'TOTAL CHECKS   ',CHECKS                                      <
? '  BALANCE      ',MDEPOSIT-CHECKS                             <
SET TALK ON
CANCEL
```

Figure 24-8

The original results of the procedure (from Figure 24-2) are reproduced here (Figure 24-9) for your convenience.

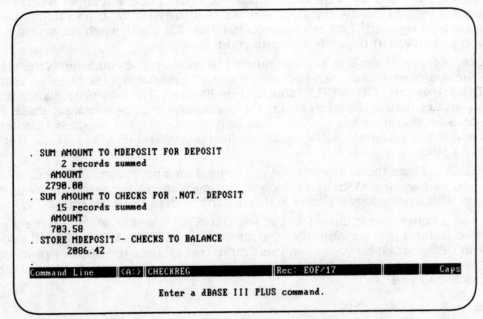

```
. SUM AMOUNT TO MDEPOSIT FOR DEPOSIT
     2 records summed
  AMOUNT
  2790.00
. SUM AMOUNT TO CHECKS FOR .NOT. DEPOSIT
     15 records summed
  AMOUNT
  703.58
. STORE MDEPOSIT - CHECKS TO BALANCE
     2086.42
.
Command Line    ||<A:>||CHECKREG         |Rec: EOF/17   ||      | Caps
```

Enter a dBASE III PLUS command.

Figure 24-9

Chapter Twenty-Four

SET TALK OFF/ON

You may have noticed that many commands — like STORE and SUM — display a response each time they are used. This is one of the ways the computer talks to you. Though this is desirable when you are working from your keyboard, it may not be so desirable when using procedures. It clutters up the screen (and/or the printer). In dBASE, the computer's visual response to a command can be turned on and off. SET TALK ON and SET TALK OFF are the commands that do this.

SKIP

The database management system actually works with only one record at a time. When the USE statement is made, the DBMS is positioned to the very top of the database — Record 1. SKIP advances the DBMS one record. When the last record is reached, the next use of SKIP will alert the DBMS that the end of the file has been reached.

DO WHILE.NOT.EOF( )

As we have seen in previous examples, the DO WHILE command applies as long as some condition is true. EOF means "end of file." The command literally means "Computer, do the following until you come to the end of the database." This command is the most common use of DO WHILE. This will automatically stop the DO loop when the end of the database is reached.

?

The question mark (?) allows you to display specific information. The single quotation marks at each end of the text — such as 'TOTAL DEPOSITS' — are called delimiters. Their presence indicates that the enclosed characters are text to be displayed. The memory variable names (DEPOSIT, CHECKS) indicate that the contents of the memory variables are to be displayed. The comma is used to separate items to be displayed. Each question mark produces one line of display.

The new sample procedure, B:BALANCE, is just a little more complicated than the original version. On the other hand, a few moments of work have produced a result more tailored to our needs. When we have the computer execute this command file, the display shown in Figure 24-10 is produced.

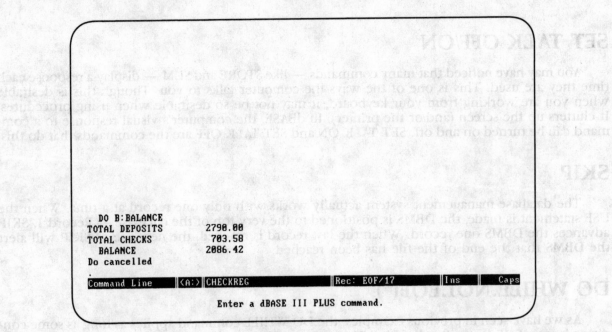

. DO B:BALANCE
TOTAL DEPOSITS   2790.00
TOTAL CHECKS   703.58
  BALANCE   2086.42
Do cancelled

Command Line	<A:> CHECKREG	Rec: EOF/17	Ins	Caps

Enter a dBASE III PLUS command.

Figure 24-10

Procedures enable you to get more work out of your computer. In this chapter we introduced some basic concepts: the accumulator, the DO loop, the decision (IF), as well as some of the dBASE commands frequently used in procedures. Procedures such as these are fun to write and ultimately save you both time and effort. In addition, they reduce the chance of error. Once a procedure is correctly written, the computer can perform a function over and over without mistake.

CHAPTER TWENTY-FIVE

MAKING A PROCEDURE WORK FOR YOU

Procedures not only save you time, effort, and money, but also often provide a more satisfactory result. Automating routine activities is one of the more useful things the computer can do for you. After all, computers are supposed to make life easier. In this chapter, we will explore a fairly comprehensive example of what a computer plus a database management system can do. Again, we'll choose a familiar example and "computerize" an ordinary checkbook. The resulting check-register process can be used to demonstrate numerous ideas.

The plan for our example database B:CHECKREG is shown in Figure 25-1.

FIELD	FIELD DESCRIPTION	FIELDNAME	TYPE	WIDTH	DECIMALS
1	Check Number	CHECKNO	N	4	
2	Paid To	PAIDTO	C	20	
3	Amount of Check or Dep	AMOUNT	N	7	2
4	Deposit or Check	DEPOSIT	L	1	
5	Deductible (Y/N)	DEDUCT	L	1	
6	Cancelled (Y/N)	CANCEL	L	1	
7	Date (mm/dd/yy)	DATE	D	8	

Figure 25-1: Check-register database plan

The fields in this plan correspond to an ordinary check register with one major exception: No field is provided for a running account balance. In a conventional checkbook, it is vital to keep a running balance. With the computer, however, this isn't true, as it is perfectly reasonable to do all of the bookkeeping each time we use the checkbook, as you saw in Chapter 23.

MAKING A MENU

There are a number of routine tasks involved in keeping any checkbook up to date. Among these are:

1. Entering a check
2. Entering a deposit
3. Changing an entry to correct a mistake
4. Checking to see whether you wrote a particular check
5. Listing deductible checks at tax time
6. Determining current balance
7. Comparing balance with bank statement

Some of these activities are performed as needed. Others are done regularly, that is, daily, monthly, or yearly. All can be accomplished from your computer keyboard using a database and query language. In the long run it is more efficient — and you will feel more confident — if your checkbook maintenance is done using procedures. The procedure establishes an appropriate process — you won't have to worry about it again.

In Chapter Twenty-Four, we discussed the basic concept of a procedure as well as the tools used in implementation. In the remainder of this chapter, we will use those tools to write a set of procedures to manage our checkbook. This set of procedures is intended to illustrate the concept, not to be a comprehensive checkbook management package.

To accomplish our objective and accommodate our routine checkbook tasks, we need a total of seven procedures. We have one of these already (Number 6, Determining current balance). Each of the seven is about the same size as our example B:BALANCE. And, because they are all part of the same process — managing a checkbook — it is reasonable to make them items on a menu.

Making a menu is even simpler than our example procedure B:BALANCE. To give a very quick and straightforward treatment to this process, we will take our list of routine tasks and make the menu directly from it. The menu procedure B:BANKMENU is shown in Figure 25-2.

Once again we have introduced a few new instructions. These are:

```
DO WHILE .T.
CLEAR
WAIT <PROMPT> TO SELECTION
TEXT/ENDTEXT

DO WHILE .T./ENDDO
```

This command means "do forever." The DO WHILE statement usually means "do while the following condition is true." In this case, .T. (for true) is always true. Since we really don't want to go

```
USE B:CHECKREG
INDEX ON CHECKNO TO B:CHECKNO
SET TALK OFF
DO WHILE .T.

CLEAR
TEXT


                    CHECK REGISTER MENU

        1.   Enter a Check
        2.   Enter a Deposit
        3.   Changing an entry to correct a mistake
        4.   Seeing if you wrote a particular check
        5.   Listing deductible checks at tax time
        6.   Determine Current Balance
        7.   Balancing (Compare with Bank Balance)
        8.   EXIT


ENDTEXT
WAIT 'Press the number for your selection ' TO SELECTION
CLEAR
IF SELECTION='1'
    DO B:CHECKENT
ENDIF
IF SELECTION='2'
    DO B:DEPOSITS
ENDIF
IF SELECTION='3'
    DO B:CHANGES
ENDIF
IF SELECTION='4'
    DO B:LOOK
ENDIF
```

Figure 25-2: Check-register menu program

Making a Procedure Work For You

```
        IF SELECTION='5'
            DO B:DEDUCT
        ENDIF
        IF SELECTION='6'
            DO B:BALANCE
        ENDIF
        IF SELECTION='7'
            DO B:CHKBANK
        ENDIF
        IF SELECTION='8'
            SET TALK ON
            CANCEL
        ENDIF
        ENDDO
```

Figure 25-2 Check-register menu program *(Continued)*

through this loop forever, we have included menu item 8, which provides an escape from the loop back to the database management system.

CLEAR

This instruction erases any existing text from the screen; that is, it clears the screen.

WAIT <PROMPT> TO SELECTION

The WAIT command causes a procedure to pause. You can restart a procedure by pressing any character. WAIT <PROMPT> TO SELECTION means to store whatever number you press for your selection in the memory variable SELECTION. The contents of SELECTION then tell the computer which procedure to do. The prompt is an optional text message that will be displayed on the screen. In Figure 25-3 and Figure 25-2, the prompt is "Press the number for your selection."

TEXT...ENDTEXT

This pair of commands is used to display the text appearing between them.

The menu procedure works like this. Entering the command DO B:BANKMENU will cause the menu to appear on the screen as shown in Figure 25-3. Figure 25-2 creates Figure 25-3.

Press the number key that corresponds to your selection. This is another case where you do not need to use the Return key. The number you press is stored in the memory variable SELECTION as a character. The IF instruction that matches your selection causes the computer to execute a procedure. For example, if you choose item 6, "Determine current balance," the computer will execute the command file B:BALANCE.

Chapter Twenty-Five

The first set of instructions in the menu procedure (Figure 24-2) will index the database according to check number. You would not actually reindex each time you used the menu. The indexing operation is shown only to point out that the procedure is based on using an indexed database.

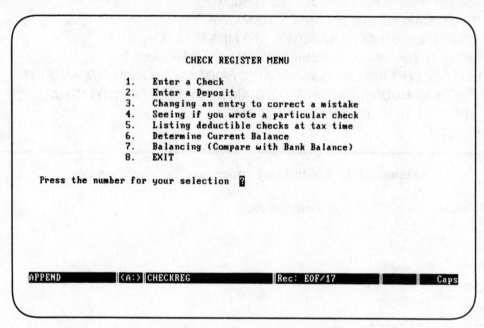

```
                    CHECK REGISTER MENU

          1.   Enter a Check
          2.   Enter a Deposit
          3.   Changing an entry to correct a mistake
          4.   Seeing if you wrote a particular check
          5.   Listing deductible checks at tax time
          6.   Determine Current Balance
          7.   Balancing (Compare with Bank Balance)
          8.   EXIT


    Press the number for your selection ▓




APPEND          ⟨A:⟩ CHECKREG              Rec: EOF/17          Caps
```

Figure 25-3: Check-register menu

MENU OPTION #1

Pressing 1 selects menu option 1, entry of a new check into your computerized checkbook. This could, of course, also be accomplished by the command APPEND, but in this example we want to illustrate a means of accomplishing the results of APPEND while providing fully descriptive prompts for each data item. One procedure that allows entry of a new check is shown in Figure 25-4.

```
APPEND BLANK
INPUT 'Enter Check Number   ' TO MCHECKNO
ACCEPT 'Paid to the Order of   ' TO MPAIDTO
INPUT 'Enter Amount of Check   ' TO MAMOUNT
ACCEPT 'Enter Date (mm/dd/yy)   ' TO MDATE
INPUT 'Is This Check Deductible (.Y./.N.)   ' TO MDEDUCT
REPLACE CHECKNO WITH MCHECKNO, PAIDTO WITH MPAIDTO, AMOUNT;
   WITH MAMOUNT, DATE WITH CTOD(MDATE), DEDUCT WITH MDEDUCT,;
   DEPOSIT WITH .N., CANCEL WITH .N.
RETURN
```

Figure 25-4: Preliminary procedure for check entry

Again, we introduce a few new commands:

ACCEPT
INPUT
RETURN
APPEND BLANK

ACCEPT and INPUT

ACCEPT and INPUT offer a means for the computer to "ask" you to enter data from the keyboard during a procedure. INPUT is used to enter numeric or logical data. ACCEPT is used to enter character data. Otherwise they are the same. The command form is demonstrated by the examples in Figure 25-4. The command displays the desired text, creates a memory variable such as MCHECKNO, and waits for you to enter the data. A weakness of this approach is that INPUT requires that you use .Y. to enter "Y" and .N. for "N."

RETURN

RETURN is similar to CANCEL in that it terminates the procedure — in this case, the check-entering procedure — returning control of the computer to the main menu program B:BANKMENU. CANCEL would terminate the entire operation, returning computer control to the keyboard.

APPEND BLANK

APPEND BLANK, often used with procedures, is a variation of the APPEND command. APPEND is used to add a record to the database. APPEND BLANK adds a blank record, but does not display the record for data entry. In this example, a blank record is created, data is entered into memory variables with ACCEPT and INPUT commands, and then the data is transferred from the memory variables into the blank record using the REPLACE command. Notice that it is not necessary to SET TALK OFF, since that has already been accomplished by the main menu procedure B:BANKMENU (Figure 25-2).

Chapter Twenty-Five

In this particular example, the prompts are displayed and the data entered one instruction at a time. From this standpoint, the procedure is not as effective as APPEND, since the cursor cannot be moved back to correct a previous data item. Because the date is entered here using the ACCEPT command, MDATE is a character variable. To convert it to a date variable, use the CTOD (character to date) function.

A computer display similar to APPEND with more descriptive prompts replacing the fieldnames would be far more desirable. In addition, for more relaxed data entry, the cursor should be movable backwards one or more fields to correct errors. This is accomplished within dBASE using special commands provided for exactly this purpose.

Alternate MENU OPTION #1

The syntax of the dBASE III @/SAY command is:

```
@ ROW,COLUMN SAY 'Whatever You Want' GET FIELDNAME
READ
```

The first of these, the @ command, allows data positioning control on the screen. Most computer terminals have a video screen with 25 rows of 80 characters each. The rows are numbered from top to bottom, 0 to 24. The columns (character positions) are numbered from left to right, 0 to 79. To display the words THIS IS AN EXAMPLE on row 5, beginning with column 10, the command reads

```
@ 5,10 SAY 'THIS IS AN EXAMPLE'
```

The text, THIS IS AN EXAMPLE, will be displayed in standard video just as the fieldnames are in APPEND. Similarly, the contents of a field named PAIDTO could be displayed with the command:

```
@ 5,10 GET PAIDTO
```

This example displays the current contents of the field PAIDTO in reverse video — as when using the EDIT command. The two examples can be combined with the command:

```
@ 5,10 SAY 'THIS IS AN EXAMPLE' GET PAIDTO READ
```

The command READ allows you to change the field contents identified with GET, in this case, the contents of the field PAIDTO. An example procedure to enter checks using these commands is shown in Figure 25-5.

```
APPEND BLANK
@ 5,10 SAY 'Enter Check Number' GET CHECKNO
@ 7,10 SAY 'Paid to the Order of' GET PAIDTO
@ 9,10 SAY 'Enter the Amount of Check' GET AMOUNT
@ 11,10 SAY 'Enter Date (mm/dd/yy)' GET DATE
@ 13,10 SAY 'Is This Check Deductible (Y/N)' GET DEDUCT
READ
REPLACE DEPOSIT WITH .N., CANCEL WITH .N.
RETURN
```

Figure 25-5: Sample check entry procedure

This procedure will cause the computer to behave in a manner similar to APPEND, except that descriptive prompts replace the field names. All the control keys for moving the cursor behave just as in APPEND. Note that all the fields in our database are not displayed — only those relevant to this procedure.

The display produced by this procedure, and specifically by the READ command, is shown as Figure 25-6. The cursor is in the first character position of the CHECKNO field — ready to enter data.

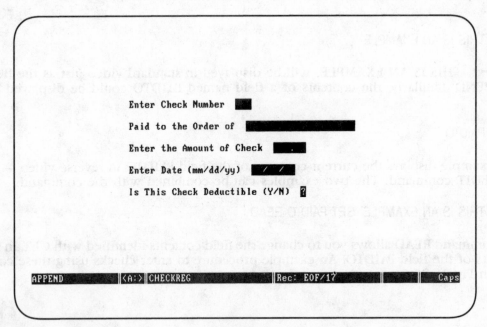

Figure 25-6

Because check numbers are usually sequential, you can save a small amount of bother by having the computer enter the check numbers for you. The revised procedure to accomplish this is shown in Figure 25-7.

Chapter Twenty-Five

```
GO BOTTOM
STORE CHECKNO+1 TO NEXTCHECK
APPEND BLANK
REPLACE CHECKNO WITH NEXTCHECK, DEPOSIT WITH .N., CANCEL WITH .N.
@ 5,10 SAY 'CHECK NUMBER' GET CHECKNO
CLEAR GETS
@ 7,10 SAY 'PAID TO THE ORDER OF' GET PAIDTO
@ 9,10 SAY 'ENTER AMOUNT OF CHECK' GET AMOUNT
@ 11,10 SAY 'ENTER DATE (mm/dd/yy)' GET DATE
@ 13,10 SAY 'IS THIS CHECK DEDUCTIBLE (Y/N)' GET DEDUCT
READ
RETURN
```

Figure 25-7: Procedure for check entry (B:CHECKENT)

The command GO BOTTOM positions the record pointer to the last record in the database. This record contains the last check number used. The check number you want to enter must be the number following that one. This new check number is temporarily stored to the memory variable NEXTCHECK by STORE CHECKNO+1 TO NEXTCHECK. A blank record is added to the database. The new check number is written in the blank record by REPLACE CHECKNO WITH NEXTCHECK.

The instruction CLEAR GETS prevents cursor movement to the fields displayed by GET commands prior to the CLEAR GETS. The display produced by this procedure is shown as Figure 25-8. Note that this display is almost the same as Figure 25-2, except that the cursor is positioned to the first character of PAIDTO and the check number is already filled in.

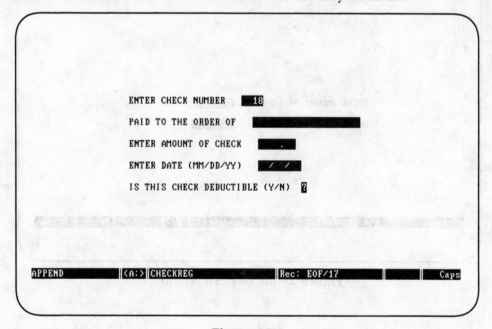

Figure 25-8

Making a Procedure Work For You

MENU OPTION #2

Our next procedure allows you to enter deposits in your electronic bankbook. Figure 25-9 illustrates the deposit entry procedure, named B:DEPOSITS.

```
APPEND BLANK
REPLACE DEPOSIT WITH .Y., PAIDTO WITH '*DEPOSIT*'
@ 9,10 SAY 'ENTER AMOUNT OF DEPOSIT' GET AMOUNT
@ 11,10 SAY 'ENTER DATE              ' GET DATE
READ
RETURN
```

Figure 25-9: Procedure for entering a deposit

It is similar to, but much simpler than B:CHECKENT, the procedure for entering checks. Figure 25-10 is the display produced by B:DEPOSITS.

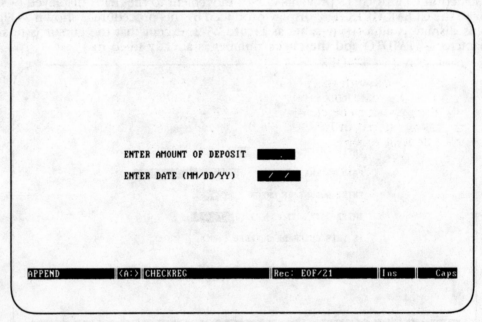

Figure 25-10: Deposit Menu

Chapter Twenty-Five

Again, the procedure is similar to APPEND, except for added detail in the descriptive prompts and the fact that all fields are not displayed.

MENU OPTION #3

The third menu selection allows *error correction*, change of a previously entered record. In dBASE, this could be accomplished with either the EDIT or BROWSE commands. As you may suspect, you can write a procedure similar to EDIT, except prompts will be descriptive text rather than fieldnames. A procedure that will do this is shown as Figure 25-11.

Our first problem is how to find the record we want. If we want to change a check entry, this is pretty simple — we have the computer find the record containing the check number for the check entry we want to change. If we have a deposit, however, we have to find the record some other way, because there is no check number field entry when entering a deposit.

In our example database, there is no unique deposit record identification (except, of course, for the record number). This points out the need for planning. Our lack of planning leads us to seek a work-around solution. Though it is tempting to use the date as our change criteria, even if we never have more than one deposit per day, we can err when entering a deposit such that there will appear to be two deposit entries per day. Our solution will be to use the record number as well as the date as the identifying criteria. Displaying all records for a particular date enables access to the appropriate record number.

The procedure has two sections, selected according to whether or not the record we wish to change is a check:

1. If it is a check, we find the record containing the desired check number and then produce the same display we used to enter data into a check record. The record is found by the SEEK command and the memory variable FINDER. SEEKVAL(FINDER) means to find the record corresponding to the check number stored in FINDER.

2. The second section deals with the need to change a deposit record, not a check record. The computer first asks for the date, displays the deposit records for that date, and then asks for the record number of the deposit to be changed. GOTO FINDER positions the database to the record with the record number stored in FINDER. The change display is the same as that used to enter information into a deposit record.

```
         WAIT 'PRESS C FOR CHECK, D FOR DEPOSIT:' TO TYPE

         IF TYPE='C'
            CLEAR
            STORE SPACE(4) TO FINDER
            @ 5,10 SAY 'ENTER CHECK NUMBER:' GET FINDER
            READ
            SEEK VAL(FINDER)
            IF EOF()
              RETURN
            ENDIF
            @ 5,10 SAY 'CHECK NUMBER:         ' GET CHECKNO
            CLEAR GETS
            @ 7,10 SAY 'PAID TO THE ORDER OF:' GET PAIDTO
            @ 9,10 SAY 'ENTER AMOUNT OF CHECK:' GET AMOUNT
            @ 11,10 SAY 'ENTER DATE (mm/dd/yy):' GET DATE
            @ 13,10 SAY 'IS THIS CHECK DEDUCTIBLE (Y/N):' GET DEDUCT
            READ
         ENDIF
         IF TYPE='D'
            STORE DATE() TO FINDER
            @ 5,10 SAY 'ENTER DATE OF DEPOSIT:' GET FINDER
            READ
            DISPLAY FOR DEPOSIT .AND. DATE=FINDER
            STORE 0 TO FINDER
            INPUT 'ENTER RECORD NUMBER TO BE EDITED: ' TO FINDER
            GOTO FINDER
            CLEAR
            @ 9,10 SAY 'ENTER AMOUNT OF DEPOSIT:' GET AMOUNT
            @ 11,10 SAY 'ENTER DATE (mm/dd/yy):' GET DATE
            READ
         ENDIF
         RETURN
```

Figure 25-11: Procedure for changing a record

MENU OPTION #4

The fourth menu item provides for looking at the check register contents to determine whether or not you wrote a particular check. Figure 25-12 is a simple procedure providing a cursory "look through" capability.

```
USE B:CHECKREG
INPUT 'ENTER MONTH  ' TO MO
INPUT 'ENTER YEAR (19XX)  ' TO YR
DISPLAY FOR MONTH(DATE)=MO .AND. YEAR(DATE)=YR
USE B:CHECKREG INDEX B:CHECKNO
WAIT
RETURN
```

Figure 25-12: Procedure to look through the check register

This procedure provides for display of all records from a particular month. In this case we use the database without the index file, because the index file separates the deposit records and check records and we would ordinarily want to see them displayed together in time sequence.

The procedure displays (in record order) the records for a designated month and year. The records are displayed one screenful at a time. (This is the way DISPLAY works.) After each screenful is displayed, the message "Press any key to continue . . ." will appear. Don't press the Esc key; it will take you out of the procedure.

The DISPLAY command compares the month entered with the month stored in DATE, and the year entered with the year stored in DATE. When the procedure is complete, the indexed file is again selected for use.

This menu item is a good candidate for a second menu, although we will not include one here. The second menu would include a selection of possible displays, in many cases the kind of REPORTS used in the liquor store inventory example of Chapter 2.

MENU OPTION #5

Menu item five — listing deductible checks — allows the opportunity to use a REPORT FORM within a command file. Figure 24-13 shows the deductible check listing procedure.

```
ACCEPT 'DO YOU WANT A PRINTED COPY (Y/N)  ' TO QUERY
IF QUERY='Y'
   REPORT FORM B:DEDUCT TO PRINT FOR DEDUCT
ENDIF
IF QUERY='N'
   REPORT FORM B:DEDUCT FOR DEDUCT
ENDIF
RETURN
```

Figure 25-13: Procedure that uses a report as output

The resulting report is shown as Figure 25-14. Reports are a convenient way to display data.

Making a Procedure Work For You

```
PAGE NO. 00001
02/01/82

                                          DEDUCTIBLE EXPENSES

    CHECK
     NO              PAID TO              DATE          AMOUNT

     208        WRACKING PAIN HOSP        6/22/81          98.50
     227        QP COMPUTERS              8/14/81        4011.04
     234        DR DENTAL,DDS (KEN)       8/21/81          91.00
     267        QP COMPUTERS             10/24/81         486.38
     289        COMPUTE-AWHILE           11/27/81          79.50
     323        LEMON MICRO              01/23/82        1257.16
     324        QP ELECTRONICS           01/23/82         344.50

 ** TOTAL **                                             6368.08
```

Figure 25-14

MENU OPTION #6

Menu item six determines the current account balance. This procedure is nearly identical to B:BALANCE (Figure 23-6 in Chapter 23). Figure 25-15 shows this variation.

Here we use the dBASE @ command for the display as shown in Figure 25-16. Another difference from the original B:BALANCE is the use of the RETURN command instead of the CANCEL command.

Because it takes less time to calculate the balance using the unindexed B:CHECKREG, we do not use the indexed database for this procedure. This time efficiency results from reading the records sequentially instead of jumping back and forth according to the index. An indexed database requires movement back and forth, and, hence, the disk read head must also move back and forth.

```
USE B:CHECKREG
STORE 0 TO MDEPOSIT, CHECKS
DO WHILE .NOT.EOF()
  IF DEPOSIT
     STORE AMOUNT+MDEPOSIT TO MDEPOSIT
  ELSE
     STORE AMOUNT+CHECKS TO CHECKS
  ENDIF
SKIP
ENDDO
@ 5,15 SAY 'TOTAL DEPOSITS' GET MDEPOSIT
@ 7,15 SAY 'TOTAL CHECKS' GET CHECKS
STORE MDEPOSIT-CHECKS TO BALANCE
@ 9,15 SAY 'BALANCE' GET BALANCE
CLEAR GETS
WAIT
USE B:CHECKREG INDEX B:CHECKNO
RETURN
```

Figure 25-15: Procedure to calculate the current account balance

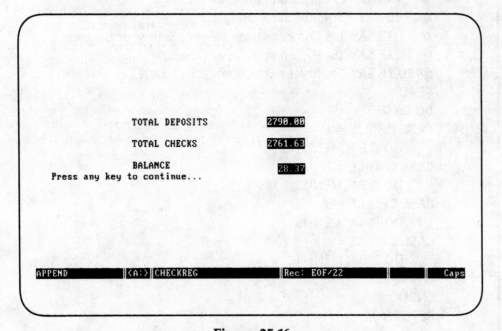

Figure 25-16

Making a Procedure Work For You

MENU OPTION #7

The seventh menu entry checks up on the bank. You need a way to monitor how well the bank is taking care of your account. This procedure is one way to do that. Balancing a checking account is sometimes called "reconciliation." Whatever it's called, it always consists of four parts:

1. Checking off cancelled checks

2. Checking off cancelled deposits

3. Entering bank charges

4. Take your final balance,
add outstanding checks,
subtract outstanding deposits, and
compare the result with the bank's balance

The procedure to reconcile your account is shown in Figure 25-17. This procedure is also a menu, allowing you to undertake each of the four parts and deal with each until you are satisfied.

```
STORE ' ' TO CHOICE
DO WHILE .NOT. CHOICE = '5'
CLEAR
@ 5,15 SAY '(1) Check off cancelled Checks'
@ 7,15 SAY '(2) Check off cancelled Deposits'
@ 9,15 SAY '(3) Enter bank charges'
@ 11,15 SAY '(4) Compare bank balance with your balance'
@ 13,15 SAY '(5) Return to the main menu'
@ 20,15 SAY 'Enter your selection' GET CHOICE
READ
DO CASE
CASE CHOICE='1'
    DO B:BALMENU1
CASE CHOICE='2'
    DO B:BALMENU2
CASE CHOICE='3'
    DO B:BALMENU3
CASE CHOICE='4'
    DO B:BALMENU4
ENDCASE
ENDDO
RETURN
```

Figure 25-17:   A menu procedure to balance a checkbook

If you compare this menu with the main check-register menu, you find a few differences. These differences illustrate the principle that you can often accomplish the same result in different ways.

The DO WHILE .T. command is replaced with the DO WHILE .NOT.CHOICE = '5' command. Entering 5 terminates the DO loop and returns you to the first (main) menu. Selection of a character which is not a menu choice will redisplay the menu.

A new command, DO CASE is introduced in this example. Similar in concept to IF, DO CASE is often used where there are a number of choices for action and the choices are exclusive. Only one of the possible cases is acted on — even if several apply. The first case to satisfy the condition is acted on. In a string of IFs, it is possible that more than one would satisfy some condition and be acted on — even if the choice is undesirable.

The way the procedures are named in this construction is preferable to that used for the main menu example. Choice of a procedure name should allow easy identification of that specific procedure, if you come across the name in some other context.

CHECKING OFF CANCELLED CHECKS

The first item on this submenu allows cancellation of checks that have cleared the bank. In the example procedure shown in Figure 25-18, the check record is found and the pertinent data is displayed on the screen so you can be sure it's what you want. If the record displayed is the one you want, you cancel the record.

```
STORE '   ' TO ENABLE
STORE 0 TO NUMBER,TOTAL
DO WHILE .NOT. ENABLE = 'X'
   CLEAR
   STORE 0 TO FINDER
   @ 5,10 SAY 'Enter Check Number' GET FINDER
   READ
   SEEK FINDER
   IF .NOT. EOF()
      @ 7,10 SAY 'Check Paid To' GET PAIDTO
      @ 9,10 SAY 'The Amount Is' GET AMOUNT
      @ 7,50 SAY 'Dated' GET DATE
      CLEAR GETS
      @ 9,50 SAY 'Cancel (Y/N)' GET CANCEL
      READ
      IF CANCEL
         STORE TOTAL+AMOUNT TO TOTAL
         STORE NUMBER+1 TO NUMBER
         @ 12,1 SAY 'Number of Checks Cancelled' GET NUMBER
         @ 12,40 SAY 'Totaling' GET TOTAL
      ENDIF
      CLEAR GETS
      @ 15,10 SAY 'Enter X When Finished - RETURN To Continue' GET ENABLE
      READ
   ENDIF
ENDDO
RETURN
```

Figure 25-18: Procedure for "cancelling checks"

A representative display from this procedure is shown in Figure 25-19.

When you have finished entering cancelled checks, the number of checks cancelled and their total value should agree with the bank's statement. If not, you need to determine why the totals do not agree. The procedure can be repeated if necessary.

Chapter Twenty-Five

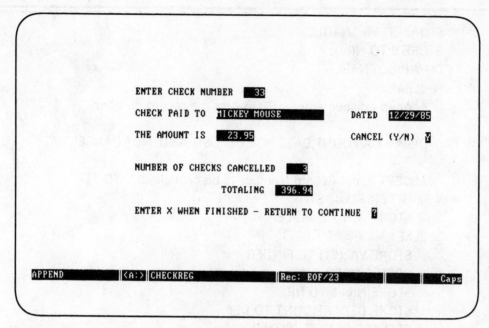

ENTER CHECK NUMBER   33

CHECK PAID TO   MICKEY MOUSE   DATED   12/29/85

THE AMOUNT IS   23.95   CANCEL (Y/N)   Y

NUMBER OF CHECKS CANCELLED   3

TOTALING   396.94

ENTER X WHEN FINISHED - RETURN TO CONTINUE   ?

APPEND   <A:> CHECKREG   Rec: EOF/23   Caps

Figure 25-19

CHECKING OFF CANCELLED DEPOSITS

Having completed the check-cancelling procedure, you move on to deposit "cancelling." The procedure to accomplish this is B:BALMENU2, which is shown in Figure 25-20.

In this example we "turn off" the DO loop from within the procedure. This loop operates as long as the memory variable ENABLE is true. Note that the .T. and .F. do not need to be enclosed in delimiters because the computer assumes them to be LOGICAL values. The .T. stands for true and the .F. for false.

Note also that the record number was stored as a character set. (ACCEPT is a way to tell the computer the data entered are characters.) If we use INPUT, we cannot enter the word "stop" into the memory variable F1.

Since we stored the record number as a character string, we need to convert it back to a number if we are to use the command GOTO. Accomplish this with the command STORE VAL (F1) TO FINDER. This means store the value of F1 to the memory variable FINDER. As you might expect, numbers can also be converted to characters.

```
STORE .T. TO ENABLE
STORE 0 TO NR,DEP
DO WHILE ENABLE
   CLEAR
   ? 'When finished enter - STOP - for the record number'
   ?
   DISPLAY AMOUNT,DATE FOR DEPOSIT.AND..NOT.CANCEL

   ACCEPT 'Enter Record Number to be cancelled   ' TO F1
   IF UPPER(F1) = 'STOP'
      STORE .F. TO ENABLE
   ELSE
      STORE VAL(F1) TO FINDER
      GOTO FINDER
      STORE NR+1 TO NR
      STORE DEP+AMOUNT TO DEP
      REPLACE CANCEL WITH .Y.
   ENDIF
ENDDO
CLEAR
@ 10,10 SAY 'Number of cancelled deposits' GET NR
@ 15,10 SAY 'Total value was' GET DEP
WAIT
RETURN
```

Figure 25-20: Procedure to "cancel" deposits

ENTERING BANK CHARGES

The third procedure in this menu allows you to enter bank charges into the database. The procedure for accomplishing this is shown as Figure 25-21.

```
CLEAR
APPEND BLANK
@ 5,5 SAY 'ENTER BANK CHARGES' GET AMOUNT
@ 7,5 SAY 'ENTER DATE (mm/dd/yy)' GET DATE
READ
REPLACE DEPOSIT WITH .N.,PAIDTO WITH 'BANK CHARGE', ;
  CANCEL WITH .Y.
RETURN
```

Figure 25-21: Procedure to enter bank charges

Since charges and checks are both debits against the account, the charges were treated as checks so the arithmetic works correctly. Charges are also cancelled at the time of entry, because they are part of the statement.

Menu item four provides for comparison of your version of the account balance with the bank's conclusion. A procedure to accomplish this is shown as Figure 25-22.

```
CLEAR
BANKBAL = 0.00
SUM AMOUNT TO SPENT FOR CANCEL .AND..NOT.DEPOSIT
SUM AMOUNT TO EARNED FOR CANCEL .AND. DEPOSIT
@ 5,10 say "Enter bank's version of balance" GET BANKBAL;
          picture '@Z ##,###.##'
READ
STORE EARNED-SPENT TO MYBALANCE
STORE BANKBAL-MYBALANCE TO BANKSERROR

@ 10,10 SAY 'My version of balance . . . . . . . . . .' GET MYBALANCE;
          picture '##,###.##'
@ 15,10 SAY "The bank's error is . . . . . . . . . ." GET BANKSERROR;
          picture '##,###.##'
CLEAR GETS
WAIT
RETURN
```

Figure 25-22: Procedure for monthly balancing

In this example we did not need to consider outstanding checks and deposits. You do this normally in a paper checkbook because of the running balance. In the computer checkbook we ignore outstanding entries and work with the same set of data the bank uses. If all the data is entered correctly, the resulting display should be like that shown in Figure 25-23.

Making a Procedure Work For You

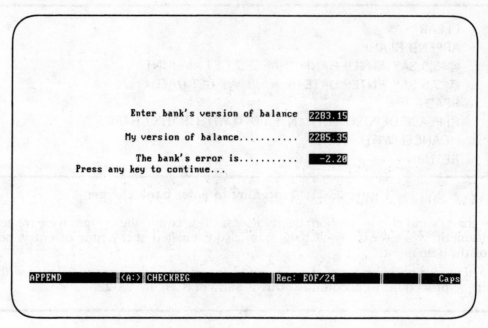

```
                    Enter bank's version of balance   2283.15
                    My version of balance..........   2285.35
                         The bank's error is.........   -2.20
              Press any key to continue...



APPEND          ║<A:> CHECKREG              ║Rec: EOF/24    ║        ║    Caps
```

Figure 25-23

In this chapter we have attempted to describe a complete database system for maintaining a check register. Some details were overlooked in the interest of describing the basic concepts involved. Also, many banks today offer interest-paying checking accounts. Because of this, a real check-register menu should also include an entry for bank credits. In any case, a menu system is a convenient way of using the computer for routine tasks to be accomplished on a daily, weekly, or other periodic basis. The menu may contain submenus for more complex tasks. As a rule, the more frequently used menu items would be on the highest or main menus and those least frequently used would be on the lowest or submenus.

CHAPTER TWENTY-SIX

SPECIAL REPORTS WITH PROCEDURES

You can use procedures to prepare special reports in just about any format you desire. Procedures can be used to prepare reports that cannot normally be obtained from the DBMS's report writer. Though procedures may take a little more effort than is required to obtain a report from the report writer, the result will be worth it.

To illustrate the use of procedures to prepare special reports, we will work through an example of a typical report that cannot easily be accommodated by the standard report writer.

An elementary school uses a database management system for student recordkeeping. At the beginning of the school year, and periodically thereafter, it is desirable to provide copies of class lists to staff members such as the school nurse, the librarian, the school secretary, and the classroom teacher.

The school database contains, among other items, fields which record each student's progress in reading and mathematics, room number, grade, teacher's name, and whether or not the student was retained in grade. The relevant parts of the database structure are shown in Figure 26-1.

FIELDNAME	FIELDTYPE	WIDTH
NAME	C	20
ROOM	C	3
GRADE	C	1
TEACHER	C	15
RETAINED	L	1
READING	N	2
MATH	N	2
GENDER	C	1

Figure 26-1: School database structure (partial)

The school wants to print and distribute class rosters which look like the one shown in Figure 26-2.

This particular example cannot be prepared in this format using dBASE III's standard report writer. The bulk of the report can be handled by REPORT, of course. It is the special annotation of

TEACHER	BOYS
ROOM	GIRLS
GRADE	READING AVERAGE
CLASS SIZE	MATH AVERAGE

that cannot be readily accommodated by REPORT.

```
                        SPECTACULAR SCHOOL

TEACHER: WISEMAN                              9 SEPTEMBER 1982
ROOM:    101
GRADE:   6


        CLASS ROSTER FOR THE 1982/1983 SCHOOL YEAR
```

NAME	READING	MATH	
Aardvark, Anthony	21	88	
Anerson, Hann	43	29	
Apple, Wise	87	29	RETAINED
.		.	
.	.	.	
Zachary, Abram	34	19	

```
CLASS SIZE: 28
BOYS:      14
GIRLS:     14

READING AVERAGE: 43.32
MATH AVERAGE:    62.67
```

Figure 26-2: Example of special report

This procedure will provide a set of printed reports with each class roster printed on a separate page. It is completely tailored to the needs and desires of the people who want it. In the following paragraphs we will go over this procedure and describe each step in some detail.

To accomplish this, we will start out with the basic element of this procedure. Then we will add new elements and continue to iterate, or repeat, until we arrive at the final procedure. At each iteration we will add the new or changed statements in boldfaced type. The most basic element is to do a loop that produces a continuous listing of all of the students in the school (this is nothing more than a procedural version of the command LIST).

```
SET TALK OFF
USE B:SCHOOL
INDEX ON GRADE+ROOM+NAME TO B:ROSTER
GO TOP
SET MARGIN TO 15
STORE  STR(DAY(DATE()),2)+'  '+CMONTH(DATE()) ;
     +STR(YEAR(DATE()),5) TO CALDATE
SET PRINT ON
DO WHILE .NOT. EOF()
?
?
?
?
?
? '                      SPECTACULAR SCHOOL'
?
? 'TEACHER: ',TEACHER,'                               ',CALDATE
? 'ROOM     : ',ROOM
? 'GRADE    : ',GRADE
?
? '          CLASS ROSTER FOR THE 1984/1985 SCHOOL YEAR' ,
? '--------------------------------------------------------------',
? ' NAME                      READING               MATH' ,
? '--------------------------------------------------------------',
?
STORE ROOM TO MROOM
STORE GRADE TO MGRADE
STORE 0 TO BOYS,GIRLS,XREADING,XMATH
DO WHILE ROOM=MROOM .AND. GRADE=MGRADE .AND..NOT. EOF()
  STORE '  ' TO RET
  IF RETAINED
    STORE 'RETAINED' TO RET
  ENDIF
? NAME, '    ',READING, '             ',MATH, '            ',RET
  IF GENDER='M'
    STORE BOYS+1 TO BOYS
  ELSE
    STORE GIRLS+1 TO GIRLS
```

Figure 26-3: Rosters.PRG

Chapter Twenty-Six

```
        ENDIF
        STORE READING+XREADING TO XREADING
        STORE MATH+XMATH TO XMATH
        SKIP
    ENDDO
    ?
    ?
    ? ' CLASS SIZE:',STR(BOYS+GIRLS,2)
    ? ' BOYS:        ',STR(BOYS,2)
    ? ' GIRLS:       ',STR(GIRLS,2)
    ?
    ? ' READING AVERAGE: ',STR(XREADING/(BOYS+GIRLS),6,2)
    ? ' MATH AVERAGE:     ',STR(XMATH/ (BOYS+GIRLS),6,2)
    EJECT
ENDDO
SET PRINT OFF
SET TALK ON


CANCEL
```

Figure 26-3: Rosters.PRG   *(Continued)*

```
        SET TALK OFF
        DO WHILE .NOT. EOF()
            ? NAME, READING, MATH
            SKIP
        ENDDO
        SET TALK ON
        CANCEL
```

Figure 26-4: Procedural version of dBASE command LIST

SET TALK OFF/ON

Nearly all procedures will begin and end with this command. Though it may be desirable for the computer to respond to you each time you issue a command from the keyboard, this is not true when using procedures. You will wish to inhibit the computer from talking except when you want it to. In this case, we want to see field contents, but we don't want to have the computer echo the record number from the command SKIP.

Special Reports With Procedures

SKIP

This command will advance the database one record each time it is used. If we had not SET TALK OFF, the computer would display the record number each time SKIP was used. If SKIP is used with a database that is not indexed, the records will be advanced in the order of the record numbers. If an indexed database is used, the records will be advanced in their *logical* order.

DO WHILE .NOT. EOF( )

This command tells the computer to repeat the commands DISPLAY and SKIP until the end of the database file is reached.

In our next step of explaining the example special report procedure, we will:

- Tell the computer which database to use
- INDEX the database by class
- Tell the computer to use the indexed database
- Display only the fields that we desire

```
SET TALK OFF
USE B:SCHOOL
INDEX ON GRADE+ROOM+NAME TO B:ROSTER
GO TOP
DO WHILE .NOT. EOF ()
    ? NAME,READING,MATH
   SKIP
ENDDO
SET TALK ON
CANCEL
```

Figure 26-5: Modified procedural version of dBASE command LIST

LIST

This procedure now produces a screen display with the students displayed alphabetically by grade and room. The ? prevents the record number from being displayed, and requires less typing than DISPLAY OFF. Only the contents of the fields NAME, READING, and MATH will be displayed.

For our next step we will add the commands to produce a simple printout of the class rosters. At this step in our development of this procedure, the resulting printout would be very crude. Each class roster would be just a list of student name, reading level and math level — beginning at the very top of the page. There would not be any left margin.

```
SET TALK OFF
USE B:SCHOOL
INDEX ON GRADE+ROOM+NAME TO B:ROSTER
USE B:SCHOOL INDEX B:ROSTER
SET PRINT ON
DO WHILE .NOT. EOF()
    STORE ROOM TO MROOM
    STORE GRADE TO MGRADE
    DO WHILE ROOM=MROOM.AND.GRADE=MGRADE.AND..NOT.EOF()
    ? NAME,READING,MATH
    SKIP
    ENDDO
    EJECT
ENDDO
SET PRINT OFF
SET TALK ON
CANCEL
```

Figure 26-6: Elementary version of class roster procedure

SET PRINT ON/OFF

This turns the printer on and off. You should usually turn the printer on after you SET TALK OFF. Similarly, turn the printer off before you SET TALK ON.

STORE ROOM TO MROOM STORE GRADE TO MGRADE

These two commands allow you to set up the DO loop for listing each class separately. They allow the computer to automatically establish the beginning and end of a class grouping.

DO WHILE ROOM=MROOM .AND. GRADE=MGRADE .AND. .NOT. EOF( )

Here we have a DO loop within a DO loop. The inner DO loop is fully contained within the outer loop. As long as each record meets the conditions:

• the room number is the same as MROOM
• the grade is the same as MGRADE
• the end of file is not encountered

the procedure will continue to print out each student's name, reading level, and math level. Note the double period between AND and NOT. Though this may look odd, this is the correct way to enter the condition.

Special Reports With Procedures

EJECT

This causes the printer paper to be advanced to the next sheet.

This procedure is relatively straightforward. The outer loop allows the entire database to be listed. Once we enter the outer loop (DO WHILE.NOT.EOF) the room and grade of the first record will be stored to the memory variables MROOM and MGRADE. Then we enter the inner loop. This inner loop will be repeated until the database is advanced to a record where ROOM and GRADE do not equal the contents of the memory variables MROOM and MGRADE. When this occurs, the paper is ejected and we go back to the beginning of the outer loop, store the new room and grade to the memory variables, and continue. If we encounter the end-of-file marker, we turn the printer off and we are through. Note that the inner loop also has .NOT. EOF( ) as a part of its condition.

At this point we are ready to add the commands that perform the actions necessary to

- Count the boys
- Count the girls
- Add the contents of the reading and math fields for each class

STORE 0 TO BOYS,GIRLS,XREADING,XMATH

This command creates the four memory variables BOYS, GIRLS, XREADING, and XMATH and sets their initial values to zero.

```
IF GENDER='M'
  STORE BOYS+1 TO BOYS
ELSE
  STORE GIRLS+1 TO GIRLS
ENDIF
```

In the inner loop we increment the value of BOYS by one if the content of GENDER is M. Otherwise, we increment GIRLS by one.

```
STORE XREADING+READING TO XREADING STORE XMATH+MATH TO XMATH
```

In addition, we add the contents of the reading field to the memory variable XREADING, and the contents of the math field to the memory variable XMATH.

At this point we have set up the procedure to be able to print this specially formatted information at the bottom of each class roster:

```
CLASS SIZE
BOYS
GIRLS
READING AVERAGE
MATH AVERAGE
```

This is accomplished by the commands:

Chapter Twenty-Six

```
SET TALK OFF
USE B:SCHOOL
INDEX ON GRADE+ROOM+NAME TO B:ROSTER
GO TOP
SET PRINT ON
DO WHILE .NOT. EOF()
  STORE ROOM TO MROOM
  STORE GRADE TO MGRADE
  STORE 0 TO BOYS,GIRLS,XREADING,XMATH
DO WHILE ROOM=MROOM .AND. GRADE=MGRADE .AND..NOT. EOF ()
  ? '          ',NAME,READING,MATH
  IF GENDER='M'
    STORE BOYS+1 TO BOYS
  ELSE
    STORE GIRLS+1 TO GIRLS
  ENDIF
  STORE READING+XREADING TO XREADING
  STORE XMATH+MATH TO XMATH
  SKIP
ENDDO
  EJECT
ENDDO
SET PRINT OFF
SET TALK ON
CANCEL
```

Figure 26-7

```
?
?' CLASS SIZE:',STR(BOYS+GIRLS,2)
?' BOYS:        ',STR(BOYS,2)
?' GIRLS:       ',STR(GIRLS,2)
?
?' READING AVERAGE:',STR(XREADING/(BOYS+GIRLS),6,2)
?' MATH AVERAGE:    ',STR(XMATH/(BOYS+GIRLS),6,2)
```

The question mark (?) when used alone will produce a blank line on the screen and/or the printer. The command line

```
?'              CLASS SIZE:',STR(BOYS+GIRLS,2)
```

will produce a printed line which looks like the one shown in the example.

Special Reports With Procedures

STR(BOYS+GIRLS,2)

This part of the command will take the sum of the memory variables BOYS and GIRLS and print the result as a two-digit character string. In this case we know that the result cannot contain more than two characters. If we were to just use the command line as:

?'CLASS SIZE:',BOYS+GIRLS

The sum would be printed as a ten-digit field. This would put eight blank spaces between the text "CLASS SIZE" and the printed sum.

?'READING AVERAGE:',STR(XREADING/(BOYS+GIRLS),6,2)

This particular version of the command is similar except that the ',2' tells the computer that we want two decimals displayed.

Now we are ready to add the commands to print the page heading and properly format the page.

STORE STR(DAY(DATE( )),2)+' '+CMONTH(DATE( ))+STR(YEAR(DATE( )),5) TO CALDATE

The date is printed in calendar form by using the date functions DATE( ), DAY, CMONTH, and YEAR. DATE( ) returns the system date, DAY extracts the day of the month from a date, CMONTH produces the calendar month, and YEAR gives the year as 19XX. DAY and YEAR are numbers. The STR function is used to "convert" these numbers to characters.

PAGE HEADING

The page heading is printed by the use of the ? command, since ? used alone will cause a blank line to be printed and/or displayed. The text enclosed by apostrophes (delimiters) will be printed as shown in the example. (The delimiters don't get printed.) Contents of memory variables or data fields will be printed when the variable name or the field name is used as shown.

? ,NAME,'   ',READING,'   ',MATH,'   ',RET

This produces the basic display format for each printed record. The blank spaces are used to position the column entries on the page. RET is a memory variable indicating whether or not the student was retained. The variable must be created and contain the proper information prior to this command line.

```
STORE' 'TO RET
IF RETAINED
  STORE 'RETAINED'TO RET
ENDIF
```

These commands show one way to set up the memory variable RET for its later use. This process must be repeated for each data record.

As you can see, there is nothing difficult about developing a procedure to prepare a special report. All that you need to do is be careful and methodical. Each step in the process must be entered into the computer. One very good approach is to add the SET PRINT ON command *after* you have the procedure working. This allows you to check out your procedure on the terminal without wasting paper.

Chapter Twenty-Six

CHAPTER TWENTY-SEVEN

A BUSINESS EXAMPLE

Now that we are expert programmers (and you thought programming was for computer experts only), Chapter Twenty-Seven illustrates how our database applications work in a practical business situation. The *Video Store* example allows us to apply our database methods to the many procedures encountered when running a business. Our database management system accommodates a variety of services, from mailing lists and inventory needs to specialized transaction recording.

The whole idea of the microcomputer and database management is to help you. One area in which they can help is in the conduct of a small business. According to a recent report, there are over three million businesses with gross revenues of less than $500,000 that employ fewer than ten people.

A video store is a prime example of this type of small business. A video store specializes in the sale and rental of TV-related items, primarily video cassette recorders (VCRs), videotaped movies, and related accessories. In addition to the sale and rental of goods, these stores often sponsor video clubs, which entitle members to reduced rates on rentals and equipment.

There are several video store operations areas that can be appropriately supported by a database management system.

- Payroll and Accounting
- Mailing Lists
- Standard Tax Reporting
- Daily Cash Register Tally
- Inventory Management
- Transaction Recording
- Flooring Charges

This list is certainly not exhaustive. However, it is fairly representative of areas easily supported by a DBMS, support that helps owners manage their operations better and with less effort. We discuss the video store because it is particularly well suited to examples which explain the support concepts. There are very few specialized skills involved.

THE VIDEO STORE RENTAL

Renting out prerecorded movies is a major part of the video store's business. The shop either purchases or leases movies for subsequent rental. Since each tape represents an investment and takes up valuable shelf space, it is important to the owner to know which movies rent well and which don't. A movie that doesn't move should be disposed of, either by placing it "on sale" or by returning it to the owner. It is also important to monitor how many times a popular movie is rented. Tapes do wear, and worn-out movies can result in unhappy (and probably, former) customers. A database management system can help monitor the number of times each tape is rented.

Many video stores operate video clubs which benefit both the store and the customer. A fixed membership fee gives significant discounts to members on movie rentals and other merchandise. A club members list often forms the basis of a mailing list. A database management system can simplify mailing list maintenance and print out mailing labels, and so on. It can also offer further support such as reminding the shop when a membership is due for renewal.

There are various other levels of recordkeeping which, without a computer, are done with pencil and paper. To be of value, a computer system must perform additional services and/or reduce the amount of paperwork. For example, receipt of new merchandise requires the addition of the items to the inventory and accounts payable systems. Sale of an item requires a record of the sale as well as inventory system modifications. A database system easily accommodates inventory management as well as helps with most routine bookkeeping tasks such as accounts payable.

"Flooring" merchandise, which is similar to having goods on consignment, is a common business arrangement. A shop would have merchandise for a period of time (often 90 days) before payment is due. Payment is due immediately if the merchandise is sold prior to the due date. Often a nominal flooring charge is paid each month on unsold flooring. Such flooring arrangements require careful recordkeeping — a task easily supported with a database management system.

What starting point might become a good basis for a computer system? Since a pencil and paper database is familiar and useful to everyone, let's start there. We will exactly replace our old-style database with a computer system database. Think first in terms of an overview of the work involved.

On a typical business day, several things might happen:

- Movies and equipment are rented
- Club memberships are sold
- Stock is sold
- Movies and equipment are returned
- Cash register transactions are balanced
- New stock is received

Each of these activities requires paperwork. For example, a "Cash Register Tally Sheet" summarizing the day's business activity and accounting for all the money must be completed each day. Such a form is shown as Figure 27-1.

Chapter Twenty-Seven

CASH REGISTER TALLY SHEET

Day _____ Date _____

Person _____

COUNT MONEY FIRST AT OPENING

1. Beginning Total (Starting cash in drawer)　$ _____

S A L E S

2. Rentals (Pre-recorded movies & equipment)　$ _____
3. Memberships (Lifetime_____ Year _____ Other _____)　$ _____
4. Services (Equipment repair & installation)　$ _____
5. NON-TAXABLE Equipment & Accessories　$ _____
6. Deposits (Prepayments)　$ _____
7. TAXABLE Equipment & Accessories (Sales Tax included)　$ _____

8. Total Sales *(2+3+4+5+6+7)*　$ _____
9. Total Cash Paid Out (attach receipts)　$ _____
10. Total Sales less Paid Out *(8 minus 9)*　$ _____

COUNT MONEY IN REGISTER AT END OF DAY

11. Cash *(15+16)*　$ _____
12. Checks (number of checks _____)　$ _____
13. Charges (MasterCard and VISA)　$ _____
14. Total Money in Register *(11+12+13)*　$ _____

17. TOTAL *(1+10)*　$ _____
18. Total Register *(14)*　$ _____

Difference if any between #17 and #18　☐ Short　☐ Extra　$ _____

Z PRINT OUT AT END OF DAY　$ _____

TOTAL CASH　$ _____

Less starting cash for drawer　$ _____

Amount for deposit　$ _____

$ 1		
$ 2		
$ 5		
$ 10		
$ 20		
$ 50		
$100		

15. TOTAL BILLS _____

1¢		
5¢		
10¢		
25¢		
50¢		
$1		

16. TOTAL CHANGE _____

Figure 27-1: Cash-register tally sheet

Since the activities summarized on this form constitute a large part of the store's day-to-day paperwork, the demonstration of appropriate database management support can begin here. As with all our previous processes, the first step is *planning*.

A Business Example

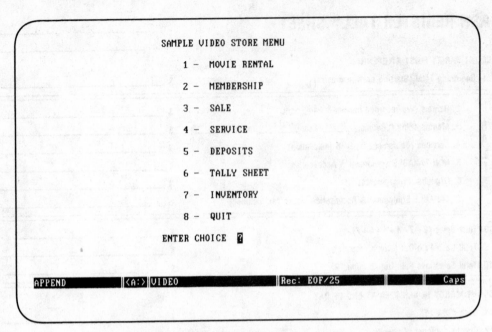

Figure 27-2: Sample video store menu system

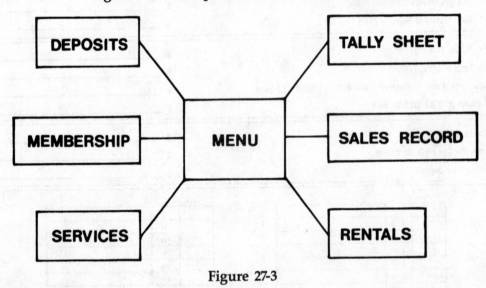

Figure 27-3

Planning must begin with a solid understanding of what is to be accomplished. So far we have identified several daily activities, represented by several pieces of paper, involved in operating the store. Duplicating each piece of paper with "electronic paper" is an uncomplicated and useful way to get started. It allows you to build the system one piece at a time. You can easily check the results against the actual paperwork, thus providing a test of your computer system operation.

In our example, the clerk begins by selecting from a menu of possible "electronic forms." The beginning menu is shown in Figure 27-2.

Chapter Twenty-Seven

A diagram of how these selections fit together is shown in Figure 27-3.

We first make the paper form into an electronic form. This requires a procedure and a database. The database plan — B:TALLY — is shown in Figure 27-4.

FIELD	DESCRIPTION	FIELDNAME	TYPE	SIZE	DECIMALS
1.	Date	DATE	D	8	
2.	Name of Employee	NAME	C	10	
3.	Starting Cash	STARTCASH	N	6	2
4.	Total Rental Income	RENTALS	N	7	2
5.	Lifetime Memberships	LIFEMEMB	N	2	
6.	Yearly Memberships	YEARMEMB	N	2	
7.	Other Memberships	SPECMEMB	N	2	
8.	Membership Income	MEMBERSHIP	N	7	2
9.	Services Income	SERVICES	N	7	2
10.	Non Taxable Sales	NONTAXSALE	N	8	2
11.	Taxable Sales	TAXSALE	N	8	2
12.	Deposits	DEPOSITS	N	7	2
13.	Cash Paid Out (total)	PAIDOUT	N	7	2
14.	End of Day Cash	ENDCASH	N	8	2
15.	No. of Checks	NOCHECKS	N	3	
16.	Value of Checks	TOTALCHECK	N	8	2
17.	VISA and MasterCard	CHARGES	N	8	2
18.	Next day starting cash	NEXTCASH	N	6	2
19.	Amount for deposit	BANKED	N	8	2

Figure 27-4: Plan for cash-register tally sheet

One tally sheet equals one record in the tally sheet database. Several items on the paper tally sheet do not have corresponding fields in the electronic form because they result from calculations on items contained in the database (they appear on the report).

Figure 27-5 shows a simple procedure allowing the clerk to fill out field entries. In this particular procedure, the clerk manually enters all the information for each day's operations, just as he or she would use the paper tally sheet. The computer, however, performs all the required calculations. Potentially, the computer can do much more — for example, help count cash and enter checks and charges similar to the check-register examples in Chapter Twenty-Five.

A Business Example

```
USE B:TALLY
SET TALK OFF
GO BOTTOM
IF .NOT.DATE=DATE()
APPEND BLANK
REPLACE DATE WITH DATE()
ENDIF
CLEAR
@ 1,10 SAY 'CASH REGISTER TALLY SHEET FOR:' GET DATE
@ 3,10 SAY 'NAME OF EMPLOYEE:' GET NAME
@ 4,10 SAY 'STARTING CASH:' GET STARTCASH
@ 5,10 SAY 'TOTAL RENT INCOME:' GET RENTALS
@ 6,10 SAY 'LIFETIME MEMBERSHIPS:' GET LIFEMEMB
@ 7,10 SAY 'YEARLY MEMBERSHIPS:' GET YEARMEMB
@ 8,10 SAY 'OTHER MEMBERSHIPS:' GET SPECMEMB
@ 9,10 SAY 'MEMBERSHIP INCOME:' GET MEMBERSHIP
@ 10,10 SAY 'SERVICES INCOME:' GET SERVICES
@ 11,10 SAY 'NON TAXABLE SALES:' GET NONTAXSALE
@ 12,10 SAY 'TAXABLE SALES:' GET TAXSALE
@ 13,10 SAY 'DEPOSITS:' GET DEPOSITS
@ 14,10 SAY 'CASH PAID OUT (TOTAL):' GET PAIDOUT
@ 15,10 SAY 'END OF DAY CASH:' GET ENDCASH
@ 16,10 SAY 'NUMBER OF CHECKS:' GET NOCHECKS
@ 17,10 SAY 'VALUE OF CHECKS:' GET TOTALCHECKS
@ 18,10 SAY 'VISA AND MASTERCARD TOTAL:' GET CHARGES
@ 19,10 SAY 'NEXT DAY STARTING CASH:' GET NEXTCASH
@ 20,10 SAY 'AMOUNT FOR DEPOSIT:' GET BANKED
READ
STORE RENTALS+MEMBERSHIP+SERVICES+NONTAXSALE+TAXSALE+DEPOSITS;
   TO TOTALSALES
STORE TOTALSALES-PAIDOUT+STARTCASH TO TOTAL
STORE ENDCASH+TOTALCHECK+CHARGES TO MONEY
CLEAR
@ 8,10 SAY 'STARTING CASH:' GET STARTCASH
@ 10,10 SAY 'TOTAL SALES:' GET TOTALSALES
@ 12,10 SAY 'AMOUNT CASH PAID OUT:' GET PAIDOUT
@ 14,10 SAY 'TOTAL MONEY IN REGISTER SHOULD BE:' GET TOTAL
@ 16,10 SAY 'TOTAL MONEY IN REGISTER IS:' GET MONEY
```

Figure 27-5

Chapter Twenty-Seven

```
DO CASE
CASE MONEY> TOTAL
STORE MONEY-TOTAL TO DIFF
@ 18,10 SAY 'REGISTER IS OVER BY:' GET DIFF
CASE TOTAL>MONEY
STORE TOTAL-MONEY TO DIFF
@ 18,10 SAY 'REGISTER IS SHORT BY:' GET DIFF
ENDCASE
WAIT
SET TALK ON
RETURN
```

Figure 27-5 *(Continued)*

We spoke briefly before of video club memberships in this type of business. When such a membership is sold, the clerk fills out a form containing:

- Member's name
- Member's address
- Member's phone number
- Video club membership number
- Membership fee
- Kind of membership (life, yearly, monthly)
- Date of membership

This form becomes a single record in your membership database file, called B:MEMBERS in this example. The B:MEMBERS database plan is shown in Figure 27-6.

FIELD	DESCRIPTION	FIELDNAME	TYPE	SIZE	DECIMALS
1.	Date	DATE	D	8	
2.	Name of Member	MEMBNAME	C	30	
3.	Street Address	ADDRESS	C	20	
4.	City	CITY	C	20	
5.	Zip Code	ZIP	C	5	
6.	Telephone Number	PHONE	C	8	
7.	Kind of Membership	KINDMEMB	C	1	
8.	Membership Fee	FEE	N	6	2
9.	Membership Number	MEMBERNO	C	8	

Note: Database is to be indexed on Membership Number to MEMBID.

Figure 27-6: Plan for video club membership

A Business Example

The database procedure allowing new member registration, B:MEMBERS, is extremely simple. It is shown in Figure 27-7.

```
USE B:MEMBERS INDEX B:MEMBID
SET TALK OFF
CLEAR
GO BOTTOM
STORE VAL(MEMBERNO)+1 TO M1
APPEND BLANK
IF RECNO()=1
REPLACE MEMBERNO WITH '10000000', DATE WITH DATE()
ELSE
REPLACE MEMBERNO WITH STR(M1,8), DATE WITH DATE()
ENDIF
@ 3,10 SAY 'SAMPLE COMPUTER MEMBERSHIP FORM'
@ 8,10 SAY 'MEMBERSHIP NUMBER' GET MEMBERNO
@ 8,40 SAY 'DATE' GET DATE
CLEAR GETS
@ 10,10 SAY 'NAME OF MEMBER' GET MEMBNAME
@ 12,10 SAY 'STREET ADDRESS' GET ADDRESS
@ 14,10 SAY 'CITY' GET CITY
@ 16,10 SAY 'ZIP CODE' GET ZIP
@ 18,10 SAY 'TELEPHONE NUMBER' GET PHONE
@ 20,10 SAY 'KIND OF MEMBERSHIP' GET KINDMEMB
@ 21,10 SAY '(L -Life Y - Year R - Renewel)'
READ
DO CASE
CASE KINDMEMB='L'
REPLACE FEE WITH 100.00
CASE KINDMEMB='Y'
REPLACE FEE WITH 50.00
CASE KINDMEMB='R'
REPLACE FEE WITH 25.00
ENDCASE

@ 22,10 SAY 'MEMBERSHIP FEE' GET FEE
READ
SET TALK ON
RETURN
```

Figure 27-7

Chapter Twenty-Seven

In establishing this procedure, we arrive at an important point. We can link the membership form (once we are sure it works correctly) back to the cash register tally sheet. Such linkage is particularly easy in this example, as both memberships data and tally sheet data were entered manually. Now a membership sale can automatically update the tally sheet. This is accomplished by a simple addition to the procedure B:MEMBERS shown in Figure 27-7. The addition inserted between READ and SET TALK ON is shown in Figure 27-8.

```
READ (Same READ as bottom of Figure 16-6)
STORE KINDMEMB TO A1
STORE FEE TO A2
USE B:TALLY
GO BOTTOM
IF .NOT.DATE=DATE()
APPEND BLANK
REPLACE DATE WITH DATE()
ENDIF
DO CASE
CASE A1='L'
REPLACE LIFEMEMB WITH LIFEMEMB+1
REPLACE MEMBERSHIP WITH MEMBERSHIP+A2
CASE A1='Y'
REPLACE YEARMEMB WITH YEARMEMB+1
REPLACE MEMBERSHIP WITH MEMBERSHIP+A2
CASE A1='R'
REPLACE SPECMEMB WITH SPECMEMB+1
REPLACE MEMBERSHIP WITH MEMBERSHIP+A2
ENDCASE
SET TALK ON (this is also from the bottom of Figure 16-6)
RETURN
```

Figure 27-8

In this membership example we add all information to the membership database B:MEMBERS. At the same time, without any effort, we are able to update the cash register tally sheet.

A Business Example

VIDEO STORE RENTALS

A major part of this business is renting of videotaped movies. These movies may be either owned or leased by the store. When a movie is rented to a customer a form is filled out and signed by the customer. The form contains:

- Customer's name
- Customer's address
- Customer's phone number
- Driver's license number or video club membership number
- Rental fee
- Amount of deposit (if any — club members avoid deposits)
- Number of movies rented
- Names of movies rented
- Date rented
- Date to be returned

When the movies are returned, the form is cancelled. The store uses this form to help keep track of these items:

- The cash transaction
- Where the movies are
- How many times each movie has been rented

At first glance, the straightforward way to handle the rental business on your computer would be to have one record for each transaction. The only problem with this approach is in keeping track of the *names* of movies rented. How do you decide about the amount of field space required to handle the names of the movies? If we do this with a paper form, we can write small. You can't write small with a computer.

The way to handle this problem is to use more than one file for the rental database. The first file will contain all the required information except for the movie titles. The title of each movie rented will become a record in a second database. The two databases will be linked with a transaction identifier. This transaction identifier must be unique for the transaction. It can require one or more fields. In this example, the unique transaction identification can be provided by the customer's driver's license number (or membership number) and the date.

The tie between the two database files is shown more graphically in Figure 27-9. The information that is to be contained in these two files is shown in two side-by-side columns.

At this point we believe that the combination of the date and the driver's license number is unique enough to identify each transaction. Each rental transaction results in a "Rental Database" record and a "Movie Title Database." This means that if a customer rents four movies, the Movie Title Database will have four movies added to it. Those titles are related to the rental record by the license number and the date.

We now have the core of the idea. However, in this example, a lot of typing is required on the part of the clerk. All the customer information as well as the movie titles must be filled in. Fortunately, in many cases, we can minimize the typing by making use of information already stored in the computer.

Chapter Twenty-Seven

RENTAL DATABASE	MOVIE TITLE DATABASE
1. Customer's Name	
2. Customer's Address	
3. Customer's Phone Number	
4. Rental Fee	
5. Amount of Deposit (if any) (club members avoid deposits)	
6. Number of Movies Rented	
7. Number of Days Rented	
8. Club Member (y/n)	
9. Driver's License Number or Video Club Membership Number	Driver's License Number or Video Club Membership Number
10. Date Rented	Date Rented
11.	Movie Title
12.	VHS or BETA

Figure 27-9

If the rental customers are members of the store's video club, the membership database can be linked to the rental database by the membership number. The membership information can then be copied to the rental database — saving the clerk both time and effort (as well as minimizing the chance of error). This is also a terrific opportunity to add nonmembers to this database — thereby increasing its use as a mailing list.

When a field is used as a tie to link two database files together, the field should be the same size and type in both database files. "Alpha " is not the same as "Alpha" to the computer. It considers the blank spaces also.

Movie titles are (or should be) a field in the Movie Rental Inventory Database. Basic inventory information includes:

Movie Title	Date Purchased or	Owned or Leased
VHS or BETA	Leased by Store	Supplier
Shelf Location	Purchase Price/Lease	Rate

The movie title is an awkward way for the store to deal with movie records. An identification number would enable the clerk to work more quickly and accurately with or without the computer. Therefore, in our example we will assume that a five-digit identification number has been assigned to each rental movie.

A Business Example

If we add a few fields to the inventory database we can use it in place of the "Movie Title Database."

Rental fee
Driver's license or membership number
Rental date
Number of times rented
Rented (Y/N)

There are a number of possible file combinations that one could use for this example. Each has advantages and disadvantages, depending upon the specific application. For the purposes of our example we will use the Inventory Database in the place of the Movie Database from now on. Figure 27-10 shows a diagram of this rental procedure (so far).

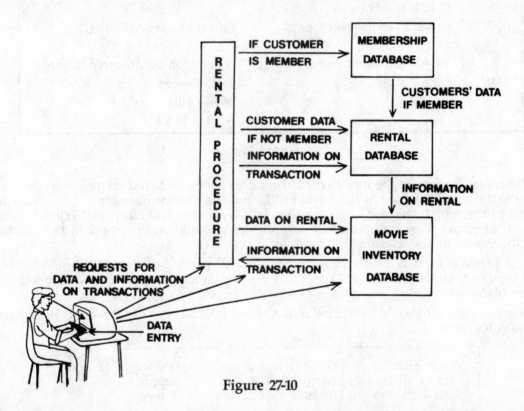

Figure 27-10

Let's take a look at where we are. When a customer rents a movie, the clerk fills out a form. This form becomes a single record in a rental database. The rental inventory database is used to identify the movies rented out. The driver's license number or club membership number and the rental date are common fields in the two database files. These two fields serve to tie the two files together. Each time a movie is rented, the "number of times rented" field gets increased by one. If the customer is a club member, much of the information is automatically retrieved from the membership database.

Chapter Twenty-Seven

Taking the inevitable next step finds the computer calculating the total rental fee and adding this to the receipt. Just as in the last example, the value of the transaction can be automatically added to the Cash Register Tally Sheet.

Now let's put all this together. A diagram of this database system is shown in Figure 27-11.

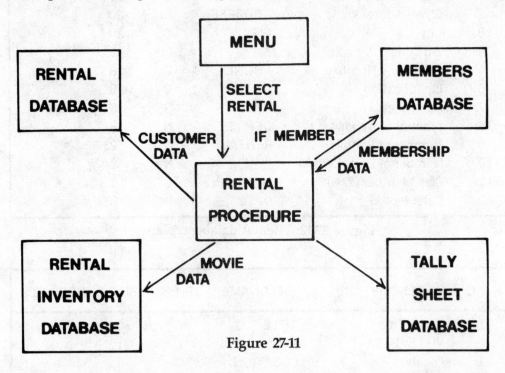

Figure 27-11

The process outlined above is a reasonable example of one way in which a computer system can be used to help with the operation of a small business. It is not the only way, and it is not necessarily the best way. However, it provides a useful demonstration of an approach to solving a business problem with a computer.

The next step is to write down the database plans for each of the database files used in this process. The plan for the membership file has already been described in Figure 27-6. The two new database files are shown in Figures 27-12 and 27-13.

FIELD	DESCRIPTION	FIELDNAME	TYPE	SIZE	DECIMALS
1.	Customer's Name	NAME	C	30	
2.	Street Address	ADDRESS	C	20	
3.	City	CITY	C	20	
4.	Zip Code	ZIP	C	5	
5.	Telephone Number	PHONE	C	8	
6.	Identification	ID	C	8	
7.	Rental Fee	RFEE	N	5	2
8.	Amount of Deposit	DEPOSIT	N	6	2
9.	Number of Rentals	RENTAL	N	2	
10.	Number of Days Rented	TIME	N	2	
11.	Club Member (Y/N)	MEMBER	L	1	
12.	Date Rented	DATE	D	8	

Figure 27-12: Rental database plan

FIELD	DESCRIPTION	FIELDNAME	TYPE	SIZE	DECIMALS
1.	Movie Title	TITLE	C	30	
2.	VHS or BETA	VHS	L	1	
3.	Location	LOCATION	C	5	
4.	Date Acquired	IDATE	D	8	
5.	Price/Lease Rate	COST	N	5	2
6.	Owned or Leased	OWNED	L	1	
7.	Supplier	SUPPLIER	C	20	
8.	Identification	RID	C	8	
9.	Rental Charge	CHARGE	N	4	2
10.	Rental Date	RDATE	D	8	
11.	No. of Times Rented	RCOUNT	N	3	
12.	Rented (Y/N)	RENTED	L	1	
13.	Movie ID Number	MOVIEID	C	5	

Figure 27-13: Inventory database

A procedure that will perform the rental process described above is shown in Figure 27-14. One word of caution: this procedure is intended to illustrate the process. It is necessarily somewhat simplified from one you might use for an actual business.

Although the procedure described in Figure 27-14 is the most elaborate in this book, there is nothing tricky or complicated about it.

Chapter Twenty-Seven

```
SET DEFAULT TO B
CLEAR ALL
SET TALK OFF
SELECT 1
USE TALLY
SELECT 2
USE INVENTRY
SELECT 3
USE MEMBERS INDEX MEMBID
SELECT 4
USE RENTAL
SET RELATION TO ID INTO MEMBERS
APPEND BLANK
REPLACE DATE WITH DATE()
CLEAR
@ 1,10 SAY 'SAMPLE VIDEO RENTAL FROM'
@ 2,10 SAY 'IS THE CUSTOMER A CLUB MEMBER? (Y/N)' GET MEMBER
READ
CLEAR GETS
IF MEMBER
   @ 8,10 SAY 'ENTER THE MEMBERSHIP NUMBER' GET ID
   READ
   GO RECNO()
ENDIF
IF ID = MEMBERS->MEMBERNO
   REPLACE NAME WITH MEMBERS->MEMBNAME,   ;
           ADDRESS WITH MEMBERS->ADDRESS, CITY WITH MEMBERS->CITY, ;
           ZIP WITH MEMBERS->ZIP, PHONE WITH MEMBERS->PHONE
ENDIF
@ 3,10 SAY 'CUSTOMERS NAME' GET NAME
@ 4,10 SAY 'CUSTOMERS ADDRESS' GET ADDRESS
@ 5,10 SAY 'CITY' GET CITY
@ 6,10 SAY 'ZIP CODE' GET ZIP
@ 7,10 SAY 'TELEPHONE NUMBER' GET PHONE
```

Figure 27-14

A Business Example

```
IF ID = MEMBERS->MEMBERNO .AND. MEMBER
    CLEAR GETS
ELSE
    @ 8,10 SAY 'DRIVERS LICENSE NUMBER' GET ID
    @ 9,10 SAY 'ENTER AMOUNT OF DEPOSIT' GET DEPOSIT
READ
ENDIF
@ 10,10 SAY 'NUMBER OF DAYS RENTED' GET TIME
@ 10,45 SAY 'NUMBER OF MOVIES RENTED' GET RENTAL
READ
CLEAR GETS

STORE 0 TO MRENTAL
DO WHILE RENTAL->RENTAL > MRENTAL
    SELECT INVENTRY
    STORE '        ' TO MOVIENO
    @ 12,10 SAY 'MOVIE IDENTIFICATION NUMBER' GET MOVIENO
    READ
    LOCATE FOR MOVIEID=MOVIENO
    @ 13,0
    IF EOF()
        @ 13,10 SAY 'Movie number '+MOVIENO+' is not in the database'
        LOOP
    ENDIF
    IF RENTED
        @ 13,10 SAY 'Movie number '+TRIM(TITLE)+' is already rented'
        LOOP
    ENDIF
    @ 13,10 SAY TITLE
    REPLACE RDATE WITH DATE(),;
            RCOUNT WITH RCOUNT+RENTAL->TIME,;
            RENTED WITH .Y.,;
            RID WITH RENTAL->ID
    SELECT RENTAL
```

Figure 27-14 (*Continued*)

Chapter Twenty-Seven

```
            REPLACE RFEE WITH RFEE + (INVENTRY->CHARGE * TIME)
            MRENTAL = MRENTAL+1
     ENDDO

     SELECT TALLY
     GO BOTTOM
     IF .NOT.DATE=DATE()
        APPEND BLANK
        REPLACE DATE WITH DATE()
     ENDIF
     REPLACE DEPOSITS WITH DEPOSITS+RENTALS->DEPOSIT,;
                 RENTALS WITH RENTALS+RENTAL->RFEE

     SELECT RENTAL
     CLEAR
     @ 5,10 SAY 'CUSTOMERS NAME' GET NAME
     @ 7,10 SAY 'MOVIE RENTAL CHARGE' GET RFEE
     IF DEPOSIT>0
     @ 7,40 SAY 'REQUIRED DEPOSIT' GET DEPOSIT
     ENDIF
     STORE DEPOSIT+RFEE TO DUE
     @ 9,10 SAY 'TOTAL AMOUNT DUE' GET DUE
     CLEAR GETS

     SELECT INVENTRY
     DISPLAY OFF TITLE,CHARGE FOR RID=RENTAL->ID .AND. RDATE = DATE()
     SELECT TALLY
     SET TALK ON
     RETURN
```

Figure 27-14 *(Continued)*

The first command SET DEFAULT TO B tells dBASE that all the files used in the procedure are on the B drive unless otherwise indicated. CLEAR ALL closes any currently open database files, their associated index files, and format files. It initializes dBASE.

A Business Example

dBASE provides ten independent work areas to be used with up to ten different database files. The next step in this procedure is to open (USE) four database files in the first four work areas. To use a file in work area one, use SELECT 1 — then open the database file with USE followed by the database name. This database name becomes the *alias* for the database. From this point on we can switch back and forth between the work areas by using SELECT followed by the database name.

When we are using multiple files, they can be linked together by the SET RELATION command. In this case we want to link the database in work area four (RENTAL) to the MEMBERS database file. Specifically, we want to link these two files by the content of the ID field in RENTAL. To do this, the MEMBERS database file must be indexed on the corresponding field — which is MEMBERNO. The linkage is accomplished by:

SET RELATION TO ID INTO MEMBERS

From this point on, each time the RENTAL database is repositioned, the MEMBERS database will be repositioned to the record where the content of the MEMBERS field MEMBERNO is the same as the RENTAL field ID. If there is no matching record in MEMBERS, MEMBERS will be positioned to its end-of-file. It will appear to be positioned to a blank record.

Our next step is to add a blank record (APPEND BLANK) to the RENTAL file and set the content of the DATE field to the system date (REPLACE DATE WITH DATE( )). Next we clear the screen and ask you or whoever is entering data if the customer is a club member. The READ command allows you to answer the question. The result is stored in the RENTAL database as a logical yes or no.

In the RENTAL file, if MEMBER is true (yes), then you will be asked for the customer's club membership number. This number is entered into the field ID. The GO RECNO( ) command repositions the RENTAL database to same record. This was done to force the MEMBERS database to be repositioned to the record matching the membership number entered into ID.

Next we compare the field MEMBERNO in MEMBERS with the field ID in the current database file RENTAL. This is accomplished with

IF ID = MEMBERS->MEMBERNO

MEMBERNO will either match ID exactly, or it will appear to be all blanks. If we get a match, we want to copy the contents of the fields MEMBNAME, ADDRESS, CITY, ZIP, PHONE from the file MEMBERS to the equivalent fields in the current work area of the RENTAL file. This is done with the REPLACE command. This command takes three lines. The semicolons indicate that the command is continued on the following line.

Next we display the customer's NAME, ADDRESS, CITY, ZIP, and PHONE using the @...SAY...GET command. If the customer is a club member we use the CLEAR GETS command to prevent the cursor from being moved into these fields. If the customer is not a club member, the ELSE is activated and the customer's driver's license number and the amount of deposit are requested.

In either case, the program will request the number of days of the rental, and the number of movies being rented. Once these items have been entered, we issue a CLEAR GETS to prevent any changes to these items.

The next step stores a zero to a memory variable MRENTAL. The DO loop will process the commands between DO WHILE and ENDDO as long as the content of the variable MRENTAL is less than the content of the field RENTAL in the database file RENTAL.

Once inside the loop we SELECT the database file INVENTRY. Then we store five blank spaces to a memory variable MOVIENO. Once the movie number has been entered, we attempt to LOCATE a record where the contents of the field MOVIEID match the contents of MOVIENO. If the search is not successful [IF EOF( )] we display an error message and LOOP back to the beginning of the DO WHILE. If the search is successful but the movie is already rented, we display an error message and again LOOP back to the beginning of the DO WHILE. If the search is successful and the movie is available for renting, we display the name of the movie. The command line @ 13,0 just prior to the line IF EOF( ) erases screen line 13 on each pass through the DO loop.

Note that you cannot get to the REPLACE command unless the search is successful and the movie is available for rental. The REPLACE command uses four lines, just for readability. (Again, the semicolons at the end of each line indicate that the command is to be continued.) Remember, the maximum length of a command line is 254 characters, and embedded blank spaces count. This REPLACE uses the system date [DATE( )] as the rental date. The number of days for the rental (the content of the field TIME in the database file RENTAL) is added to the content of RCOUNT. We then set the rental flag RENTED to "yes," and enter the customer's ID code into RID, the rental ID field.

Next we switch back to the RENTAL database. When we switch, we maintain our place in the database we have just left. We must be selected to the database we are changing. We moved here so that we could add the rental fee (from the inventory database) times the number of days the movie is being rented to the content of the field RFEE.

Now we increment the variable MRENTAL by one and jump to the beginning of the DO WHILE. If the number stored in MRENTAL is now larger than the content of the field RENTAL, we jump to the first command line following the ENDDO. Otherwise we go through the process until the MRENTAL is larger than RENTAL.

Next, we SELECT our tally sheet TALLY (See Figure 27-14). If the content of the DATE field in the last record is *not* the same as the system date DATE( ), we add a record and enter the system date into the DATE field. Then we add the amount of the deposit from this customer (if any) to the content of the DEPOSITS field and the rental fees to the content of the RENTALS field.

Finally, we SELECT our RENTAL file, clear the screen, and display a summary of this customer's transaction. The bottom line is the amount of money the customer must pay. To cap off the program, we SELECT the INVENTRY file, and display the names and per day charge rates for each movie being rented.

As you can see, there is nothing complex about this example. The procedure is just a step-by-step list of instructions for the computer to execute. All the program did was describe the actions you would take if you were to undertake the same process using pencil and paper.

This example is particularly significant. There are four separate database files used. The procedure isolates you (and the clerk) from the database activity. As the information is filled in, the database management system moves from database to database adding and changing information as necessary.

The procedure B:RENTAL covers the basic elements in managing the movie rental aspects of this business. You should *not* consider it adequate for operating the movie rental business. The procedure has not considered all possible details that should be covered in a business procedure. Some elements were omitted in order to better illustrate the concepts of working with video screen forms and multiple database files.

Appendix A

FORMATTING A DISK

For a disk to be useable by your computer it must be *formatted*. This is the process of preparing the disk to accept data from the computer. Formatting is accomplished with the help of FORMAT.COM. This program is one of many utility programs that come with your computer's operating system. Incidentally, you can format a previously formatted disk. Doing so, however, will destroy anything stored on that disk.

Computers with fixed disks:

If your computer has a fixed (hard) disk, the formatting program is probably kept on the hard disk. Use the CD (change directory) command to select the directory containing FORMAT.COM. Place a blank floppy disk in drive A. Format the disk in drive A with the command

```
C> FORMAT A:
```

Caution: Failure to include the A: in the command will result in your hard disk being reformatted — with the loss of all its data and programs.

Computers with only floppy disks:

Place the floppy disk containing the program FORMAT.COM in the A disk drive (the left-hand drive). Insert a blank floppy disk in the B disk drive. Format the disk in drive B with the command

A> FORMAT B:

Caution: If you do not add the disk-drive identifier for the disk being formatted, the format command will format the logged disk drive—destroying all the data.

APPENDIX B

CUSTOMIZING WITH CONFIG.DB

The configuration file CONFIG.DB is used to customize dBASE to suit your own taste and needs. CONFIG.DB must be located on the same disk and directory as the overlay file DBASE.OVL. The file can be used to establish your own default values for most of the SET commands, the function keys, as well as some processing parameters that can not be set within dBASE.

```
bell = off              margin = 10
escape = off            menu = on
device = screen         safety = off
F2 = ;                  talk = off
F3 = ;
F4 = ;                  PROMPT = $
F5 = ;
F6 = ;                  WP = WP.EXE
F7 = ;                  TEDIT = WS.COM
F8 = ;
F9 = ;                  command = do MENU
F10= ;
help = off
```

Sample Configuration File CONFIG.DB

The SET commands are issued with an equation using the command's *keyword* and the desired setting. **set talk off** becomes **talk** = off in the configuration file. The function key **set** commands **set function** *n* to *setting* become **F***n* = setting. Note that quotes are not used around the function key assignment.

You can issue *one* dBASE III command from within CONFIG.DB. In the sample, the program system developed in this book is brought up automatically by issuing the command **do MENU** from within the configuration file. If more than one *command* is issued, only the last command is actually executed.

The configuration file allows you to set seven processing parameters that cannot be *set* at all from within dBASE. These are BUCKET, GETS, MAXMEM, MVARSIZ, PROMPT, TEDIT, and WP. The sample program makes use of the last three of these special setup controls.

PROMPT allows you to substitute a prompt of your own choosing for the dot prompt normally used by dBASE. The prompt is not to be enclosed by delimiters. If you create or edit the configuration file with WordStar or any other word processor that allows you to enter control characters into the text, you can use a prompt that is not one of the keyboard characters. For example, you can use a heart, or a happy face, or any other exotic character that is available from the extended ASCII set. If you edit the file with WordStar, place the cursor on the character position occupied by the dollar sign in the above example configuration file — then press Ctrl-P followed by Ctrl-C. This will give you a heart as the dBASE prompt. In your WordStar file, the result of this operation will be ^C.

WP allows you to substitute an external word-processing program for the internal word processor that is normally used to edit **memo** fields. In this example, we have substituted the editor WORD PERFECT for the internal dBASE editor for editing memo fields. The easy way to find out if your favorite editor will work with dBASE is to try it.

TEDIT lets you substitute an external word processor for the internal word processor used for **modify command.** In this example we have substituted WordStar for the internal dBASE editor. If you use another editor, such as WordStar, you should follow whatever installation procedure — or usage control — as is necessary to insure that it is used in the correct mode. The **modify command** processor *must* be set to edit standard ASCII files. In WordStar this means that it must be set to automatically edit in the *non-document* mode.

BUCKET controls the number of 1Kb blocks of memory dedicated to handling the **picture** and **range** options for **get** commands. The normal memory allocation for these options is 2Kb. If you have trouble with **picture** and **range**, increase the memory allocation (up to 31Kb). To set the memory allocation to 4Kb, use

```
BUCKET = 4
```

GETS limits the number of active GETS. An active GET is one which may be accessed by a read command. Normally, the number of active GETS is limited to 128. To increase this number to 217 use

```
GETS = 217
```

MAXMEM controls the amount of memory retained by dBASE when calling another program via the RUN command. The normal memory retained is 256K bytes. Increase MAXMEM when using more than the normal amount of memory with either BUCKET, GETS, or MVARSIZ.

Appendix B

MVARSIZ controls the amount of memory allocated to dBASE memory variables. The default allocation is 6,000 bytes. You can increase this allocation to 31Kb. The additional memory is above and beyond the 256 Kb normally required by dBASE. If you do use added memory and you want to use the **run** command, change the memory retention with MAXMEM.

APPENDIX C

INSTALLING dBASE ON A HARD DISK

The process of moving dBASE from the floppy disks that it comes on to your hard disk is called *installing*. The dBASE people make it easy to do by providing you with a program to help you do it. dBASE has to be installed because it is copy protected. Copy protection, unfortunately, has become necessary because too many folks copy the software without bothering to pay for it.

To install dBASE on your disk, place system disk #1 in floppy disk drive A. Select drive A by typing A: after an operating system prompt. The operating system prompt will change from C> to A>. Then type INSTALL C: and press Return. The transaction looks like

```
C> A:
A> INSTALL C:
```

This starts the process of installing dBASE onto your hard disk. As the program INSTALL progresses, it will guide you through each step. There is a counter on system disk #1. When the software has been successfully moved from disk #1 to your hard disk the number stored in this counter will be decremented (reduced by one). Save this floppy disk. It contains the counter as well as a program UNINSTAL, which is needed if you ever want to move dBASE from this hard disk to another computer.

Note: The installation program copies dBASE on the current directory on your hard disk. If you want to move dBASE into a particular subdirectory, you should select that subdirectory with the CD command prior to beginning the installation procedure. If you are not completely familiar with disk directories, you may wish to read the first part of Chapter 21 before installing dBASE. To move the installed copy of dBASE from one subdirectory to another, you should UNINSTALL the copy and re-INSTALL dBASE into the desired subdirectory.

APPENDIX D

ASCII Chart

Binary	Hex	Decimal	Character	Code	Symbol	Description
00000000	00	0		^@	NUL	Null
00000001	01	1	☺	^A	SOH	Start of Heading
00000010	02	2	☻	^B	STX	Start of Text
00000011	03	3	♥	^C	ETX	End of Text
00000100	04	4	♦	^D	EOT	End of Transmission
00000101	05	5	♣	^E	ENQ	Enquiry
00000110	06	6	♠	^F	ACK	Acknowledge
00000111	07	7	•	^G	BEL	Bell
00001000	08	8	◘	^H	BS	Backspace
00001001	09	9	○	^I	SH	Horizontal Tabulation
00001010	0A	10	◙	^J	LF	Line Feed
00001011	0B	11	♂	^K	VT	Vertical Tabulation
00001100	0C	12	♀	^L	FF	Form Feed
00001101	0D	13	♪	^M	CR	Carriage Return
00001110	0E	14	♫	^N	SO	Shift Out
00001111	0F	15	☼	^O	SI	Shift In
00010000	10	16	►	^P	DLE	Data Link Escape
00010001	11	17	◄	^Q	DC1	Device Control 1
00010010	12	18	↕	^R	DC2	Device Control 2

Binary	Hex	Decimal	Character	Code	Symbol	Description
00010011	13	19	‼	^S	DC3	Device Control 3
00010100	14	20	¶	^T	DC4	Device Control 4
00010101	15	21	§	^U	NAK	Negative Acknowledge
00010110	16	22	▬	^V	SYN	Synchronous Idle
00010111	17	23	↨	^W	ETB	End of Transmission Block
00011000	18	24	↑	^X	CAN	Cancel
00011001	19	25	↓	^Y	EM	End of Medium
00011010	1A	26	→	^Z	SUB	Substitute
00011011	1B	27	←	^[	ESC	Escape
00011100	1C	28	∟	^\	FS	File Separator
00011101	1D	29	↔	^]	GS	Group Separator
00011110	1E	30	▲	^^	RS	Record Separator
00011111	1F	31	▼	^_	US	Unit Separator
00100000	20	32				
00100001	21	33	!			
00100010	22	34	"			
00100011	23	35	#			
00100100	24	36	$			
00100101	25	37	%			
00100110	26	38	&			
00100111	27	39	'			
00101000	28	40	(			
00101001	29	41	)			
00101010	2A	42	*			
00101011	2B	43	+			
00101100	2C	44	,			
00101101	2D	45	-			
00101110	2E	46	.			
00101111	2F	47	/			
00110000	30	48	0			
00110001	31	49	1			
00110010	32	50	2			
00110011	33	51	3			

Binary	Hex	Decimal	Character	Binary	Hex	Decimal	Character
00110100	34	52	4	01010110	56	86	V
00110101	35	53	5	01010111	57	87	W
00110110	36	54	6	01011000	58	88	X
00110111	37	55	7	01011001	59	89	Y
00111000	38	56	8	01011010	5A	90	Z
00111001	39	57	9	01011011	5B	91	[
00111010	3A	58	:	01011100	5C	92	\
00111011	3B	59	;	01011101	5D	93	]
00111100	3C	60	<	01011110	5E	94	^
00111101	3D	61	=	01011111	5F	95	_
00111110	3E	62	>	01100000	60	96	`
00111111	3F	63	?	01100001	61	97	a
01000000	40	64	@	01100010	62	98	b
01000001	41	65	A	01100011	63	99	c
01000010	42	66	B	01100100	64	100	d
01000011	43	67	C	01100101	65	101	e
01000100	44	68	D	01100110	66	102	f
01000101	45	69	E	01100111	67	103	g
01000110	46	70	F	01101000	68	104	h
01000111	47	71	G	01101001	69	105	i
01001000	48	72	H	01101010	6A	106	j
01001001	49	73	I	01101011	6B	107	k
01001010	4A	74	J	01101100	6C	108	l
01001011	4B	75	K	01101101	6D	109	m
01001100	4C	76	L	01101110	6E	110	n
01001101	4D	77	M	01101111	6F	111	o
01001110	4E	78	N	01110000	70	112	p
01001111	4F	79	O	01110001	71	113	q
01010000	50	80	P	01110010	72	114	r
01010001	51	81	Q	01110011	73	115	s
01010010	52	82	R	01110100	74	116	t
01010011	53	83	S	01110101	75	117	u
01010100	54	84	T	01110110	76	118	v
01010101	55	85	U	01110111	77	119	w

ASCII Chart

Binary	Hex	Decimal	Character	Binary	Hex	Decimal	Character
01111000	78	120	x	10011010	9A	154	Ü
01111001	79	121	y	10011011	9B	155	¢
01111010	7A	122	z	10011100	9C	156	£
01111011	7B	123	{	10011101	9D	157	¥
01111100	7C	124	¦	10011110	9E	158	₧
01111101	7D	125	}	10011111	9F	159	ƒ
01111110	7E	126	~	10100000	A0	160	á
01111111	7F	127	⌂	10100001	A1	161	í
10000000	80	128	Ç	10100010	A2	162	ó
10000001	81	129	ü	10100011	A3	163	ú
10000010	82	130	é	10100100	A4	164	ñ
10000011	83	131	â	10100101	A5	165	Ñ
10000100	84	132	ä	10100110	A6	166	ª
10000101	85	133	à	10100111	A7	167	º
10000110	86	134	å	10101000	A8	168	¿
10000111	87	135	ç	10101001	A9	169	⌐
10001000	88	136	ê	10101010	AA	170	¬
10001001	89	137	ë	10101011	AB	171	½
10001010	8A	138	è	10101100	AC	172	¼
10001011	8B	139	ï	10101101	AD	173	¡
10001100	8C	140	î	10101110	AE	174	«
10001101	8D	141	ì	10101111	AF	175	»
10001110	8E	142	Ä	10110000	B0	176	░
10001111	8F	143	Å	10110001	B1	177	▒
10010000	90	144	É	10110010	B2	178	▓
10010001	91	145	æ	10110011	B3	179	│
10010010	92	146	Æ	10110100	B4	180	┤
10010011	93	147	ô	10110101	B5	181	╡
10010100	94	148	ö	10110110	B6	182	╢
10010101	95	149	ò	10110111	B7	183	╖
10010110	96	150	û	10111000	B8	184	╕
10010111	97	151	ù	10111001	B9	185	╣
10011000	98	152	ÿ	10111010	BA	186	║
10011001	99	153	Ö	10111011	BB	187	╗

Appendix D

Binary	Hex	Decimal	Character	Binary	Hex	Decimal	Character
10111100	BC	188	╝	11011110	DE	222	▐
10111101	BD	189	╜	11011111	DF	223	▀
10111110	BE	190	╛	11100000	E0	224	α
10111111	BF	191	┐	11100001	E1	225	β
11000000	C0	192	└	11100010	E2	226	Γ
11000001	C1	193	┴	11100011	E3	227	π
11000010	C2	194	┬	11100100	E4	228	Σ
11000011	C3	195	├	11100101	E5	229	σ
11000100	C4	196	─	11100110	E6	230	μ
11000101	C5	197	┼	11100111	E7	231	τ
11000110	C6	198	╞	11101000	E8	232	Φ
11000111	C7	199	╟	11101001	E9	233	θ
11001000	C8	200	╚	11101010	EA	234	Ω
11001001	C9	201	╔	11101011	EB	235	δ
11001010	CA	202	╩	11101100	EC	236	∞
11001011	CB	203	╦	11101101	ED	237	φ
11001100	CC	204	╠	11101110	EE	238	ε
11001101	CD	205	═	11101111	EF	239	∩
11001110	CE	206	╬	11110000	F0	240	≡
11001111	CF	207	╧	11110001	F1	241	±
11010000	D0	208	╨	11110010	F2	242	≥
11010001	D1	209	╤	11110011	F3	243	≤
11010010	D2	210	╥	11110100	F4	244	⌠
11010011	D3	211	╙	11110101	F5	245	⌡
11010100	D4	212	╘	11110110	F6	246	÷
11010101	D5	213	╒	11110111	F7	247	≈
11010110	D6	214	╓	11111000	F8	248	°
11010111	D7	215	╫	11111001	F9	249	·
11011000	D8	216	╪	11111010	FA	250	·
11011001	D9	217	┘	11111011	FB	251	√
11011010	DA	218	┌	11111100	FC	252	ⁿ
11011011	DB	219	█	11111101	FD	253	²
11011100	DC	220	▄	11111110	FE	254	■
11011101	DD	221	▌	11111111	FF	255	

ASCII Chart

INDEX

Index

Index

Physical records, 44, 131
Picture function, 224
Picture template, 224
Plain page, 198
Position menu, 254
Positioning commands, 103
.PRG., 271
Primary keys, 44, 128
Printing,
 printing reports, 202, 206
 print server, 142
 printer, 128
 printing items vertically, 203
 printing selected labels, 213
 PRINT command,
  SET PRINT ON/OFF, 307
  SET PRINTER TO, 145
  TO PRINT option, 35, 202, 206, 213-214
Procedural query languages, 96
Procedure, 265
 LIST, 306
 command file, 267
 DO WHILE...ENDDO, 273, 280
 initializing a loop, 274
 accumulator, 274
 IF, 275
 SET TALK ON/OFF, 277, 305
 SKIP, 277, 306
 Making a menu, 280
 CLEAR, 282
 WAIT, 282
 TEXT...ENDTEXT, 282
 APPEND, 284
 INPUT, 284
 RETURN, 284
 error corrections, 289
Prompt, 10
PrtSc, 47

Q

Queries, 239, 242
Query, see *Database management–using a database*
query language processor (QLP), 96
QUIT, 14

R

Random access, 128
READ, 285
RECALL, 83
Record lockout, 143

Records, 7, 10
 Record number, 9, 88
Relate menu, 248
Relational database system, 115, 133
Relational operators, see *Operators–relational*
REPLACE, 89
Reports, 193
 liquor store inventory example, 194
 preparing, 196
  page layout, 196
 report generator, 29, 193
REPORT command, 35, 96, 193, 206
 column headings, 204
 Columns menu, 30, 32-34, 199-201
  Contents, 32, 200
  Heading, 32, 201
  Width, 32, 34, 202
  Decimal places, 32, 202
  Total this column, 32, 202
 Exit menu, 35, 202
  Save, 35, 202
  Abandon, 35, 202
 grouping data items, 205
 Groups menu, 31, 198
  Group on expression, 199
  Group heading, 199
  Summary report only, 198
  Page eject, 199
  Sub-group, 199
  Sub-group heading, 199
 Locate menu, 34, 202
 Options menu, 30, 196, 197
  Page title, 30, 197
  Page width (positions), 197
  Left margin, 197
  Right margin, 197
  Lines per page, 198
  Top margin, 198
  Double space report, 198
  Page eject before printing, 198
  Page eject after printing, 198
  Plain page, 198
 page heading, 206
 printing items vertically, 203
 printing reports, 206
 report form, 29, 193
 reports from multiple databases, 205
 REPORT TO PRINT, 35, 206
 saving report output to a disk, 206-207
 selecting records, 206
 special reports, 301-310
 substituting text, 204

Index

Index